Nietzsche Against the Crucified

Nietzsche Against the Crucified

Alistair Kee

SCM PRESS

Copyright © Alistair Kee 1999

0 334 02783 7

This edition first published 1999 by
SCM Press,
9-17 St Albans Place London N1 0NX

SCM Press is a division of
SCM-Canterbury Press Ltd.

Printed in Great Britain by
Biddles Ltd, Guildford and King's Lynn

Contents

Preface

In 1888 Friedrich Nietzsche wrote a short book, completed in three weeks, a work of 'deliberate self-mythologization'[1] in which he reviewed the course of his publications over the previous sixteen years and the development of his Dionysian philosophy of life. He was not to know that it was the last book he would write: already it displays the first signs of the insanity which was soon to overtake him. The title was *Ecce Homo*, the words of Pontius Pilate as he presented Jesus of Nazareth to the crowd before condemning him to crucifixion and to death: 'Behold the man.'[2] Nietzsche may have intuited that his own public life – full of suffering and rejection – was also coming to an end. The book, and with it the main writings of Friedrich Nietzsche, concludes with this one last defiant cry: 'Have I been understood? Dionysos against the Crucified.'[3]

'Dionysos against the Crucified' is indeed the way in which he has been understood and remembered, sometimes with awe, sometimes with anger, and sometimes with not a little anxiety. Nietzsche, bitter opponent of the Crucified Christ, to the death. Nietzsche, atheist, critic of Christianity, sometime student of theology who like many before him turned his familiarity with the tradition into a scathing denunciation of the faith. Nietzsche, who according to one of his best informed and sympathetic expositors, 'launched what may be the most merciless assault upon Christianity in our time'.[4] Nietzsche, who while lesser critics, men of little insight, fearful of the implications of their outbursts, raised doubts about secondary matters, saw with searing clarity what had to be said if mankind were to survive two thousand years of religious control. 'Have I been understood?' Without doubt! What could be clearer?

How could he have been *mis*understood? By the world at large? They had heard nothing of this nomadic eccentric who flitted by the season from France, to Italy, to Switzerland, like some migrating bird, afraid of the cold breath of reality that might catch up with it. Misunderstood? By the academic community? They, who had first welcomed the brilliant philological genius, were soon offended by his criticism of the discipline and his disturbing philosophical assertions which undermined all other disciplines. Misunderstood? By his friends and former colleagues? But he had spurned them, one by one, for failing to support his work. Misunderstood? Who was left in the European cultural and intellectual world of the day to misunderstand him – except perhaps himself? As the end approached he could no longer maintain this abrasive, assertive, dismissive posture: even if he were indeed Dionysos, or at least the last disciple of the Greek god who affirmed life. He could not at the last be understood as the enemy of the one Christian, the only Christian, that disturbing figure who could not be deflected from his grasp of life by the intimidating threat of death, the lover of life who in his single-minded commitment to abundant life merited the enmity of the destroyers of life, the Galilean whose outstretched arms welcoming the despised and rejected must be nailed to the cross in a last but ultimately ineffectual attempt to suppress his message and nullify his power.

'Have I been understood?' A meaningless, unnecessary question – if Nietzsche was indeed the enemy of Christ crucified. 'Dionysos against the Crucified.' Is this not the most appropriate of all mottoes – as crystal clear as it is elegant – to hang above his collected works? It is a beautifully crafted metaphor which seems to capture and express his philosophical project, his life's work, the achievement without rival which he bequeathed to those unborn future generations who would someday be liberated by his thought, treasure his words and honour his name – the characteristically pithy, if premature epitaph of one of the most lucid and creative minds of the modern age. Why then was this redundant question asked, if not that at the end Nietzsche took fright at the thought that some gullible, misguided, immature young mind might read the motto – and believe it!

Edinburgh
St Robin's Day

Introduction

In the last decade there has been a proliferation of books on Nietzsche, often on marginal or rather precious aspects of his thought. An author might well feel obliged to offer a defence of adding to the list, not least in view of the harsh words of Nietzsche himself on the subject. 'Writers ought to be treated as malefactors who deserve to be freed or pardoned only in the rarest cases: this would be a way of preventing the proliferation of books.'[1] This book has been written for three reasons.

The first arises from lecturing to undergraduate students on the thought of the great man. When I look at any page of my lecture notes I see that in developing a single point I am quoting from perhaps half a dozen of his books. Nietzsche is a most unsystematic writer in the sense that his aphorisms on any subject are spread throughout his works. Do you want to know what he says about truth, about rank, about race, about women, about European unity, about art, about music? The material is scattered about in a variety of contexts and not even a concordance would help. In this book I have therefore sought to connect the most important themes in his works in a systematic way. This does not mean imposing a system against the will of the author, against the grain of the material. His writings are unsystematic, but it is possible to trace the relationship among the most important elements in his thought.

There are several useful introductions to Nietzsche's thought, and so I must offer a second justification for this book. It could be broached in several ways, but I choose to do so by reference to academic freedom. Many scholars may spend their lives working in universities without ever having to reflect on this subject. In the USA the culture of 'publish or perish' may have threatened the quality of research which anxious academics have felt constrained to produce. In the UK the Research Assessment Exercise may have led to premature publication and a driving down of standards. But neither context threatens academic freedom. Those of us who have worked in police states are aware of the political pressures which can be brought to bear to censor research into certain subjects. Fortunately such external censorship is relatively rare – certainly in Western countries. I have in mind, however, another kind of censorship, self-censorship. Under the banner of academic freedom scholars sometimes decide that because a subject, or an aspect of a subject, does not interest them, it can be ignored. In Europe we may associate censorship with East European countries (prior to 1989). In this we might well be mistaken, as the following example illustrates. In 1979 I spent a few weeks in the Institute of Sociology at the University of Warsaw. Poland was at that time a communist country and the state ideology included a programme of secularization, to undermine and eliminate religious faith among the people. However, I was struck by the amount of research undertaken into religion. Academics were not allowed to take the position that if they themselves were not interested in religion, it need not be studied. Religion was an important element in Polish society and therefore must be studied, regardless of the personal predilections of sociologists. The same was true with regard to psychology. At the Jagiellonian University of Krakow there was important research being carried on in the psychology of religion. The personal position of researchers was not a criterion of whether the work should be undertaken or not. It was objectively important in the private and societal lives of individuals and therefore must be investigated.

I have chosen this rather indirect way of approaching the second reason for writing this book. Although there have been many books published on Nietzsche in recent years, few of them have dealt with religion. Through the self-censorship which is permitted under the banner of academic freedom, scholars who are not personally interested in religion have decided that it is entirely possible to expound Nietzsche or dialogue with Nietzsche without reference to his views on religion. Nietzsche, this German philosopher of impeccable Prussian ancestry, wilfully declared himself to be of Polish origin. It is necessary to take account of religion when studying Polish society, regardless of the predilections of sociologists. It is necessary to take account of religion when studying the position of Nietzsche, regardless of the predilections of philosophers. This is what I miss in most books on Nietzsche; the omission of this element distorts otherwise insightful introductions to his work. This is not at all the same as saying that everything that was important to Nietzsche must be included in every book on his thought. Music was immensely important to him: in his youth he even thought it might be the career which he should follow. It thrilled and enriched his life from his days at school; it was the one strand of human culture which kept him in touch with his diminishing social world when insanity had dissolved his reason. Yet more fundamental to his life and thought was religion. It is possible to deal with Nietzsche while ignoring his thoughts on religion, but not without distortion. His critique of Christianity runs throughout the entire corpus of his writing. Loss of religious faith is the beginning of his journey, a loss which projects him against his will into a quest for an alternative faith by which to live. That in itself would justify the necessity of dealing with religion in the exposition of his position, and yet the situation is more complicated than that. The alternative faith by which to live, that faith which point for point rejects Christian values, is not in fact the faith by which Nietzsche himself lived. As he tells us in that last poignant work, *Ecce Homo*, 'I am one thing, my writings are another.'[2] And if we still required a justification for dealing in detail with religion in his works, it emerges that this self-styled Anti-Christ who attacked Christianity with such vehemence throughout his life, could at the last defend Jesus of Nazareth against his greatest enemy – the Christian church. As his life as a writer came to an end, this last disciple of the god Dionysos cannot be understood simply by the epitaph: 'against the Crucified'. The casual, personal decision to deal with Nietzsche without reference to religion is academic licence, not academic freedom.

There is, more briefly, a third reason for writing this book. Nietzsche considered *Thus Spoke Zarathustra* to be his greatest work. It is not simply a vehicle for his own position: he does not identify himself with the prophet. Indeed he can speak as if Zarathustra came to him, unannounced, unbidden. Without a trace of romanticism we can say that Nietzsche comes similarly to us, unexpected and unwelcome. He was truly one of the great nineteenth-century prophets of European culture. He came too soon. Many, indeed most, of his observations have taken decades to become true, from the decline of religion to the political and economic integration of Europe. As the twentieth century has unfolded Nietzsche has come to us, again and again. In the 1960s the exponents of the theology of the death of God found themselves in dialogue with him. More recently he has come to us with his critique of modernity, lending authority to the devotees of postmodernism.

In this study we begin with Nietzsche, with the loss of religious faith and the development of an alternative faith. We consider his historical relationship to Christianity and his curious claim that 'the most serious Christians have always been well disposed towards me'.[3] Finally, it is because of his continuing involvement with religion that we can call in question the assumption that he is the father of postmodernism. In spite of himself I believe that Nietzsche would have been entertained by an observation made by Erich Heller, one of his most insightful expositors. '"Postmodernism" is the most unimaginative term of "periodization" that was hit upon by an enfeebled age.'[4] Nietzsche does not deserve to be accused of paternity in the case of this ill-constituted foundling.

I

Ecce Homo

Most philosophers stand apart from their work: we need not be introduced to them to understand or evaluate their writings. This is as it should be. However, there are exceptions to this rule. It is not simply voyeurism: details of their travels, their drinking habits, their love life. In the case of this small group of thinkers we believe that their lives will throw light on their philosophy. Life is an *issue* for them, and the course of their lives is in turn the source of their philosophy and the outworking of that philosophy. This is nowhere better illustrated than in the case of Friedrich Nietzsche. In a letter to his loyal friend Peter Gast, only three weeks before his final collapse, he declares, 'I never write a sentence now in which the whole of me is not present …'[1] If truth be told, Nietzsche's career was not very interesting: its high point was his appointment to a university chair at the age of twenty-four, from which he resigned for health reasons after ten years. But the fascination is with his life rather than his career, with his personal crises rather than his public responsibilities. The events of his life can be simply told: they are not in dispute.[2] Our interest lies rather in evidence which he provides about his inner life, in turn of tragedy, despair and joy.

'I was born on October 15, 1844, on the battlefield of Lützen.'[3] So Nietzsche begins a review of his life, and later he was to describe himself as 'more a battlefield than a man'.[4] As Middleton observes, 'throughout this curriculum vitae Nietzsche is striking a martial and heroic pose, creating an image of himself as anything but a Saxon provincial'.[5] Nietzsche never settled for information when metaphor would do. He was born in the peaceful, rural village of Röcken, but his family in any case were far from being bucolic. His paternal grandmother, Erdmuthe Krause, had been associated with the Goethe-Schiller circle in Weimar. She was a great admirer of Napoleon, as was her grandson. There is an early photograph of Nietzsche as a schoolboy, right hand tucked into the front of his morning coat, in the slightly menacing manner of one who could take control of Europe if he so desired – immediately after Latin prep.[6] His great-uncle was Professor of Theology at Königsberg, later superintendent of the churches of the duchy of Weimar. Nietzsche's father, a Lutheran pastor, lived in the castle of Altenburg as tutor to four princesses. It was from Friedrich Wilhelm IV that he received his appointment to Röcken, and it is not surprising that he named his son after his patron, the King of Prussia. A distinguished Saxon-Prussian family, and yet Nietzsche never missed an opportunity to insist on his Polish origins. His early home life was therefore marked by a deep sense of piety as well as nationalism. On both sides of his family he came from a long line of Lutheran clergy, and ironic as it may now seem, his family had hopes that the 'little pastor'[7] might follow in this tradition. His father, whom he admired and respected, died in 1849 and an acceptance of tragedy and suffering can be seen in a passage in which the thirteen-year-old describes his religious faith.

> I have already experienced so much – joy and sorrow, cheerful things and sad things – but in everything God has safely led me as a father leads his weak little child … I have firmly resolved within me to dedicate myself for ever to his service. May the dear Lord give me strength and power to carry out my intention and protect me on my life's way. Like a child I trust in His grace: He will preserve us all, that no misfortune may befall us. But His holy will be done! All He gives I will joyfully accept: happiness and unhappiness, poverty and wealth, and boldly look even death in the face, which shall one day unite us

all in eternal joy and bliss. Yes, dear Lord, let Thy face shine upon us for ever! Amen.[8]

The precocious youth, looking back over his childhood, prays that God will give him the power to serve Him. Was there ever such an example of unanswered prayer! But as we shall see, it is entirely possible that Nietzsche has exercised a more profound and positive influence on Christians as a critic of religion than he ever could have as a local pastor.

Nietzsche grew up in Naumburg in a household consisting of his sister, mother, grandmother and two aunts. He never married. More to the point, Küng believes that this had an important influence on his view of religion. 'The family atmosphere and his education solely at the hands of gentle, pious women could have been a first factor in the genesis of Nietzsche's anti-Christianity. Christianity always seemed to him a soft, feeble, unmanly, decadent affair ...'[9] In one of his early works he declared that there is 'something feminine in Christianity'.[10] Being Nietzsche, this is intended as a criticism. Much later he was to describe Islam as a religion for men, contemptuous of Christianity 'which it feels to be a woman's religion'.[11] From 1858–1864 Nietzsche attended the Landes-Schule Pforta, Germany's most famous Protestant boarding school, founded in 1543. It compensated for the loss of his father, whose death had deprived the boy of what he subsequently described as 'the strict and superior guidance of a male intellect'.[12] Although his work was outstanding in German literature, classics and religion, Nietzsche as he set out on his academic career reflected that at Pforta he had been well taught, but badly educated.[13] However, it was there that his life-long love of music developed. He tells us that from the moment there was a score of *Tristan and Isolde* he became a devotee of Wagner and even contemplated a career as a musician and composer.

During this period his own personal religious faith reached its most intense level, as witnessed by the recollection of his schoolboy contemporary and life-long friend, Paul Deussen, on the occasion of their confirmation in 1861.

When the candidates for confirmation went in twos to the altar, where they knelt to receive their consecration, Nietzsche also knelt, and as his closest friend, I knelt with him. I remember well the sense of holiness and detachment from the world that filled us during the weeks before and after confirmation. We would have been quite prepared there and then to die in order to be with Christ, and all our thinking, feeling and activity was resplendent with a more than earthly serenity – this of course was an artificially reared little plant, which could not endure very long.[14]

Away from the school hothouse, in the cooler atmosphere of the University of Bonn, the little plant did indeed wither. However, the experience itself was formative for Nietzsche, as he was to acknowledge later. 'Do not underestimate the value of having been religious.'[15] It distinguishes him from those reductionist critics of religion who are its unworthy adversaries. As we shall see, his vehement rejection of religion is also mixed with a more liberal view. 'One must have loved religion and art like a mother and nurse – otherwise one cannot grow wise. But one must be able to see beyond them, outgrow them; if one remains under their spell, one does not understand them.'[16]

Nietzsche matriculated at the University in 1864 and began a life which for all its uniqueness also included two experiences not at all remarkable. He encountered relations with women (as distinct from women relations) and historical criticism. The effects of both were to remain with him for the rest of his life. In February of the following year, in his leisure time, he visited a brothel in Cologne, where he contracted syphilis. In this he was the victim of bad luck rather than a dissolute lifestyle. It was from its long term-effects that he eventually suffered insanity and progressive paralysis. Meanwhile, in his academic life he was introduced to historical criticism of the Bible, notably through the monumental work of David Strauss *The Life of Jesus: Critically Examined*. I have placed these two facts together because they may well have been in the young man's mind as he returned home to celebrate Easter in Naumburg. He shocked and distressed his mother by refusing to take communion at that most sacred moment in the Christian year. At this time the young Nietzsche was turning away from the faith of his family and we might have expected him to produce some undergraduate arguments against religion. His actual position is therefore entirely more interesting. Reflecting on the situation many years later he was to say that he had 'no experience of actual *religious* difficulties', and more specifically that atheism for him was not the outcome of a rational process.[17] In an aphorism penned several years later Nietzsche reveals to us his thoughts on that period of his life.

> He who wants to desert a party or a religion believes it is incumbent upon him to refute it ... We did not attach ourself to this party, or religion, on strictly rational grounds: we ought not to affect to have done so when we leave it.[18]

His alienation from the Christian religion did not immediately lead to irreligion, but rather to a desire to devote himself to something else. In a poem written in 1864 he writes to 'the unknown God', 'I want to know you – even serve you.'[19] The loss of traditional religion would not eliminate devotion from his life, but it was not yet clear where this devotion would lead him – nor at what personal cost.

His loss of faith should not have been a surprise to his sister Elisabeth, to whom he wrote a few weeks after the Easter incident, 'If you want to achieve peace of mind and happiness, then have faith; if you want to be a disciple of truth, then search.'[20] However, I wish to suggest that there might well have been another aspect to this incident, moral rather than intellectual. I shall propose, towards the end of this book, that Nietzsche was offended by those who *did* take communion. In public life he could see political leaders who had long since ceased to believe anything in the creeds, but who felt no need to change their lives in consequence. They were 'practical anti-Christians through and through',[21] yet they called themselves Christian and went to communion. He, the recent and unfortunate patron of a brothel, may well have thought himself unworthy of communion, but what of those who brazenly, thoughtlessly and hypocritically came forward, unconcerned about the dire warning expressed in the awesome words of the King James version that he who 'eateth and drinketh unworthily, eateth and drinketh damnation to himself, not discerning the Lord's body'?[22] Nietzsche continued his study of theology but concentrated now on philology. As the young man made the transition from school to university he experienced a transition from the faith which originally enfolded him, to a new one, yet to be discovered. 'And so the human being outgrows everything that once surrounded him. He does not need to break the fetters; unexpectedly, when a god beckons, they fall away. And where is the ring that ultimately encircles him? Is it the world? Is it God?' This quotation from the nineteen-year-old Nietzsche in his autobiography is claimed by Heidegger as presaging the doctrine of eternal return.[23] This seems unlikely. The full impact and implications of the loss of Christian faith had yet to dawn upon him. An alternative to it would come much later.

It was in the field of philology that Nietzsche was first to come to prominence. While still an undergraduate he began to publish studies on philological topics, in addition to his dissertation on *Theognis, the Aristocratic Poet of Megara*. This brought him to the attention of the University of Basel, who contacted his teacher, Friedrich Wilhelm Ritschl, whom he had followed from Bonn to Leipzig. In recognition both of his loyalty and his outstanding ability Ritschl recommended him to Basel for appointment to the vacant chair in Classical Philology. He described the young scholar as a 'prodigy' and declared, 'he will accomplish anything he puts his mind to'.[24] Nietzsche did not even have time to undertake his doctoral studies, which would have made him a more conventional candidate for academic life. When in April 1869 he signed his letter to Carl von Gersdorff 'Friedrich Nietzsche Dr' it was because Leipzig had hastily conferred upon him the degree – without examination. Surely such a prodigious talent would dominate the discipline for a generation to come. Nietzsche taught in Basel for ten years, from 1869 to 1879, interrupted in 1870 by a short time when he volunteered to serve as a medical orderly in the Franco-Prussian war. As a condition of employment he had become a Swiss citizen, and therefore could not be a combatant. No doubt the young man considered that he could have fought with distinction. Three years earlier, in 1867, he had been drafted into the Fourth Regiment of the Field Artillery. A photograph taken at this time shows Nietzsche in the uniform of an artilleryman, gripping a long cavalry sword in his right hand. The haughty pose is somewhat compromised by the rather camp position of the left hand on hip. Perhaps the photographer was reluctant to make this observation.[25] At that time he signed letters to his friends 'Artilleryman'. Indeed when as a philosopher he pounded the positions of his intellectual opponents he returned to the use of this metaphor, for example signing a letter to Erwin Rohde, 'The Mounted Gunner with the Heaviest Gun'.[26] There are alarmingly enthusiastic references to war and militarism in Nietzsche's writings, as for example when he claims that 'so highly cultivated and for that reason necessarily feeble humanity as that of the present-day European requires not merely war but the greatest and most terrible wars – thus a temporary relapse into barbarism – if the means to culture are not to deprive them of their culture and their existence itself'.[27] However, such views issue from his philosophy, as we shall see: the reality of his own experience of war was very different and its effects were always with him. As a medical orderly he witnessed at first hand scenes of appalling suffering and destruction. In a letter to Wagner he gives a graphic account of travelling for three days and nights in a cattle truck with the wounded. After only four weeks of service he was discharged, suffering from dysentery and diphtheria.[28] His health was permanently damaged, adding to the migraine which he had suffered from childhood, the syphilis which he contracted as a student and the failing eyesight which at the end he described as three-quarters blindness.

Ironically, even as a student at Leipzig he had begun to voice criticism of the narrowness of classical philology, writing to

Rohde of 'the seething brood of philologists' and having to
observe 'their moleish polluting, the baggy cheeks and the blind
eyes, their joy at capturing worms and their indifference to the
true problems, the urgent problems of life ...'[29] Philology did not
provide him with resources to address the growing crisis within
his own life. At Basel he lectured to university students and also
taught Greek in the local grammar school. Although he was
rather pleased with his ability to motivate these young pupils, and
satisfied with the numbers of students who enrolled for his
lecture courses, he soon came to doubt the value of this work. 'I
would like to be something more than a drillmaster for competent
philologists ...'[30] Not long after his appointment to Basel these
doubts led him increasingly to turn his attention to questions of
philosophy. Having been appointed to one chair without the
requisite qualifications, he clearly thought he could repeat the
process, and applied for appointment to the chair of philosophy!
This in turn led to an alienation from his colleagues in the discipline. Wagner, whom Nietzsche first met in 1868, was a powerful
influence on him at this stage and it is of some significance that
the composer welcomed with enthusiasm the publication in 1872
of Nietzsche's first book, *The Birth of Tragedy from the Spirit of
Music*, the book which was to ruin his reputation among philologists and academics more generally. Even Ritschl could do no
better than describe an advance copy of the book as 'inspired
dissoluteness'.[31] Nietzsche wrote to Wagner to report that for the
winter semester no students had enrolled for his classes.

The alienation, personal and professional, continued as he
began to publish his first philosophical works, *Untimely
Meditations* and *Human All Too Human*. It was as a philosopher
that he was able to address the most important and pressing
questions of existence. By comparison, in his present post he felt
that he was impersonating a philologist. In fact there was more of
a connection between the two fields than he allowed, since as a
philosopher he constantly refers to Greek thinkers such as
Heraclitus, Epictetus and especially Plato. However, in retrospect
he distanced himself from this period of his life. 'It is the humour

of my situation that I should be mistaken for the former Basel professor Dr Friedrich Nietzsche. The devil take him! What has this fellow to do with me!'[32] During the next few years his health steadily deteriorated and it was officially for this reason that in 1879 he finally resigned his chair in Basel. The University provided him with a pension for the next six years, during which he lived nomadically. He wrote as he travelled, from Germany to Italy to France, to Switzerland, keeping in touch with a small number of colleagues at the University of Basel, Wilhelm Ritschl, Jacob Burckardt the historian, Franz Overbeck the church historian, and a group of friends, including Paul Rée the psychologist, Erwin Rohde a fellow philologist from student days at Leipzig, Paul Duessen his schoolboy friend now Indologist, Carl von Gersdorff, Malwida von Meysenbug and of course Peter Gast (Henrich Köselitz), whom he first met in 1875 when Köselitz, a music student, had come to Basel to attend Nietzsche's lectures. Gast was loyal to the end, a confidant, something of a disciple and as a scribe perhaps the only person who could read Nietzsche's handwriting in that frantic, final period. It is not surprising that most of his friends were men. Malwida von Meysenbug was almost thirty years older than Nietzsche: they first met at Bayreuth in 1872, the year of the publication of *The Birth of Tragedy*. She expressed interest in his work and was one of those who helped to bring attention to his writings. It was she, together with Paul Rée, who introduced Nietzsche to Lou von Salomé. Like Malwida, this young Russian woman was of a Huguenot family: her father had been a general under Czar Alexander. She came to the West for her education and was introduced to Nietzsche in 1882 with the intention that she should become his pupil and study his philosophy. She was certainly capable of it. In a letter to Gast, Nietzsche describes Lou as 'keen as an eagle, brave as a lion, and yet a very girlish child'.[33] To Overbeck he reports that 'Lou is by far the most intelligent person I have become acquainted with'.[34] (So much for his colleagues in Basel!) However, in other respects she seems to have been too much for Nietzsche. As Michael Tanner observes, 'Lou was an immensely gifted woman, who went on to become Rilke's mistress and later one of Freud's most valued disciples; he pays tribute to her in uncharacteristically generous terms for her discoveries in the area of anal eroticism.'[35] There is a photograph of her standing in a cart being pulled by Rée and Nietzsche. The innocent scene is of three friends on holiday. However, a more intense photograph of Lou von Salomé survives, in which she stands in a drawing room, leaning against a sideboard in a masculine way, dressed in black. Her hair is cut severely, emphasizing the cold and calculated stare of her dark, piercing eyes.[36] Whatever the lads between the shafts thought, the young woman standing above them brandishing her whip looks to be too much for either or both of them. 'Are you visiting women? Do not forget your whip!'[37] It was hardly surprising that she declined Nietzsche's proposal of marriage (twice), but the rejection had a devastating effect on him. In his plans for marriage to Lou were invested his hopes to overcome at last the loneliness which was such a feature of his life, a loneliness aggravated by his nomadic travels, his increasing alienation from the academic community, his elitist philosophy. In a letter to Lou, only four months after their first meeting he confides in her: 'I want to be lonely no longer, but to learn again to be a human being.'[38] It is sometimes said that his affair with Lou von Salomé was the only romantic relationship of Nietzsche's life: it was not his only proposal of marriage. Six years earlier, in Geneva, he had met Mathilde Trampedach and within days wrote to her, proposing marriage. 'Will you be my wife? I love you and feel that you already belong to me.'[39] The greatest wordsmith of the German language certainly had a way of approaching women! He was nothing if not resilient, and the following year, 1877, was again planning marriage. There was no one specific in mind, but the two qualities of this ideal bride were that she must be good and rich. We might speculate, good and rich, but not necessarily in that order. Nietzsche was in continual dispute with his publisher and, never receiving any royalties, was frequently dependent on the generosity of his friends. Perhaps the most significant woman Nietzsche counted as a friend was Cosima

Wagner. While in Basel Nietzsche spent some of the most creative and enjoyable times in his life in the company of the Wagners, visiting them over twenty times in a three-year period at Tribschen, near Lucerne. The maestro was born in the same year as Nietzsche's father, and in addition to his influence on the young man through his music and his views on art and aesthetics, he was also something of a father-figure. We can only speculate on the corresponding role of Cosima. Like the young Russian she was too much for Nietzsche, but more so. The illegitimate daughter of Franz Liszt, she had married Hans von Bülow, one of her father's piano students. Within a few years she formed an adulterous affair with Wagner, and in 1866 left her husband for the maestro. This did not prevent the now conductor Hans von Bülow from conducting the first performances of *Tristan* and *Meistersinger*. (He was later to reject Nietzsche's symphonic meditation *Manfred*.) If Freud was impressed by Lou von Salomé, he would have been fascinated by Nietzsche's relationship with Frau Wagner. And in the best Freudian tradition, in the last few days of his active life, as he lost control of his mind and therefore of the concealment of his innermost feelings, he penned a note to Cosima Wagner: 'Ariadne, I love you. Dionysos.' Even more convolutedly, after his mother had arranged for him to be taken to a psychiatric clinic in Jena he told his doctors 'my wife Cosima brought me here'.[40] Scattered throughout his works are references to women, most – but by no means all – chauvinistic in character, in which Nietzsche claims knowledge of his subject. In his last book he remarks that he had 'never striven after *honours*, after *women*, after *money*. Not that I could not have had them.'[41] He did have honours and at least some money at Basel, but as for women, this claim is laddish bravado. There is a marked contrast between his attraction to strong, independent women and the scattered reference in his writings to mother-love.[42] He was certainly a shrewd observer of human behaviour and motivation, frequently referring to himself as a psychologist rather than a philosopher, but we may doubt if he had any knowledge of women at the most intimate and personal level. His remarks on the subject are testimony to the continuing influence on his thought of the nihilistic philosopher Arthur Schopenhauer, who could have captained Germany to victory in the Misogynist World Cup.[43] (It is for this reason that I have used politically incorrect language throughout the book. To do otherwise would have been a constant criticism rather than exposition of Nietzsche).

It was during this nomadic existence that he was to write his major works. Cutting himself off from settled society and in turn one by one from the circle of his closest friends, he set himself to develop not a system of philosophy, but a philosophy by which to live. Yet herein lay the irony, if not the tragedy, that the life he was living was hardly an advertisement for it. It was as if he had a vocation which took him away from the common, social life: 'life has proposed my duty to me with the terrible condition that I should fulfil that duty in *solitude*'.[44] To busy academics the idea of solitude might seem idyllic – but only for a limited period. In a very perceptive review of *Beyond Good and Evil*, Widmann commented on the cost at which the new philosophy was being developed. 'Nietzsche is the first man to find a way out, but it is such a terrifying way that one is really frightened to see him walking the lonely and till now untrodden path!'[45] In a letter reflecting on his forty-third birthday he observes that he has no more friends now than on the first day he entered the world. He had no 'interests' and tells his mother that there is no one alive about whom he cares very much. The fact that his work was not accepted or even discussed in academic circles was very hurtful to him. He had no advocates, no disciples, no heirs. It is hardly surprising that his copious letters of the time indicate great swings from ecstasy at his achievements to depression about the value of his life of suffering and rejection. His works display the genius of the man who single-mindedly devotes his waking hours to his work, but also the eccentricity of one who has removed himself from the community of scholars and the creative power of critical dialogue. As Jens observes, 'Nietzsche was a pastor without pulpit, a professor without a chair.'[46] Nietzsche was gratified that

Georg Brandes, Professor of Literature at the University of Copenhagen and a prolific scholar, had lectured on his work in Warsaw, St Petersburg and Moscow. However, it was small consolation to learn that he was becoming well known in the Slavic countries, when his work was never mentioned in Germany. They engaged in a very polite exchange of letters. Brandes was deferential, though not uncritical of Nietzsche. For his part Nietzsche did not see Brandes as a significant thinker, although he was taken by the latter's description of his position as 'aristocratic radicalism'[47] and, with a hint of vanity, declared it 'the cleverest thing I have yet heard about myself'.[48] Clever, even perceptive, but then *any* academic observation about him would have soothed Nietzsche's desperate craving.

Nietzsche even became alienated from his family, especially from his sister, initially because of her jealousy of Lou von Salomé, and then in 1885 with her marriage to Berhard Förster, who in his anti-semitism embodied so many of the traits that led Nietzsche to turn his back on Germany. For this reason Nietzsche took to claiming Polish ancestry – not of course of peasant stock! 'Consider my name: my forebears were Polish aristocrats – even my grandfather's mother was Polish.'[49] Niezky certainly is sufficiently unpronounceable to be Polish, and there has been a good deal of scholarly debate on the matter. Nietzsche himself would have been exasperated at those who took the powerful metaphor literally. To lose health, friends, family, country, looks like misfortune, carelessness, tragedy. Edwin Rohde saw him for the last time in 1886, and afterwards reported to Overbeck, 'it was as if he came from a land which no one else inhabits'.[50] There is the distinct impression that as the purist, single-minded Nietzsche ploughs his lonely furrow, the disappointments and discomforts of this present moment count as nothing compared with the affirmation of his new world-view which is just about to break forth upon an unsuspecting and unworthy Europe – *and yet* he would gladly have deserted it all for a more human life. His new life philosophy might promise to become the eighth wonder of the existentialist world, but he would gladly have exchanged it all for the love of a good woman and the embrace of a true friend. In one letter to Overbeck he says that it 'hurts frightfully that in these fifteen years not one single person has "discovered" me, has needed me, has loved me'.[51] In an earlier letter he wrote poignantly, 'my life is now comprised in the wish that the truth about all things be different from my way of seeing it. If only someone could convince me of the improbability of my truth!'[52] The twentieth century has stood in awe – whether in admiration or in dismay – of Nietzsche's construction. How tragic that at least in his darker moods he hated it, and would have blessed anyone who could have convinced him that life need not be thus. The popular image of Nietzsche is of an entirely self-sufficient man, despising the common life of hearth and health, work and leisure, standing outside and above the society of his time and place, condemning and threatening, a prophet of dissolution and destruction. But if this comes from his works, his life was very different, as Jaspers indicates. 'The picture of Nietzsche as a hero of steel-like hardness, who relies on himself and moves through the world untouched and unshaken, is false. Nietzsche's heroism is of another kind. He had to suffer a human fate from which all forms of natural human fulfilment are withheld.'[53] In its originality and brilliance his philosophy has been a wonderful gift to Europe and the world, but it seems to have been bought at a terrible personal cost.

Perhaps for this reason Nietzsche was greatly impressed by the life and works of Fyodor Mikhailovich Dostoyevsky. It has been said by Stefen Zweig that the suffering of the Russian writer's life made 'his biography a tragedy'. This close relationship between experience and writing was a feature of Nietzsche's own work. There is a tragic incident in one of Dostoyevsky's works which has come to have a particular interest in relation to Nietzsche's own biography. In *Crime and Punishment* Dostoyevsky tells us that his leading character, Roskolnikoff, had a strange dream. It concerned an incident when he was seven years old, out walking with his father in his home town. A group of peasants suddenly emerged from a tavern, and were invited by one of them, Nikola,

to get into his cart and be drawn by an old mare. The burden was
beyond the strength of the unfortunate animal, and it was beaten
first of all with whips, and then clubbed with a flat board and
finally struck down with an iron bar. In a drunken rage Nikola
would rather kill the animal than be shamed by its inability to
fulfil his boast. From the crowd which had gathered he was
chided for such un-Christian actions, but no one intervened.
'The poor boy thought not of himself, and made his way through
the crowd to the dead mare; he embraced her blood-stained head
and kissed it, then he leaped up and rushed frantically at Nikola
with closed fists.'[54]

In 1888 Nietzsche discovered Turin, a city of culture and
aristocracy where he felt strangely on the verge of recognition. He
anticipated the end of his longing and waiting. Indeed it was the
end of his tormented journey. His health improved, he began to
take an interest in his appearance. At last he was able to sleep,
even as the carriages rumbled past the windows of his lodging in
Via Carlo Alberto – an image which we shall meet again as a
powerful metaphor of his own significance. People were deferential to him as a distinguished writer and he notes that he is
accepted as a distinguished military figure, a foreign visitor –
Polish and certainly not German! Given his love of rank he was
particularly gratified to be treated like royalty and an object of
some fascination. His lodgings were central and to his liking. The
proprietor and his family were impressed by this guest, who
played the piano for hours, especially the works of – yes,
Wagner.[55] His philosophical works, so brilliant, so incisive, so
original and disconcerting, were all but complete. *Ecce Homo* was
dashed off confidently, carelessly, but around the horizon of that
bright winter's scene were massing the clouds which would soon
overtake his mind. A race against time. In his letters instructions
were issued, increasingly absurd and strident. His letters are
signed 'the Monster', 'the Phoenix', 'Caesar', 'Dionysos', 'the
Anti-Christ'. The contents are increasingly eccentric, beginning
from October 1888. 'I am strong enough to break the history of
mankind in two.' 'The world will be standing on its head for the

next few years: since the old God has abdicated, *I* shall rule the
world from now on.' '... in two months I shall be the foremost
name on earth.' 'I hold, quite literally, the future of mankind in
the palm of my hand.' 'I have ordered a convocation of princes in
Rome – I mean to have the young emperor shot.'[56] Writing to his
former colleague Jakob Burckhardt reminds him of his two lives,
one pleasant, the other so demanding. 'Actually I would much
rather be a Basel professor than God; but I have not ventured to
carry my private egoism so far as to omit creating the world on his
account. You see, one must make sacrifices, however and wherever one may be living.'[57] We know what is about to happen:
Nietzsche is oblivious to it. It looks to us as if the pit opens up in
his path, but the opposite is true for him. Here in Turin is the end
of the terrible lonely journey. Now there is friendship and recognition. He has fulfilled the burden laid upon him. In his last
letter to Peter Gast he writes as one who has kept the faith, who
anticipates the great *eschaton*, who experiences the ecstasy of that
welcome and reward which comes only to those who suffered and
triumphed. To the composer friend he writes simply (simply!):
'Sing me a new song: the world is transfigured and all the
heavens rejoice,' signed, 'The Crucified'.[58]

His works remained, but he himself fell back from them, losing
touch with reality, falling metaphorically and at the end falling
quite literally, falling in such a bizarre way that his action was a
metaphor of life, of fate, of philosophy itself. On 3 January 1889
he fell in the street in the Piazza Carlo Alberto, throwing his arms
round the neck of a cab-horse which was being beaten, like the
innocent young Roskolnikoff protecting a living creature from an
un-Christian act. With this last and possibly symbolic act his
mind and his health finally broke. He lived on till 25 August 1900,
during a decade in which his reputation and fame grew, but he
was unaware of such matters, insane and semi-paralysed. The
Madman came too early: now the madness came too soon.

Karl Jaspers, the Swiss philosopher who has written one of the
classic studies of Nietzsche, was himself a professor of psychiatry
before becoming a philosopher. He has given a detailed

description of the organic brain disorder and progressive paralysis which overtook Nietzsche.[59] On the morning of that fateful day Nietzsche wrote down on a piece of paper these prophetic words: 'I am taking narcotic after narcotic in order to drown my anguish; but still I cannot sleep. Today I will certainly take such a quantity as will drive me out of my mind.'[60] Franz Overbeck hurried to Turin and took Nietzsche to a psychiatric clinic in Basel. From there his mother conveyed him to Jena. By May he was sufficiently stable to go home to Naumburg, to that place which during his working life he declared had never been home. As the fame of Friedrich Nietzsche grew, he lived quietly as a man of the same name, quite unrelated to his previous life, unaware of his growing significance, deprived both of the satisfaction of recognition and the capacity to engage in that dialogue which had been so sadly absent from his active life. As a boy he had offered to devote himself to an unknown god. As Stern observes, 'it was as if the unknown god had used him and had done with him'.[61] Sad, tragic: but there was one further and final misfortune which was to overtake him, or rather his reputation. At least he was spared all knowledge of it.

His sister Elisabeth had accompanied her husband to Paraguay in 1886 to found a colony of racially pure German settlers. After he committed suicide she returned to Germany. In 1893 she founded the Nietzsche Archives in Naumburg, and on the death of their mother in 1897 she took over the care of her brother. More ominously she sought to control the publication of his works, including the voluminous unpublished notes, the *Nachlass*. She soon moved her brother and the Nietzsche Archives to Weimar, to parallel Cosima Wagner's establishment of the Wagner Archives. Her objective was to use her brother's growing reputation in the furtherance of her late husband's anti-semitism. Her approach did not neglect tampering with documents and blatant forging of letters, 'generally in line with a characteristic of hers, that in sensitive areas of her brother's biography her memory for convenient detail improved as she got older'.[62] Kaufmann notes her guiding principle.

If one wanted a symbol of his sister's unfitness for her later role as his apostle, one might find it in the name which she assumed in this capacity: Förster-Nietzsche. The irony of this name suggests almost everything that could be said against her: the gospel she spread was indeed Förster first and Nietzsche second.[63]

In this she had considerable success, culminating in the day when she received Adolf Hitler at the Archives. Georges Bataille sees her as a betrayer of her brother. 'November 2, 1933, in the house where Nietzsche died, Mrs Elizabeth *Judas*-Förster received Adolf Hitler, Führer of the Third Reich. On that solemn occasion she attested to the family's anti-semitism by reading a text by – Bernard Förster!'[64] It is further reported that she presented a gift to the Führer – her brother's walking stick – before inviting him to visit the Nietzsche Archives. 'Taking the walking stick in hand, Mr Hitler strode through the crowd to great huzzahs.'[65] Indeed scarcely two years later Adolf Hitler returned to the Archives to attend a memorial service for Elisabeth Förster-Nietzsche. Such was the power of the Nietzsche name. To be denied fame and recognition in Germany was not the worst thing that could have happened to him.

2

The Death of God

Nietzsche's family were shocked when he refused to take communion at Easter 1865. A more gracious son would have made some excuse to his mother: he did after all suffer from migraine. But not Nietzsche: no concessions to the feelings of others. He did not spare her, or himself, and in this we see the evidence of his integrity. Nietzsche was far from unique in his loss of religious beliefs: many of his contemporaries experienced the same thing. He was distinguished by openly declaring himself. If he no longer believed, then he would not pretend that he did. However, this was the least of it. If he had lost his faith then he would not continue to live in a world built upon religious presuppositions, as if nothing had fundamentally changed. Nietzsche came to describe himself as an atheist, but we should not try to understand him within that long tradition of philosophers who have joined battle with theologians over the traditional proofs for the existence of God. As we shall see, his position is so much more profound and complex that to describe him as an atheist, while not false, is liable to mislead. The position invites comparison with the protest of his older contemporary, Ludwig Feuerbach: 'He who says no more of me than that I am an atheist, says and knows nothing of me.'[1] We have already noted that for Nietzsche few people enter a religion on rational grounds, and those who leave should not feel constrained to show that they depart from it on rational grounds. If participation in religion comes about primarily through socialization, then it is likely that the loss of religion comes about through the same forces. In some centuries the vast majority of people participate in religion. Later, relatively few. Nietzsche was living at a time when the balance was still in favour of the religious, but prophetically he could anticipate a coming age in which the balance would tip in favour of the irreligious. 'It is our taste which now decides against Christianity, not our reason.'[2] Our taste: participation in religion or lack of it is not an essentially rational matter, but a function of the culture within which we live, the period in which we live. As Jaspers notes, '"taste" is conceived by Nietzsche as something which substantially precedes any thought, any insight, and value-judgment', and he goes on to quote a letter Nietzsche sent to Peter Gast in November 1886. 'I have a taste, but it rests upon no reasons, no logic, and no imperative.'[3]

This movement in Western culture which Nietzsche intuited we now call secularization. Its most obvious feature is a loss of religious beliefs and consequently participation in institutional forms of religion. Most people who become secular or irreligious in this sense are still content to live within the same world-view as before – except for belief in God. As Jaspers observes, 'as modernism becomes godless, it regards morality as a solid ground upon which it still stands and by whose laws it lives'.[4] But Nietzsche saw that the ramifications were much more extensive. Irreligious people would still like to be moral, to distinguish between good and evil. But in Western culture morality is based on religious assumptions. There are people who would find life in this world unendurable 'if its foundation lacked an ethical significance',[5] and that is precisely the situation they would find themselves in without a creator God. Nietzsche was more honest, more consistent about the loss of a complete world-view. 'If one breaks out of it a fundamental idea, the belief in God, one thereby breaks the whole thing to pieces ...'[6] This halting between two ways is for Nietzsche a lack of imagination – mankind can do with itself whatever it wishes. This is the basis of his attack on the later work of David Strauss. The old man now admitted that he was no longer a Christian, but drew no conclusions about the basis of ethics. 'Here was an opportunity to exhibit native courage: for here he ought to have turned his back on his "we" and boldly derived a moral code for life out of the *bellum omnium contra omnes* and the privileges of the strong ...'[7] This was to be the lonely path of Nietzsche himself. Eminent writers again and again refused to recognize the implications of their atheism. A good example was George Eliot. It was she who translated Feuerbach's *Das Wesen des Christentums* into English. English Romantics found in that book a path by which they could neglect the claims of Christian doctrine, without giving up their religious heritage. 'They have got rid of the Christian God, and now feel obliged to cling all the more firmly to Christian morality.'[8] It is this clinging which disgusts Nietzsche. He calls it naivety, but it is surely not so innocent. 'The "beyond" is absolutely necessary if faith in morality is to be maintained.'[9] The religious tradition is that morality comes from elsewhere: it is not possible to cling to morality as an absolute if its justification, its transcendent setting, has been removed.

However, the foundation which has been removed supported more than morality. Irreligious people assume that knowledge is possible, that there are facts, fixed points in our understanding of reality. They assume that there is such a thing as 'the truth'. But such a world-view stems from belief in an absolute and unchanging God. As Jaspers explains, 'truth is not at first pursued merely for the sake of the objective validity that it acquires in science; its pursuit is incited by belief', and he goes on to quote Nietzsche, who says that 'all actual striving for truth has entered the world as a result of the struggle for a sacred assurance'.[10] And thirdly, the loss of foundation also affects those who still wish to make aesthetic judgments about creativity and beauty. But these too are based on a religious tradition. Nietzsche is consistent across the board: '*The* beautiful exists just as little as does *the* good, or *the* true.'[11] For Nietzsche, to lose religious beliefs is to lose the foundations of life itself: truth, moral values and aesthetic judgment. A common distinction today is between people who are religious and those who are secular in their beliefs and behaviour. Nietzsche certainly anticipated a secular culture, but not one in which religious and secular people continue to share the same world-view, take or leave one supernatural being. If there is no difference, there certainly should be. For him the loss of religious beliefs involves the loss also of every moral landmark, every aesthetic point of reference, the loss of that epistemological framework in which we know the world and ourselves.

It is not difficult to see why people who lose religious beliefs ignore the full implications of their new situation. It could be inconvenient: they do not want to lose the familiar and the comfortable elements in their social lives, or their careers and professional status. Nietzsche had specific examples before him. In a letter to Carl von Gersdorff he characterizes the quiescence of the famous historian at the University of Basel, Jacob Burckhardt, 'that elderly, highly original man, given not to distorting truth, but to passing it over in silence'. And in a telling metaphor he claims that Burckhardt knew very well that the religious foundations and legitimation of life had been undermined. 'He continued to eat the bread and drink the wine, and called them by the names of culture and tradition.'[12] Thus the irreligious life continued to depend on its religious foundations. Nietzsche was clearly offended that so many of his contemporaries chose this path. Perhaps intuitively they suspected that if they stepped outside the world which is legitimated by religion there would be nothing on which to stand: no land, no assured place. This is indeed the metaphor which Nietzsche uses to describe his situation. But the power of the metaphor derives from the fact that for Nietzsche this is no debating point: it is an experience of existential terror.

We have quit the land and gone on board ship. We have cut off the bridge behind us – more than that, the land behind us. Now, little ship, be careful. Alongside you lies the ocean. True, it does not always roar, and sometimes it stretches out as silk and gold, like a comforting dream. But there will be times when you will realize that it is infinite and that there is nothing more dreadful than infinity. Oh, the poor bird that felt itself

free but now beats against the sides of the cage. Alas, if you
should be seized by homesickness for land, as if there had been
more freedom there – and there is no 'land' any more.[13]

For Nietzsche there is no going back: we have burned our
bridges. We have sailed away, but not along a God-given course.
Now we are cast adrift on an ocean without God's heaven by
which to chart our way. We cannot return to the religious age of
innocence, like a bird which beats its wings against the outside of
the cage, desperate to return to its old but safe prison, as if there
had been more freedom there. The loss of religious beliefs is not
just socially inconvenient. It brings existential terror. It would be
easy to avoid this by dishonesty, by pretence, by cowardice, by a
culpable loss of human dignity. All of that is but a small price to
pay in the eyes of the many, but too great a price for Nietzsche.

It sounds like masochism, to entertain and then embrace the
unthinkable – and to what end? What is to be gained? What is
wrong with living within the old world, as if it were still our
home? What is the alternative? Nothing could better mark off the
difference between the nihilism of Schopenhauer, the quiescence
of Burckhardt – and the courage and integrity of Nietzsche. They
come to the abyss and turn back: he takes the plunge. They
attempt to salvage what is left to them: he is prepared to lose his
life, and strangely finds it. How Galilean! Some have claimed that
Nietzsche was hostile to Hegelian philosophy,[14] but as Nietzsche
attempts to make sense of his experience, and map out his future
path there is a very clear dialectical movement in his thought.
This is well illustrated in two long passages, which I shall repro-
duce below in full. In each case he begins from the recognition of
the crisis (personal, cultural, historical, societal) and its full
acceptance. Staring into the abyss, plunging into the abyss, he
discovers that the outcome is not at all as he anticipated or feared.
These two passages begin from the death of God. Religion existed
and thrived in our culture, but now it has come to the end of its
natural term. Nietzsche is not going to argue with anyone, not
those of previous generations who lived the religious life, not

those who continue with religion in the present age, and certainly not those who wish to debate the existence of God. The death of God is a dramatic metaphor by which he refers to a hugely complex cultural movement which is spreading inexorably over the contemporary landscape. It is a cultural fact, not a rational conclusion. The clock is ticking, even if people stop their ears against its insistent beat: the countdown has begun and its outcome cannot be prevented simply by the testimony of individual believers. This towering wave which is set to engulf Europe cannot be dissipated on the shores of modern times by the religious subjects of King Canute. In such extremities who in his right mind would experience anything but terror and despair? But we know of such a man. In *The Gay Science*[15] we find a passage entitled 'The Meaning of Our Cheerfulness'.

> The greatest recent event – that 'God is dead', that the belief in the Christian god has become unbelievable – is already beginning to cast its first shadows over Europe. For the few at least whose eyes – the suspicion in whose eyes is strong and subtle enough for this spectacle, some sun seems to have set and some ancient and profound trust has been turned into doubt; to them our old world must appear daily more like evening, more mistrustful, stranger, 'older'. But in the main one must say: The event itself is far too great, too distant, too remote from the multitude's capacity for comprehension even for the tidings of it to be thought of as having arrived as yet. Much less may one suppose that many people know as yet what this event really means – and how much must collapse now that this faith has been undermined because it was built upon this faith, propped up by it, grown into it; for example, the whole of our European morality. This long plenitude and sequence of breakdown, destruction, ruin and cataclysm that is now impending – who could guess enough of it today to be compelled to play the teacher and advance proclaimer of this monstrous logic of terror, the prophet of a gloom and an eclipse of the sun whose like has probably never yet occurred on earth?

Religion has a cosmic dimension to it, and it is fitting that Nietzsche describes a cultural event as if it were a cosmic happening, something taking place on earth, in Western societies, as if it were an upheaval at the edge of the universe, a human event as if it occurred originally without reference to mankind. A prophet is not a person who makes eccentric guesses about the future, but one whose antennae are so sensitive as to be able to pick up the first tremors, the earliest hints of events which one day will become manifest. Nietzsche writes of the beginnings of a social revolution which will not in fact come to public notice for two further generations. Most people know nothing of such a movement; some know better, but refuse to face the 'logic of terror'. But a few, such as Nietzsche, do know and try to face this period of 'gloom and eclipse' in all its horror. But is it only gloom and eclipse?

> Even we born guessers of riddles who are, as it were, waiting on the mountains poised between today and tomorrow, we firstlings and premature births of the coming century, to whom the shadows that must soon envelop Europe really should have appeared by now – why is it that even we look forward to the approaching gloom without any real sense of involvement and above all without any worry and fear for ourselves? Are we perhaps still too much under the impression of the initial consequences of this event – and these initial consequences, the consequences for ourselves, are quite the opposite of what one might perhaps expect. They are not at all sad and gloomy but rather like a new and scarcely describable kind of light, happiness, relief, exhilaration, encouragement, dawn.

We see here the dialectic in his thinking. Hope lies not with those who are oblivious to the catastrophe and will be unprepared for it when it comes, comes with an apparent suddenness. Hope lies not with those who know better, with the nihilists who see no point in acknowledging what is going on if they have nothing to put in its place. Hope lies only with those who honestly face up to the situation, who pursue its 'logic of terror', for only they can see in the destruction of one world the possibility of the creation of another.

Indeed, we philosophers and 'free spirits' feel, when we hear the news that 'the old god is dead', as if a new dawn shone on us: our heart overflows with gratitude, amazement, premonitions, expectation. At long last the horizon appears free to us again, even if it should not be bright: at long last our ships may venture out again, venture out to face any danger; all the daring of the lover of knowledge is permitted again: the sea, *our* sea, lies open again; perhaps there has never yet been such an 'open sea'.

Many will refuse to recognize the death of God, the end of religion, the removal of the religious foundations of epistemology, morality and aesthetics, yet those who follow the consequences to the end discover that the death of the old heralds the birth of the new. But Nietzsche was no romantic. This new world which is to be brought into being, this world which is to be the responsibility of man, not God, will not be perfect. It will not be safe or comfortable. The future in such a world 'is not bright', *but* – and it is with this 'but' that the new age of human liberation begins – this sea is *our sea*. Mankind has always charted its way by looking to the heavens. Never did such a 'open sea' exist. And this is 'the meaning of our cheerfulness'. Only those who accept the loss will experience the joy.

There is a more famous passage in *The Gay Science*[16] which deals with the same movement, but in a more existential mode. 'The Madman' displays the now familiar dialectical sequence.

Have you heard of that madman who lit a lantern in the bright morning hours, ran to the market place, and cried incessantly: 'I seek God! I seek God!' As many of those who did not believe in god were standing around just then, he provoked much laughter. Has he got lost? asked one. Did he lose his way like a child? asked another. Or is he hiding? Is he afraid of us? Has he gone on a voyage, emigrated? Thus they yelled and laughed. The madman jumped into their midst and pierced them with his eyes. 'Whither is God?' he cried: 'I will tell you. We have killed him – you and I. All of us are his murderers. But how did we do this? How could we drink up the sea? Who gave us the sponge to wipe away the entire horizon? What were we doing when we unchained this earth from its sun? Whither is it moving now? Whither are we moving? Away from all suns? Are we not plunging continually? Backward, sideward, forward, in all directions? Is there still any up or down? Are we not straying as through an infinite nothing? Do we not feel the breath of empty space? Has it not become colder? Is not night continually closing in on us? Do we not need to light lanterns in the morning? Do we hear nothing as yet of the noise of gravediggers who are burying God? Do we smell nothing as yet of the divine decomposition? Gods too decompose. God is dead. God remains dead. And we have killed him.'

Once again there is an event, as yet undetected by the majority of people. But now it is assigned to human actions. All those who have had a part in the creation of the coming secular culture, the culture of irreligion, the time of the death of God – all such like assassins have had a hand on the knife which killed God. But those who have happily participated in the deed have yet to understand its terrible consequences. Darkness has fallen on the human world: the light of knowledge, which came from the heavens, has been extinguished. Those who have cast themselves about on this wild sea cannot look beyond themselves to determine which way is forward, or up or down. All objective standards, all moral and aesthetic judgments have been dissolved. As long as they fail to see what they have done and take responsibility for it, its consequences will come upon them in a disorienting and destructive way. But is that the last word – or merely the first?

'How shall we comfort ourselves, the murderers of all murderers? What was holiest and mightiest of all that the world has yet owned has bled to death under our knives: who will wipe the blood off us? What water is there for us to clean ourselves?

What festivals of atonement, what sacred games shall we have to invent? Is not the greatness of this dead too great for us? Must we ourselves not become gods simply to appear worthy of it? There has never been a greater deed: and whoever is born after us – for the sake of this deed he will belong to a higher history than all history hitherto.'

The emphasis now moves from the awfulness of the deed to its implications, to responsibilities and possibilities implicit in the new situation. Instead of looking to religion to deal with moral matters such as guilt and forgiveness, people must find a new and human basis for such matters. The transition marks not the end of history, but the beginning of a new history. Those born after the death of God will be born into a higher history. Nietzsche has yet to tell us why it is "higher", but we can sense the same cheerfulness, anticipation, hope: nihilism can be transcended. But now the mood of the passage changes. The one who comes bearing this message is treated like a madman – although he is the only one in touch with the new reality. Or in Heller's fine turn of phrase, 'he is the madman, breaking with his sinister news into the marketplace complacency of the pharisees of unbelief'.[17]

Here the madman fell silent and looked again at his listeners: and they too were silent and stared at him in astonishment. At last he threw his lantern on the ground, and it broke into pieces and went out. 'I have come too early' he said then; 'my time is not yet. This tremendous event is still on its way, still wandering; it has not yet reached the ears of men. Lightning and thunder require time; the light of the stars requires time; deeds, though done, still require time to be seen and heard. This deed is more distant from them than the most distant stars – and yet they have done it themselves.' It has been related further that on the same day the madman forced his way into several churches and there struck up his *requiem aeternam deo*. Led out and called to account, he is said always to have replied nothing but: 'What after all are these churches now if they are not the tombs and sepulchres of God?'

We can see from these passages just how complex is the meaning of the phrase 'God is dead'. It has led to a too hasty description of Nietzsche as an atheist. That he was, but such a categorization is misleading when it places him superficially in the same bag as the irreligious. Heidegger asks the question, 'Which God is dead?' 'The God of "morality", the Christian God is dead – the "Father" in whom we seek sanctuary, the "Personality" with whom we negotiate and bare our hearts, the "Judge" with whom we adjudicate, the "Paymaster" from whom we receive our virtues' reward, that God with whom we "do business".' Nietzsche does not belong with the irreligious who deify progress to bestow meaning on their meaningless lives. He is not one of the godless who, as Heidegger concludes, 'have never struggled to find a god, and never can'.[18] We have deplored the lack of interest among philosophers in the place of religion in Nietzsche's life and thought. It is of some significance that Erich Heller, one of the most perceptive writers about Nietzsche, declares that Nietzsche's philosophy begins with the death of God. He catches the gulf which separates Nietzsche at this point from a merely intellectual scepticism or, in Heidegger's phrase, 'supercilious atheism'.[19] Heller concludes, 'it is like a cry mingled of despair and triumph, reducing, by comparison, the whole story of atheism and agnosticism before and after him to the level of respectable mediocrity and making it sound like a collection of announcements by bankers who regret they are unable to invest in an unsafe proposition'.[20]

Autobiographically speaking, Nietzsche's philosophy begins with the loss of religion, not an argument against the existence of God, but with the death of God. It is not simply irreligion, nor simply atheism. Above all it is not nihilism. There must be a new philosophy for life, a new basis on which the truly human life can be lived. Religion was an obstacle to this new philosophy, but the end of religion achieves nothing in itself. It merely clears the decks for what must now come about. The great critic of religion sets himself the task of replacing religion, providing an alternative to it. Against all expectations, the death of God is experienced not as a cause for despair, but as the occasion of hope. The outcome is not Schopenhauerian pessimism, but Dionysian affirmation. The death of God is the loss of foundation. In consequence, as we noted above: '*the* beautiful exists just as little as does *the* good, or *the* true.' In the following three chapters we shall follow the path by which Nietzsche seeks to provide a new foundation for truth, morality and aesthetics. Without them there can be no meaning and significance in human life and nihilism beckons.

3

The Shadow of God

In the context of our day-to-day lives any intellectual enquiry is likely to be focussed on gaining new knowledge, whether it be knowledge about computers or vacation destinations. And having come by knowledge in a variety of ways, we occasionally have to verify that what we think we know is true. In an academic context it is disconcerting to be confronted by epistemological questions concerning how we know what we know, and the conditions required for truth-claims to be meaningful. Philosophers can and have managed to get themselves into contradiction and error in such matters, especially when they have formulated definitions for the verification of propositions and tests for the meaningfulness of language – formulations which themselves fail the definitions and tests. A particularly blatant case was that of Logical Positivism. Warnock uses a dramatic metaphor and a concluding pun to describe the process by which the author of the *Tractatus Logico-Philosophicus* finally came to recognize the inner contradiction on which the whole movement was based.

> Thus Wittgenstein was led to, and heroically drew, the conclusion that most of what he himself had said was senseless; in an odd way, to understand his own book was to see that this was so, and to realize that, although perhaps he had succeeded in *showing* something, he had not really *said* anything at all. This thesis, laid quite early like a sort of time-bomb in the basement of Logical Atomism, escaped notice, or was nervously disregarded, for a number of years; when it went off its inventor and fortunately many others had already transferred themselves to other premises.[1]

Nietzsche seems to get himself into a comparable position by his denial that there is such a thing as truth at all, but this is only one of many major contradictions which appear throughout his works. His critics have been quick to point these out: they cannot be ignored, even by his most sympathetic expositors. However, his contradictions, unlike those in the example just given, seem to arise not as simple mistakes but from his treatment of his subject and his own premises. As Jaspers concedes, 'self-contradiction is the fundamental ingredient in Nietzsche's thought ...'² Nietzsche admitted as much. 'This thinker needs no one to refute him: he does that for himself.'³ But of his many contradictions his pronouncements on truth seem particularly damaging. It is not a single instance of contradiction: it threatens to undermine every statement which he makes since presumably he believes them all to be true. Maudemarie Clark is representative of many who have observed this point. 'Nietzsche's apparent nihilism in regard to truth thus threatens the coherence of his critique of morality, and of his entire philosophy – insofar as the latter commits Nietzsche to certain truths while at the same time it denies that there are any truths.'⁴ Since Nietzsche must himself have been aware of this point, we have to conclude that the contradiction has its own significance within his overall project. Erich Heller assures us that 'his contradictions are far too obvious to be looked upon as mistakes or oversights. They are the outcome of his fear of curtailing articulation; and such curtailment is, lamentably and unavoidably, the result of logical consistency, as it is of any imposition of a philosophical system upon the totality of things.'⁵ While the first part of this statement is true, Heller fails to identify the fundamental reason for contradiction in Nietzsche. As Jaspers advises, 'instead of being occasionally provoked by contradiction, one should pursue contradictoriness to its source'.⁶ What then is the source?

Nietzsche's rejection of the idea of truth does not arise from epistemology, but theology – or rather from the loss of it. For Nietzsche the very idea of truth arises from metaphysical and theological assumptions. With the death of God, with the loss of religious belief in its Christian and Platonic forms, we are now cast adrift on a sea of becoming. 'Everything has become: there are no eternal facts, just as there are no absolute truths.'[7] Instead of the death of God he might as well have written of the death of being, though that expression loses something of its power, shock and impact in the metaphysical translation. As we bob about on the sea of becoming we experience flux, change, uncertainty – the very features of the ancient Greek philosophy of Miletus, developed by Leucippus and Democritus, the father of materialist philosophy, a philosophy of becoming which was defeated by Socrates and his assistant, Plato the master metaphysician of being. Increasingly Nietzsche attacked the figure of Socrates as the source of degeneracy in European philosophy.

We should note that as an undergraduate Nietzsche had read F.A. Lange's *History of Materialism*. He knew of the works of Feuerbach, the so-called (erroneously so-called) 'father of German materialism', whose turning of Hegel on his head, the critique of idealism as projection, pointed Marx towards materialism. Marx had published his *Capital* three years before Lange's work appeared. As Karl Fortlage observed about the growing influence of materialism, 'a new world is settling itself in the minds of men. It goes about like a virus.'[8] However, the most radical materialism in Germany at that time was not left-wing Hegelianism, but medical materialism, and it is of some significance that Nietzsche attempted to trace such phenomena as morality and religion back not to anthropology but *physiology*. More of this later, but for once Nietzsche is too modest as he describes his reversal of the great tradition. As Heidegger correctly observes, it is much more radical than 'standing all of Plato's statements on their heads, as it were'.[9] It is for this reason that Heidegger's insistence that Nietzsche's primary concern is for being seems not so much mistaken as wilful. However, Heidegger is not above having it both ways. 'All Being is for Nietzsche a Becoming.'[10] But is this Nietzsche or is it Heidegger? Later he admits that the ontological question 'remains as foreign to Nietzsche as it does to the history of thought prior to him',[11] adding rather candidly that his goal in reading Nietzsche is not simply exposition, but 'to bring his thought out into the open and *make it fruitful* ...' (italics added).[12] But in this homely metaphor of everyday gardening folk we must ask which is the rooted tree and which the alien graft.

What we see depends on where we stand: what we know depends on where we are at this time and place. The case of mathematics might seem an exception. Indeed in a letter written to his sister only a few weeks after that fateful Easter occasion, Nietzsche responds to her view that truth lies with those things that are more difficult to believe. 'With respect to your axiom that truth is always on the more difficult side, I am willing to concede this to you at least in part. Even so, it is difficult to conceive that $2 \times 2 \neq 4$. Is it on that account more true?'[13] Perhaps we should say that it is correct, rather than true. We have just quoted Nietzsche's view that 'there are no eternal facts, just as there are no absolute truths'. This comes from *Human All Too Human*, published in 1886. Some eight years previously Friedrich Engels had published his *Anti-Dühring*, including a chapter on 'Eternal Truths'. These, he admits, tend to be platitudes. In his *Materialism and Empirio-Criticism* Lenin recalls that even this was not enough for Bogdanov. Engels had given the example, 'Napoleon died on May 5, 1821,' to which Bogdanov replies in some exasperation, 'What sort of truth is that?' 'Are platitudes truths? Truth is a vital organizing of experience; it leads us somewhere in our activity and provides a point of support in the struggle of life.'[14] This distinction catches something of Nietzsche's concerns. Statements of fact may be said to be correct: they hardly merit the description 'true'. Truth is proved in 'the struggle of life'. In such a struggle Nietzsche was deeply and existentially involved. Indeed this becomes something of a criterion of authentic philosophy as opposed to professional work-a-day philosophy: 'the epitaph of university philosophy – "it disturbed nobody"'.[15] For Nietzsche the trouble began with Socrates, 'the great exemplar of that theoretical man',[16] the man who believed that it was possible by reason alone to 'plumb the

farthest abysses of being ...'[17] The divorce between reason and
life leads him to a simile worthy of Kierkegaard. 'The man of
theory, having begun to dread the consequences of his views, no
longer dares to commit himself freely to the icy flood of existence,
but runs nervously up and down the bank.'[18]

Modern philosophy begins with Descartes, with a man who
sought the truth by first of all secreting himself within the belly
of a wood-burning stove. (Freud, Freud, thou shouldst have been
here at this time!) Nietzsche stands within this question-
ing tradition. He wishes 'to implant a sense of suspicion and
reductionism into the souls of man'.[19] This master of suspicion
apparently follows the Cartesian example by insisting that 'all
that exists that can be denied deserves to be denied'[20], but
Nietzsche eventually turns the whole approach through 180
degrees: *vivo ergo cogito*.[21] With the death of God, with the demise
of theology, the ancient 'queen of the sciences', philosophy steps
forward to catch the sceptre as it falls. But it does not represent a
quest for truth pursued in the struggle of life. Its struggle is with
the grammar of the word 'perhaps', and as such attracts the
derision of the combatant for whom life is an issue.

> Philosophy reduced to 'theory of knowledge', actually no
> more than a timid epochism and abstinence: a philosophy that
> does not even get over the threshold and painfully *denies* itself
> the right of entry – that is philosophy at its last gasp, an end,
> an agony, something that arouses pity. How could such a
> philosophy rule![22]

At the outset, in attempting to distance himself from religion,
Nietzsche expressed great confidence in the method of natural
science,[23] but as his philosophy developed he came to see that
even modern science is dependent on the previous world-view. It
has 'erroneous articles of faith',[24] including the belief that there
are things, substances and bodies.

> But you will have gathered what I am driving at, namely, that
> it is still a metaphysical faith upon which our faith in science

rests – that even we seekers after knowledge today, we godless
and anti-metaphysicians still take our fire from the flame lit by
a faith that is thousands of years old, that Christian faith which
was also the faith of Plato, that God is truth, that truth
is divine. But what if this should become more and more
incredible, if nothing should prove to be divine any more
unless it were error, blindness, the lie – if God himself should
prove to be our most enduring lie?[25]

Other writers have since then pointed to the difficulty faced by
science in establishing its own foundations. Husserl, for example,
in his essay on 'Philosophy as Rigorous Science', warns against
'naturalism'. The decision to adopt the scientific method and use
it is not itself a scientific decision.

He is, however an idealist, who sets up and (so he thinks)
justifies theories, which deny precisely what he presupposes
in his idealistic way of acting, whether it be in constructing
theories or in justifying and recommending values or practical
norms as the most beautiful and the best.[26]

Similarly Heidegger, who knew less about science and more
about metaphysics, addressed the question of 'The Ostensibly
Scientific Procedure of Proof'. 'What are the "facts" of natural
science and of all science, if not particular appearances interpreted according to explicit, tacit, or utterly unknown metaphysical principles, principles that reflect a doctrine concerning
beings as a whole?'[27] However, Nietzsche presses on beyond
Husserl and Heidegger and this simple though important point.
Jaspers, in more existentialist mode, assures us that 'scientific
cognition can provide no goals whatever for life'.[28] But in
presenting Nietzsche's position, he has to go even beyond the
philosophy of existence, to religion itself. 'Truth is not at first
pursued merely for the sake of the objective validity that it
acquires in science; its pursuit is incited by *belief*.'[29] This
accurately represents Nietzsche: 'All actual striving for truth has
entered the world as a result of the struggle for sacred
assurance.'[30] It is in this sense that for Nietzsche the crisis in

epistemology begins – like every other crisis in his philosophy – with theology, or the loss of it, that is with the death of God. As Jaspers sums up Nietzsche's position, 'once godlessness becomes a reality, the interest in truth will finally cease'.[31] This is an extraordinary claim, and if it had been made by a theologian it would have been hailed as epistemological imperialism on a cosmic scale. However, the claim is made not by an advocate of theology, but by its most profound critic. Unlike its more superficial critics, the profundity of this analysis is as disconcerting as it is incisive.

What if 'God himself should prove to be our most enduring lie'? It is tempting to think as follows. There is truth and there is error, and then there is the lie. The lie is distinguished by being a human construct. Truth and error are opposites, but they stand together as the lineaments of reality, a reality which is there to be explored, discovered, uncovered, comprehended. By comparison the lie is neither truth nor simple error: it is a deliberate attempt to disguise the truth, to invent a truth, to impose a false image upon reality. It is the projection of human subjectivity with the intention that it should replace the divine objectivity. It is tempting to think thus, but nothing could be further from Nietzsche's understanding. What if there is no such distinction? What if the human projection and the divine objectivity are one and the same, what if 'God himself should prove to be our most enduring lie'? What if in this respect at least there is no essential difference between the truth and the lie: both are human projections upon an indifferent reality. Once the premises of the projection have been accepted, the conclusions seem to follow inevitably. 'What are man's truth ultimately? Merely his irrefutable errors.'[32] For Nietzsche there is no truth lying there to be discovered: truth has to be created.[33] Using a recurring metaphor we might say that like a spider man spins truth from within himself and spreads it upon the external world to entrap and control it. In an early essay Nietzsche draws the conclusion that there is a play-back effect: in science man discovers comforting and confirming structures in the world, uncovering only that which he has unconsciously placed there in the first place – 'so that it is we who thereby make the impression on ourselves'.[34]

With this temptation out of the way, with this last vestige of security denied, the way is clear for Nietzsche to attack a now defenceless position in the most shocking, threatening and apparently destructive terms. This is the time for passion and even contradiction: stand clear. The truth does not describe the real, but dishonestly disguises reality from us. It does not deserve to be called 'error' and let off with a caution. No, viewed in this way the truth is itself the lie. There is no truth – and that is the truth of it. '*We have need of lies* in order to conquer this reality, this "truth", that is, in order to live.'[35] 'Metaphysics, morality, religion, science' – he tells us – 'merit consideration only as various forms of lies: with their help one can have *faith* in life.'[36] All of them take their fire from that ancient idealist faith. But now that faith, which revealed the truth, is exposed as itself based on the great lie. Does that mean the end of faith? No, that way lies nihilism. Now with 'cheerfulness' Nietzsche seeks a new 'faith in life', a faith which arises in the struggle of life. The question for a new truth begins by doubting all previous truths. 'Truth will have no other gods beside it. Belief in truth begins with doubt as to all truths believed in hitherto.'[37]

There is no fixed, timeless, changeless divine frame of reference any more, which formerly achieved several things at once: the integrity of the subject, the guarantee that there is a true knowledge of the subject, and the availability of a norm against which our partial provisional knowledge can be judged. The way we view language discloses the religious and metaphysical context in which it was developed: 'every word is a prejudice'.[38] Knowledge is always an interpretation or, in his favourite metaphor, 'every word is also a mask'.[39] Nevertheless it is possible to hold that this perspectivism is true, while rejecting the possibility of truth in its old religio-metaphysical form. There were no truths: it came to be assumed that the image and the reality were one. As Nietzsche turned his attention from philology to philosophy, one of his first essays, written in 1873, was entitled 'On

Truth and Falsity in Their Extramoral Sense'. In it he tells us that 'truths are illusions of which one has forgotten that they are illusions; worn-out metaphors which have become powerless to affect the sense; coins with their images effaced and now no longer of account as coins but merely as metal'.[40] But as we saw from the 'Cheerfulness' passage quoted in full in Chapter 2, with Nietzsche no cloud is unlined, no disaster unmitigated. The collapse of the old clears space for the building of the new. When Nietzsche claims that 'nothing is true, everything is permitted'[41] he is welcoming the clearing of the decks to explore new possibilities which were previously ruled out. This striking aphorism, this slogan of 'the invincible Society of Assassins',[42] like so many other unguarded statements by Nietzsche, is liable to abuse. But Jaspers points us through the distortions to its precise meaning. 'Taken by itself it expresses complete lack of obligation; it is an invitation to individual caprice, sophistry, and criminality. But to Nietzsche it represents the emancipation of the deepest and therefore truest of human motives, unimpeded by any of those forms of so-called truth which, being fixed and final, are actually untrue.'[43] In the variety of contexts in which these matters are discussed, the word 'truth' is being used in different ways. They seem contradictory – are contradictory – if they are viewed in isolation from Nietzsche's total project, if they are reduced to an exercise in logic. With the death of being, there is no truth any more, no metaphysical truth. But by this Nietzsche means that the supposed metaphysical truth is now shown to have been delusion. The loss of such truth might be a shock initially, but it frees us to enter a new experience of becoming, which has its own truth, truth of a very different order. It is an end to 'the tyranny of the true'.[44]

As we have seen, the shock may be an obstacle to giving up the comforting world of being. This 'demand for certainty', as Nietzsche identifies it, is to be seen as a form of scientific positivism, which in its desire for a 'prop' is happy to be assured by evidence which is less than sound. It is the expression of an instinct 'which, to be sure, does not create religious, metaphysical

systems, and convictions of all kinds – but conserves them'.[45]
This is a constant theme in Nietzsche, that even after the death of
God and the rejection of religious doctrine and practice, it is
virtually impossible to be rid of the remnants of this view of
reality. In several of his works, following the example of
Schopenhauer, but no doubt under the more direct influence of
Paul Deussen, Nietzsche refers to Indian religion and philosophy,
but especially to Buddhism. In *The Gay Science* he mentions the
shadow of the Buddha, without elaborating. It is worth reflecting
on its source. The reference is to a legend from North India,
found in several Sanskrit sources, describing how the Buddha
overcame the evil naga king Gopala. Gopala, under the influence
of the Buddha, forsook his previous ways, but in his new life was
dismayed when the time came for the Buddha to leave. However,
to preserve him in his new path, the Buddha left the imprint of
his shadow on the wall of Gopala's cave, a shadow which was not
dark, as might have been expect, but luminous.[46] Nietzsche
concludes that even after his death, God will cast a shadow for
thousands of years. God is dead, but 'we still have to vanquish his
shadow too'.[47] This continuing influence preserves many in a
religious way of thinking of which they may be unaware. The
assumption that truth is truth is truth, in forgetfulness of
Wittgenstein's warning, 'let the use teach you the meaning',[48] is
evidence that not a few critics are still living in the metaphysical
world of being. As we have seen, Nietzsche was well acquainted
with contemporaries who thought themselves sufficiently
sophisticated to have rooted religion from their lives: they had yet
to root it out of their minds. As he observed, 'I fear we are not
getting rid of God because we still believe in grammar.'[49] He
might have said, logic. As Michel Haar observes, Nietzsche's
discourse is 'an attempt to encourage disbelief in the laws of logic
and the rules of grammar (the final refuge of a defunct theology)
…'[50] Josef Simon comments on the same point, though I fear
he distorts Nietzsche's analysis as, for his own reasons, he
translates from Platonic to Aristotelian categories.

Thinking in traditional categories, as for example in the categories of substantiality and causality, therefore results not directly from language but from a specific interpretation of language that we believe to be justified. This is the 'belief in grammar' with which as is well known Nietzsche associates belief in God. Whoever 'believes' in the ontological relevance of the categories of substantiality and causality will necessarily 'believe' in a highest substance of all substances and in a cause of all causes. Nietzsche does not say that this belief is overcome, but fears we would 'not get rid of God, because we still believe in grammar'.[51]

4

Revaluation of All Values

The death of God means an end to truth, to absolute truth in its religious and metaphysical forms, though not to truth in its perspectival form. The death of God also means the end of moral values, values which come to us from elsewhere, from religion and from idealism. We have already noted in Chapter 2 that even among those who are aware of this situation the majority would like to continue as if nothing had changed. Nietzsche dismisses philosophers who construct a 'rational ground of morality', which is in reality only 'a scholarly form of *faith* in the prevailing morality'.[1] The actual values look all too familiar. 'Naiveté: as if morality could survive when the *God* who sanctions it is missing! The "beyond" is absolutely necessary if faith in morality is to be maintained.'[2] Actually the situation is more complex and convoluted than that. Such people hope that morality will occupy the place of God. 'Those who have abandoned God cling that much more firmly to the faith in morality.'[3] In this context we might reflect on the number of 'causes' which have sprung up in modern secular society, from the friends of the natterjack toad to the mink liberation front. It is not whether such actions might reasonably be undertaken, but their transformation into 'causes' to which people can 'devote' themselves. If the shadow of the absent God continues through language, it is also present through the new devotion.

The death of God removes the basis for all traditional codes of morality. Recognition of this fact may be too disturbing or alarming for the many, but Nietzsche is concerned above all to liberate mankind – or at least that minority who are capable of responding to the possibility and challenge of freedom. It is important that they face up to the crisis and know how to respond to it. 'The entire idealism of mankind hitherto is on the point of changing into nihilism – into the belief in absolute *worth*lessness, i.e. *meaninglessness*. The destruction of ideals, the new desert.'[4] When the death of God can no longer be denied or ignored, when its full consequences are at last experienced, then those foolish virgins who are not prepared for it will fall into nihilism, will fall into the arms of Arthur Schopenhauer and his solution – suicide. Nihilism does not arise from 'epidemics of being fed-up' (*Satthaben*):[5] it is not the outcome of feeling down, unhappy or sorry for oneself. It is a state in which life has no aim, in which the question '"why?" finds no answer'.[6] This loss of hope, loss of energy, this loss of control is nihilism, *passive* nihilism. The 'nothing' in this nihilism refers to the negative experience which follows from the death of God, it is unmitigated loss, without compensation.

This is Nietzsche in free-fall: no pit too bottomless, no picture too black, no prediction too apocalyptic. He believes it, this 'logic of terror', and wishes us both to believe it and experience it without any amelioration. But we also know that he has an alternative waiting, there is a way back; in certain circumstances 'cheerfulness' can break out. By calling this *passive* nihilism he raises in our minds the possibility of an alternative, *active* nihilism.[7] When as a student in Leipzig Nietzsche read *The World as Will and Idea*, it seemed as if Schopenhauer had written it with him in mind. It spoke to his condition. Together with Wagner, Schopenhauer was a powerful influence on his development as he moved from philology to philosophy. As late as 1870 he could write to Carl von Gersdorff: 'For me, all that is best and most beautiful is associated with the names of Schopenhauer and Wagner ...'[8] Yet in both cases it was even more important that he make a break with these two luminaries of a previous situation. As so often with Nietzsche, his criticism is less that a thinker has gone in the wrong direction than that he has stopped short. With respect to the truth, Schopenhauer still continued as an atheist to seek the absolute truth, the truth which only belongs to God. And now with respect to the value of life, Schopenhauer could not conceive of the necessary turn. By continuing to accept the morality of religion the death of God led to the loss of meaning in life. This was the parting of the ways. 'At the same time I grasped that my instinct went in the opposite direction from Schopenhauer's: toward a *justification of life*, even at its most terrible, ambiguous, and mendacious; for this I had the formula "Dionysian".'[9] If Nietzsche can call himself a 'thorough-going nihilist'[10] it is as good as rejecting nihilism – or at least insisting that nihilism is a stage along the way, but not the outcome. With the experience of the death of God, only those who go through it, who fully experience and accept it, only they can supersede it. So too with nihilism. The death of God leads to the end of all truth – in its traditional religio-metaphysical context – but that opens up the possibility of truth in another context, the truth of becoming, a truth created by man, a truth which comes from this world and not from elsewhere. The death of God means the end of all values – those of the religio-metaphysical world-view – but that opens up the possibility of moral values which come from this world and not from elsewhere. Nietzsche has a name for this project: 'the revaluation of all values'. The revaluation of all values is 'a movement that in some future will take the place of this perfect nihilism – but presupposes it, logically and psychologically, and certainly can come only after and out of it'.[11] Only those who have experienced life bereft of the meaning, worth and value bestowed upon it from another world, only they can undertake this momentous task – the replacing of traditional moral values with another set of values. These new values must have their own basis and justification, not only independent of religious values but in all probability standing in stark contrast, even contradiction to those which have had to be surrendered.

Nietzsche's *magnum opus* was to be entitled *The Revaluation of All Values*. It was not completed, but throughout his writings we can recognize elements of this project. 'Everything is false!

Everything is permitted.'[12] Nihilism opens up the door to any kind of behaviour, without consideration or restraint – if it has the energy for it. But Nietzsche will not rest content with this licence or anarchy. He rejects external constraint, heteronomous ethics, but as with truth, he affirms the morality which comes from within life itself. Rather provocatively he can refer to himself as an 'immoralist',[13] but by this he refers to his rejection of traditional morality, not to a rejection of all moral values. When the old religious truths are set aside, a new form of moral life is possible for the first time. As Jaspers says, this represents 'the emancipation of the deepest and therefore truest of human motives, unimpeded by any of those forms of so-called truth which, being fixed and final, are actually untrue'.[14] The 'thou shalt' is a voice to which he still responds: 'we too are still *men of conscience*'.[15]

Nietzsche has set aside passive nihilism. He will favour active nihilism. However, we could imagine a form of active, virulent, nihilism which sets aside the merest remnants and vestiges of morality and restraint. By comparison with *this* active nihilism, Nietzsche looks like a sheep in wolf's clothing. Be that as it may, he seeks a new basis for moral judgments, without reference to religion or metaphysics. Previously these values had been given to mankind as the will of God, or eternal Platonic forms. The two go together: he reckons that 'Christianity is Platonism for the people',[16] and judges that Plato 'is still Europe's greatest misfortune'.[17] As we have seen, the emancipation from the rule of God does not lead to an easy life. Now emancipation from the divine law will bring its own demands. 'The time has come when we have to pay for having been Christians for two thousand years ...'[18]

If Nietzsche rejects the supernatural origin of values, what then might be their natural basis? Kaufmann suggests a starting point. 'Nietzsche was aroused from his dogmatic slumber by Darwin, as Kant had been by Hume a century earlier.'[19] As Nietzsche asks in his earliest book, 'what kind of figure does ethics cut once we decide to view it in the biological perspective?'[20] If moral values arise from the earth rather than descend from the heavens, then what are their physiological and social origins and functions? If we reject the idealist account of moral values, what are their materialist origins? At what level must the question begin? Nietzsche tells us that we require 'a chemistry of the moral, religious and aesthetic conceptions and sensations'.[21] What is going on here? What has morality to do with chemistry? In 1882 he wrote to Erwin Rohde of his plan to become a full-time student again, studying science at the University of Vienna. He wished to 'consecrate' the rest of his life to this study.[22] Science of course was not his fundamental interest: it was the path to a deeper interest. This plan was not carried out, and we can only speculate on the prospect of a young instructor faced with a tutorial group which included F. Nietzsche.

In his quest for the natural, human basis of moral values Nietzsche is drawing on an assumption which he makes again and again, an assumption the implications of which are much wider than this immediate subject of morality. The assumption is that values express needs, needs of a physiological or even chemical nature. He discusses his attempt 'to understand moral judgments as symptoms and sign languages which betray the processes of physiological prosperity or failure ...'[23] This is throughgoing materialism, but it is not dehumanizing. It is reductionist, but is it merely clearing the decks of an unnecessary religio-metaphysical superstructure? He can also say that 'moralities too are only a *sign-language of the emotions*',[24] but this simply begs the question about the physiological basis of the emotions. Heller writes of 'the persistent suspicion that all "higher values" are merely satisfactions of psychological needs, dams built against the onrush of emptiness, of the "nihil", the spiritual vacuity created by the "death of God"'.[25] This is true so far as it goes, but Nietzsche presses beyond psychology to physiology and also implies that this unconscious process has a long history – which *ends* with the death of God. Beyond a psychological account of the origins of morality, is there a chemical account, which 'would end up by revealing that in this domain too the most glorious colours are derived from base, indeed from despised materials'?[26] Is it possible that those elements in human existence which were previously suspect and condemned are in fact the roots of the 'spiritual' values? Not for the first time the offsprings which had made good and become socially acceptable would be embarrassed at the lives of their parents.

An action is moral because it meets certain moral criteria – but what makes criteria moral? There are certain primary levels of discourse which cannot rely on reference to further levels. Moral criteria, according to Nietzsche, have to refer to non-moral factors. It is for this reason that he claims that 'there are no moral phenomena, there is only a moral interpretation of these phenomena. This interpretation is of extra-moral origin':[27]indeed we stand on the threshold of a period which should be called 'extra-moral'.[28] There are no moral facts, only interpretations, but for Nietzsche up till now these were 'misinterpretations',[29] semiotics which were mistaken for literal accounts. Following Feuerbach before him, he saw the value in morality to be its embodiment of human self-understanding.[30] Stated in this way, it is clear why values will have to be revalued. The new values will stand in contradiction to the old. As Jaspers indicates, Nietzsche 'wishes to substitute "nature" for duty, the "innocence of becoming" for what the Christians call grace and redemption from sin, and the historical reality of the individual for what is accepted as universally valid by men in general'.[31] The new moralist will seem to conventional morality to be indeed an 'immoralist'. Having said that, Nietzsche is not entirely consistent in dealing with the relationship between the old and new moralities. He obviously wishes to get away from the idea of morality as 'submission'[32] or obedience to heteronomous law tables. 'To speak of right and wrong *per se* makes no sense at all. No act of violence, rape, exploitation, destruction is intrinsically "unjust", since life itself is violent, rapacious, exploitative, and destructive and cannot be conceived otherwise.'[33] The point with which he begins is reasonable. A slap might be immoral if with it a man intends to coerce a woman into complying with his will. A slap might be an act of concern if it is to bring a sufferer out of a hysterical fit. But rape is always immoral, if only because the word by definition describes a violation for which there can never be any moral justification. Common sense supervenes.

> It goes without saying that I do not deny – unless I am a fool – that many actions called immoral ought to be avoided and resisted, or that many called moral ought to be done and encouraged – but I think the one should be encouraged and the other avoided *for other reasons than hitherto*. We have to *learn to think differently* – or at least, perhaps very late on, to attain even more: *to feel differently*.[34]

We shall presently discuss these other reasons and other feelings, but as we shall see, there are still many actions which will be revalued, so that what was previously called evil will not be called evil *for other reasons*, but will be called *good*.

Nietzsche rejects the metaphysical scheme that there is a higher world than this one. Similarly he rejects the corollary that human beings are most human when they have divested themselves of their animal natures. His whole philosophy requires an end to this devaluing of the material and the natural: his intention is 'to "naturalize" humanity'.[35] 'We no longer trace the origins of man in the "spirit", in the "divinity"; we have placed him back among the animals.'[36] 'The body,' he tells us, 'is a more astonishing idea than the old "soul".'[37] Nietzsche therefore begins not with the supposed weaknesses of animal life, but with its strengths. An example is aggression. An animal requires aggression and assertiveness in order to survive and in order to achieve its goals. Without this aggression it would die and the species would die out. In its animal context, aggression is a virtue, it has value. It is good, and its absence or loss would be bad. Instead of seeing an idealist opposition between the animal and the human, Nietzsche concentrates on the continuity between them. Instead of condemning aggression, as in conventional morality, he claims that it is a virtue, a moral good. Thus in Zarathustra's Discourses, the prophet tells his hearers, 'once you had passions and called them evil, but now you have only your virtues: they grew out of your passions.'[38] 'Good actions are sublimated (*sublimirte*) evil ones ...'[39] However, the transition from animal to human is marked by sublimation. The instinct or power of aggression in its animal form now assumes a different human form. But there is continuity. The animal is not condemned but transcended: 'I too speak of a "return to nature", although it is not really a going-back but a going-up ...'[40] Nietzsche is claiming that the animal virtues are not set aside or rejected: this would be fatal. Rather they continue, but in a transformed, refocussed way, as appropriate for human life. The self-assertiveness will now involve self-control. Nietzsche is making an important distinction between his position and conventional morality. It condemns the passions. He is not advocating that human beings simply return to animal forms of existence, but rather that the passions are recognized, sublimated and put to use in human life.

> Overcoming of the passions. The man who has overcome his passion has entered into possession of the most fertile grounds, like the colonist who has mastered the forests and swamps. To sow the seeds of good spiritual works in the soil of the subdued passions is then the immediate urgent task. The overcoming itself is only a means, not a goal; if it is not so viewed, all kinds of weeds and devilish nonsense will quickly spring up in this rich soil now unoccupied and soon there will be more rank confusion than there ever was before.[41]

This imagery is strangely reminiscent of the warning of Jesus about a demon cast out, who since nothing is put in its place, returns 'and brings seven other spirits more evil than himself ...'[42] We can see here the revaluation of existing values, but also the natural basis of the new values. 'All virtues are really redefined passions and enhanced states.'[43] When we hear self-assertiveness praised we are perhaps uncomfortable, because it is against conventional morality. We should love our neighbour. Nietzsche begins at another point, criticizing the idea of the neighbour as very weak in our lives. 'Egoism is not evil ...':[44] love of self is

natural. Rather provocatively, therefore, Zarathustra in his
teaching 'glorified selfishness, the sound healthy selfishness that
issues from a mighty soul'.[45] He declares 'the ego healthy and
holy' and declares 'selfishness glorious'.[46] *The Gay Science* opens
with a further point, reminiscent of an argument in Adam Smith's
work on *The Theory of Moral Sentiments* [Part IV]:

> Even the most harmful man may really be the most useful
> when it comes to the preservation of the species; for he
> nurtures either in himself or in others, through his effects,
> instincts without which humanity would long have become
> feeble or rotten.[47]

The new virtues, the natural virtues, begin with the passions,
which of course are sublimated and transformed. It will be clear
from this that Nietzsche is not substituting a new set of concepts
by which to judge behaviour. The new values relate to new ways
of living. As Deleuze puts it, 'evaluations, in essence, are not
values but ways of being, modes of existence of those who judge
and evaluate, serving as principles for the values on the basis of
which they judge'.[48] He goes on to tell us that a moral system will
not make the break with the past evaluations: 'morality is the continuation of religion but by other means'.[49]

For conventional morality the natural is always a source of
suspicion and condemnation. 'Christianity,' Nietzsche declares in
The Anti-Christ, 'has excommunicated all the fundamental
instincts.'[50] By contrast, in *Twilight of the Idols*, he tells us that 'all
naturalism in morality, that is, all healthy morality, is dominated
by an instinct of life ...'[51] For the new order, 'one acts perfectly
only when one acts instinctively ...'[52] It is for this reason that he
claims 'one must destroy morality if one is to liberate life'.[53]
Conventional morality has persuaded us that we should distrust
our instincts in favour of our reason, but our reason operates
within a religious or metaphysical world-view. And as we have
seen, Nietzsche welcomes the death of God and the end of metaphysics. In an echo of Francis Bacon, *Novum Organum
Scientiarum* (1620), he sees the ideal world as a world of idols:[54]

the time of the death of God marks the end of the age of idols, the ideals or truth of another world.[55] The *Götterdämmerung* and the *Götzendämmerung* go together, Wagner's *Twilight of the Gods* and Nietzsche's *Twilight of Idols*.

In the revaluation of all values Nietzsche therefore begins with the question, 'can all values not be turned round, and is good perhaps evil …?'[56] What we find disturbing in Nietzsche arises from the fact that he is posing an alternative to conventional moral judgments. In aesthetics, as in morality, the higher values have been those which derive from the presupposition that the spiritual is to be preferred to the material, the human to our previous animal life, a set of opposites which reveal 'a prejudice as to what spirit is'.[57] Nietzsche's revaluation calls noble what is natural and what was previously condemned: 'noble values have been designated temptations'.[58] He is therefore seeking to return to the natural life of mankind, the instinctual life, liberated from the inhibitions of conventional morality. Everywhere he sees interference. Religion condemns the natural, idealism devalues it, socialism exhibits a secular form of religious condemnation. He therefore rejects 'the entire morality of improvement',[59] which begins with Socrates, 'the pied piper of Athens'[60] and runs through Christianity into its modern metamorphoses. Nietzsche enters as a defender of mankind. He gives us an assurance in the Foreword to *Ecce Homo*: 'The last thing I would promise would be to "improve" mankind.'[61] However, as we shall see he does in fact wish mankind to change, but in the sense of fulfilling its potential, not in the sense of rejecting its nature to wander down an alien path. If previously truth was not discovered, but created, in the struggle of life, now values are not received but created in the struggle to liberate life. There are, however, various struggles going on and we shall examine the place of three such struggles in the formation of moral values.

First of all, there is the struggle against idealism in its metaphysical and religious forms. The implication is that the natural life of mankind has been distorted by the advent of the improvers, those who observe life and condemn it, those who compare the

natural life with an ideal – a non-existent ideal life as lived in a
non-existent ideal world. The values which Nietzsche advocates
are found in the struggle against the distorting influence of the
ideal world. Again and again he defends the individual against the
undue influence and interference of groups or institutions, and in
particular coercion by moral codes which are imposed from elsewhere, arbitrary rules alien to individuals but enforced by
authority, often religious authority. It is for this reason that
Zarathustra challenges his hearers to be responsible for creating
their own moral values. 'Can you furnish yourself with your own
good and evil and hang up your own will above yourself as a law?
Can you be judge of yourself and avenger of your law?'[62] When
dealing with the natural basis of morals, he therefore concentrates
on the individual over against social constructs which distort and
undermine life. This is the first struggle of life.

The second is the struggle of small communities in earlier
times simply to preserve life. Here Nietzsche turns from physiology to anthropology. The individual is now understood as an
integral part of the social group. He does not exist over against the
community, indeed could not survive without being a member.
This might at first seem a very unlikely scenario for Nietzsche,
but it leads him to offer an account of the social basis of moral
values. This is a natural community: the social influence is not
one of improvement. Up to this point Nietzsche has been
describing elements in animal and human nature, such as aggression, self-assertiveness, egotism, instinctual behaviour. But why
should these things be described in moral categories, as if natural
behaviour was morally good? His answer is that the terms 'good'
and 'bad' first arose within natural human communities, and it is
in this context that they received their meaning. In *Human All
Too Human* he tells us that,

> Morality is first of all a means of preserving the community
> and warding off its destruction; then it is a means of preserving
> the community at a certain height and in a certain quality of
> existence.[63]

Nietzsche no doubt has in mind communities living on the edge, threatened by natural disasters and human enemies. In these harsh conditions there is a ruthlessness and single-mindedness about the communal good. Sentiments more typical of easier times would be inappropriate and even dangerous, and therefore bad. One such sentiment to which Nietzsche returns again and again is pity. Pity for conventional morality is good, but in a natural community it is bad. One of his earlier works is entitled *Daybreak: Thoughts on the Prejudices of Morality* (1881). In it he describes the values evident in:

> Decisive eras of history which determined the character of mankind: eras in which suffering counted as virtue, cruelty counted as virtue, dissembling counted as virtue, revenge counted as virtue, denial of reason counted as virtue, while on the other hand well-being was accounted a danger, desire for knowledge was accounted a danger, peace was accounted a danger, pity was accounted a danger, being pitied was accounted an affront, work was accounted an affront, madness was accounted godliness, and change was accounted immoral and pregnant with disaster.[64]

What preserves and enhances the life of a community is good: what threatens or diminishes it is bad. The individual's interests are subordinated to those of the community. Individuals pursuing their own advantage in ways which endangered the tradition or custom would be judged bad.

As we have noted, Nietzsche's critics see his work as full of contradictions. It could be claimed that we have now reached a further example, the contrast of his presentation of the individual in the natural context and the context of social custom. Earlier he approved of the individual who is responsible for creating and achieving his or her own moral values, over against the conventional morality of society. Now he is saying that originally the individual would be immoral if he or she followed their own interests rather than those of the community. However, if we wish to deal with Nietzsche's work sympathetically, it is not difficult to see how these contradictions are overcome. The life-affirming values of the early community are also the values which encourage the individual's affirmation and fulfilment. By contrast the values of the improvers, far from affirming life, deny and condemn it and in consequence prevent the fulfilment of the life of the individual. The individual should therefore espouse the values of life against the values of death, the values of enhancement against those of degeneracy.

There is, however, a third struggle of life, a context very different from that of the improvers or the marginal community. This context is much more familiar to us, namely a society divided into socio-economic classes. Here the struggle is between a ruling class, perhaps an alliance of political and religious interests, and a weaker and impoverished class. This struggle also has an influence on the development of moral values within a society, and the development introduces an important new element. Previously Nietzsche had described an integrated community in which certain life affirming values were called good, but now he enters a distinction which runs throughout his work. He does not regard human societies as uniform. He has a special interest in communities ruled by powerful, noble, aristocratic individuals or classes – even races. Numerically such people are in the minority, but they are strong and wilful enough to control their own lives and also the destinies of the majority. There is no doubt where Nietzsche's sympathies lie, and he describes the majority in turn as the masses or more pejoratively as the 'herd'. Those of the herd are without power or direction for their own lives. Individually they behave as members of a herd, accepting their lot, trying to make the best of it, and submitting to the common will. Not surprisingly the two social classes or ranks give rise to two forms of morality, two contrasting perspectives on moral values: the morality of the master and the morality of the slave. There is no one morality for society: 'there exists an order of rank between man and man, consequently also between morality and morality'.[65]

What is good for the rulers, the noble aristocratic class, is the definition of the moral good. However, their interests are not narrowly defined – tax concessions, box seats at the pantomime of life. Their goods are those life-affirming sentiments and actions which we discussed earlier. In their lives the natural passions are recognized, affirmed, indeed glorified, sublimated and used. This is in stark contrast to, lives of the majority, the 'base, low-minded, and plebeian',[66] the herd. These are the 'ruminants', who without imagination, creativity, courage or authority simply chew over the tradition. Zarathustra hears the Voluntary Beggar preach a crude parody on the Sermon on the Mount. 'If we do not alter and become cows, we shall not enter into the kingdom of heaven. For there is one thing we should learn from them: rumination.'[67] The terms used exhibit clearly the essential elitism of Nietzsche's philosophy. It is not difficult to see why Brandes described his position as 'aristocratic radicalism', or why Nietzsche in spite of himself was charmed by the phrase.[68] There is an ambiguity in the description which implies that Nietzsche is part of the aristocracy he describes. There is no doubt that Nietzsche loved to attach himself to the highest class in society, but that is not entirely relevant to the present exposition. In fairness to him, he admired those noble and aristocratic members of the ruling class who possess and display the life-affirming virtues only when and insofar as they *do* possess and exhibit these features. He is quite clear that at the French Revolution the same class utterly failed to exhibit such qualities.[69] By the same token, the leader of a slave revolt might embody the noble values more evidently. As Nietzsche points out, Epictetus was a slave.[70] He has in mind those who are slaves in their minds, in their souls rather than simply in the eyes of the law. Strictly speaking, when Nietzsche says that those of noble lives should despise the herd, he is speaking about the contempt due to the values of the herd, a recognition of the unworthiness of such a condition. However, in the wrong hands it is easy to quote Nietzsche in support of the ruling class against the oppressed classes, indeed the colonial race against the subject peoples.

Nietzsche's concern is not so much with two different types of morality, as with two very different attitudes to life itself. There is the self-confident attitude of the rulers, the aristocratic self-directed life which affirms the natural values. In contrast, there is the attitude of the slaves: they do not affirm life as it is, because they suffer under it. It is not in their control and they are apprehensive towards it. They are fearful of the rulers who ride roughshod over them; they do not show initiative, they are reactive. More ominously, they watch and wait, they observe and bide their time. They harbour sentiments of revenge.[71] Nietzsche has a term for this attitude, *ressentiment.* He borrows and persistently uses the French form, perhaps because it retains its original intensity: perception through the senses and not simply reflection in the mind. But by using the French term he ensures that it always carries the connotations he intends. *Ressentiment* is a mixture of frustration and fear, it is indignation but always with an element of jealousy. And now the nightmare has come to pass. In the modern world the herd have come to power. They the ruled are now the rulers: their moral judgments govern society. It is from their perspective that the natural values are outlawed and declared evil. The aristocratic and noble values are condemned. But the herd by definition cannot achieve final victory over their previous rulers. They have defeated them in the streets by sheer force of numbers, they have displaced them in parliament by the weight of their votes, but they have not been able to get them out of their minds. The morality of the rulers is consistent: good and bad. But the morality of the herd is more ambiguous. If the rulers look only to themselves, the herd understand themselves only in relation to the rulers. Theirs is the morality not of good and bad, but of *good and evil.*[72] That which was previously called good is now called evil: this is the morality of *ressentiment*, jealousy and the spirit of revenge. As Magnus points out:

In the moral sphere *ressentiment* arises out of the experience of powerlessness, dependency, lack of self-direction and self-control. It finds expression as contempt for the body, beauty and power. In the metaphysical sphere, vengeance becomes aversion to transience, to becoming; aversion to time and temporality.[73]

We seem to have come full circle. On Nietzsche's view it is the aristocratic, noble values which are condemned not only by the herd, but by the improvers, both philosophical and religious. Those who affirm life will be condemned by the herd as evil, out of *ressentiment*, and by religion as sinners. Either way they will be immoralists.

Nietzsche is clearly outlining different forms of life, personal and societal. In his terms the natural life might be called moral, but it is far from clear why its values should also be designated 'higher'. This issue concerns Irving Zeitlin. 'Higher! What ground does Nietzsche have for calling either the pre-herd or the post-herd morality higher? Nowhere does he provide any such ground, nor can he, since he claims to have rejected both metaphysical and rational means of doing so.'[74] If this is the case, then we should have to consider again the quotation from Nietzsche with which this chapter began: 'we too are men of conscience'. To decide to live the 'natural' life rather than the life of social convention is interesting, perhaps in some circumstances courageous, but is the choice a moral one? Is the choice made because of the call of conscience? Unlikely. If there is a call, if there is a voice of conscience, then it is more likely that it is the call to live a certain kind of life for reasons that are – *extra-moral*. It is of some significance that Nietzsche, in distinguishing the two forms of life falls back on an even more traditional concept than conscience. 'We, who have a different faith ... whither must we direct our hopes?'[75] In spite of his claims to radicalism, in spite of his condemnation of Schopenhauer, is Nietzsche's new morality still inspired by idealism? This would seem to confirm the suspicion expressed by Deleuze that a moral system, no matter how 'immoral', will not make the break with the past: 'morality is the continuation of religion but by other means'.

5

Lest the Bow Break

The death of God means the loss of foundation, the loss of any justification for belief in the truth, any credible choice of moral values and also any adherence to aesthetic judgments. Nietzsche experienced the despair and terror of such a conclusion and he confronts us like some Ancient Mariner who will not let us pass. He springs out into our path, a Madman with an in-your-face dysangel.[1] But that is not quite the whole story. Like some Epistemological First Officer on the Starship Enterprise he pronounces on the situation: 'It's truth, Jim – but not as we know it.' It is possible there can be truth, differently understood, raised up on a new foundation – the struggle of life. There is no morality any more, or at least not as it was previously understood. It is possible there can be moral values, but so different that they look at first sight to be immoral values, because they are raised up on a new foundation – the affirmation of the natural life of mankind. And now we come to our third casualty. '*The* beautiful exists just as little as does *the* good, or *the* true.'[2] The old foundation has gone and with it any thought of aesthetic standards of judgment that come from elsewhere. We have imposed 'our aesthetic anthropomorphisms' on the world, he tells us, but 'none of our aesthetic and moral judgments apply to it'.[3] Aesthetics are possible in the future, but beauty on its new foundation will have a very different meaning and will be judged by very different criteria. Only when the terms are redefined can we make sense of Nietzsche's claim. 'Truth is ugly. We possess *art* lest we perish of the truth.'[4] What on earth could the new aesthetic standard be?

What on *earth*. As with truth and morality, the beautiful will be 'what is useful, beneficent, life-enhancing'.[5] Like truth and morality, beauty will be in the *life* of the beholder. It will be perspectival in one sense, but it will objectively relate to the enhancement of the life of the individual. It will be that which contributes in a particular way to the struggle of life. With the end of obedience comes the dawning of responsibility.

Religion, the loss of religion, the alternative to religion: this is the heart of Nietzsche's philosophy. Like Marx before him, this critic of religion is primarily a moral philosopher, who is concerned also with epistemology. He wrote little on aesthetics, nevertheless it could be argued that this is more fundamental to his life than anything else. As we have seen, music was important to him as a schoolboy. He and two other sixteen-year-olds founded a little school society called *Germania*. They used their pocket money to subscribe to the *Zeitschrift für Musik*, the only musical journal to espouse the work of Wagner. In the winter of 1862 they bought an arrangement of *Tristan und Isolde*. This was Nietzsche's first encounter with the work of Wagner. Much later he was to reflect: 'From the moment there was a piano score of *Tristan* ... I was a Wagnerian.'[6] He would happily have made music his career. The importance of the artistic in his life began with Wagner, became articulated with Wagner, was raised to its highest expression only in his break with the maestro, but at the end, at the very end when he was no longer in touch with social reality, it was still variations on Wagner which he played to himself in his narrowed and narrowing world: 'Wagner, the great benefactor of my life.'[7]

And what a young life it was! On 9 November 1868 he wrote from Leipzig to Edwin Rohde expressing his intention to begin his *Habilitation*, little knowing that two months later, before he could even begin, it he would be offered the chair at Basel. In the letter he gives an account of his meeting the previous day with Richard Wagner. Later, when illness forced him to resign, when he travelled alone, isolated and alienated, he seems a sad and pathetic figure, but at this stage, when his self-confidence was

high and life opened up before him, we see a very different side
to the young student. By chance a new suit he had ordered was to
be ready on the morning of day they were to meet. He describes
how the afternoon wore on, but still no sign of the suit. At
6.30 p.m. a messenger brought it. The suit fits and the messenger
requires payment. The haughty student declares he will only pay
the tailor.

> The man becomes more insistent; the time grows shorter and
> shorter. I lay hold of the garments and attempt to put them on;
> the man seizes them and prevents me from carrying out my
> intention. Display of force on my side; display of force on his
> side. Farce![8]

The man goes off with the suit, leaving Nietzsche in shirt-tails to
contemplate his meagre wardrobe. What do you wear when
meeting a legend for the first time? A nice sense of humour,
entirely lacking in the seriousness with which Nietzsche later
takes himself.

Nietzsche was thrilled to meet Wagner, the more since they
shared a common interest in Schopenhauer. Even before his
inaugural lecture at Basel he had visited Wagner and Cosima von
Bülow (as she was then) at Tribschen, their home near Lucerne.
It was the period in which he turned from philology to philosophy. In retrospect he confessed to his sister: 'Certainly those
were the best days of my life: the ones I spent with him at
Tribschen ...'[9] He associated with one of the great cultural forces
of the day. More than that, he was welcomed as a coming man.
They shared music, but also ideas about art and culture and
values. When in his early writings Nietzsche speaks of the artist,
it is Wagner he has in mind. His first book, *The Birth of Tragedy
from the Spirit of Music,* arose from many discussions they had at
Tribschen, and it begins with a *Preface to Richard Wagner.* Art is
not 'a merry diversion', but 'the highest human task, the true
metaphysical activity such as it is understood by the man to
whom, as my great precursor on that path, I now dedicate these
pages'.[10] Attention has focussed on the distinction he makes

between the plastic Apollonian arts and non-visual art of music, inspired by Dionysos, but Nietzsche makes important points about aesthetics.[11] In the Dionysian rites individuation is overcome and the bond of man and man is renewed, as is the reconciliation of man and nature. The aesthetic is also the expression of the struggle of life: the artist 'has himself become a work of art ...' [12]

As Nietzsche's philosophy developed, he designated truth and morality simply as interpretations laid upon the world. It is different with aesthetics. Here man acts directly upon the world. His relationship to the world is 'an aesthetic relation'.[13] More particularly, the artist is the creator, who creates himself and the world, as if 'art, rather than ethics, constituted the essential metaphysical activity of man ...'[14] This is the meaning of art, and of the world. 'Only as an aesthetic product can the world be justified to all eternity ...'[15] Nietzsche had not yet developed his genealogy of morals, his sublimation and supersession of the natural, but already we can see the first evidence of this thought. 'Art is not an imitation of nature, but its metaphysical supplement, raised up beside it in order to overcome it.'[16] Art is not the meaning of life: *l'art pour l'art*. Yes, art has to be defended against those who would use it for their own religious, moral or ideological ends. But that is not the end of the matter, as if art existed for itself, as if it were an end in itself. It has its own true and proper end. The artist directs himself towards the meaning of art – which is *life*. I am reminded of a graduate in English Literature who asked me to supervise his research into something he had found in Alexander Solzhenitsyn, Graham Greene and Saul Bellow. After discussion we concluded that his subject was, broadly, 'spirituality'. I began to advise him to seek supervision in a department of Comparative Literature, but he had already decided against that. He told me that there he would be encouraged to study form, character development, the use of metaphor – but not the issue, not that burning issue in the struggle of life which had driven these authors in their very different contexts to create their novels. Which is the artist's concern? *L'art pour l'art?* 'Is his basic instinct directed toward art, or is it not rather directed towards the meaning of art, which is *life*?'[17]

It is significant, then, that Nietzsche's philosophy begins to develop through contemplation of aesthetics. He had before him the example of Wagner himself, this man who in his youth had been a follower of Feuerbach, and who in Paris had been caught up in the spirit of revolution. Wagner had congratulated the young professor on *The Birth of Tragedy*: they both saw it as a tribute to his life and work. And now Wagner had decided to make the break with the irritating constrictions of German culture-philistinism, as Nietzsche called it.[18] He would establish his own tradition at Bayreuth. Nietzsche was caught up in the excitement of this project and visited the festival site with Wagner several times before its formal opening. In July 1876, four weeks before the launch, with the first performance of *The Ring of the Nibelung*, Nietzsche wrote an 'untimely meditation' entitled 'Richard Wagner in Bayreuth'. The young intellectual – acolyte of the composer – writes in suitably heroic terms. 'To us, Bayreuth signifies the morning consecration on the day of battle.'[19] The new work of Wagner was not intended to entertain. His message was to be inscribed on the souls of men. It could not be heard by theoretical man, the man of science or of conventional morality. 'And where are the free and fearless, those who in innocent selfishness grow and blossom out of themselves, the Siegfrieds among you?'[20] Where is the natural man, the Dionysian man, the man of intuition and instinct, the man who with passion affirms life? Such a man will suffer in this life, but he will not be ground down by it; he will be attacked by lesser beings, but will not be overcome by them. When the burden and the blows are greatest, it will not be to science or morality that he will look for strength and inspiration. 'Art exists so that the bow shall not break. The individual must be consecrated to something higher than himself ...'[21] We can imagine with what anticipation Nietzsche attended the first cycle of *The Ring*. But we can scarcely comprehend the disillusionment he experienced at the performance. He immediately left Bayreuth having suffered a crisis second only to the death of God. The University of Basel granted him a year's leave of absence on health grounds. Later that year in Sorrento he encountered Wagner, in what proved to be their last meeting. In the following year Nietzsche reflected on the parting of the ways with the two great influences on his life. His philosophy developed as he made the break with Schopenhauer: his aesthetics develop as he makes the break with Wagner.[22]

However, as we have already noted, no cloud for Nietzsche is unlined. As he reflected on his creative time with Wagner it became clear to him that he had made a mistake. The aesthetics, the ideas, the values which they had discussed belonged not to both but only to one. Nietzsche had mistaken which one.

> I similarly interpreted Wagner's music in my own way, as the expression of a Dionysian powerfulness of soul, I believed that I heard in it the earthquake with which a primitive force of life, suppressed for ages, finally relieves itself, indifferent as to whether all that at present calls itself civilization is shaken thereby. It is obvious what I misunderstood, it is obvious in like manner what I *bestowed upon* Wagner and Schopenhauer – myself.[23]

Perhaps understandably the young man had assumed that in their discussions the Dionysian view of life and art came from the older man. He anticipated that at Bayreuth the Dionysian revolution would break forth upon an unprepared and unworthy audience. Art and the artist coincided. For Nietzsche Wagner was himself the embodiment of many of the Dionysian qualities: a man of destiny, self-made, self-willed, a sensuous man beyond the conventional morality of good and evil, riding roughshod over the interests of others, a free spirit constricted only by the culture herd. He could write for their approval, but the time had come for him to confront the values of the new *Reich* and call the Prussian people to a higher destiny. Who better to unleash these values through the spirit of music? This was the promise of Bayreuth and especially *The Ring of the Nibelung*. Germany should turn from the West with its demeaning, debilitating love of gold, turn from the West with its degenerate morality. It should turn, or rather return, to the East, to the old Nordic sagas, to myths which are more powerful than facts, to myths which are more truthful than descriptions. This was to be the message of August 1876. The production of *The Ring of the Nibelung* was immensely powerful, even hypnotic. *Rhinegold* points to the source of current woes, the love of gold which leads from theft to deceit, to envy and to fratricide. *The Valkyrie* is the celebration in heaven of the old natural passions – loyalty in the struggle, courage in face of danger, honour in life and the fierce and fearless embracing of death. In *Siegfried* we have the hero, born of adultery and incest, who embodies these passions, affirming life in a society which is weary of life. And in *The Twilight of the Gods* there is both the destruction of the old heaven and the possibility of a new earth. In 'Richard Wagner at Bayreuth' Nietzsche had declared:

> This music is a return to nature, while being at the same time the purification and transformation of nature; for the pressing need for that return arose in the souls of men filled with love, *and in their art there sounds nature transformed into love*.[24]

From his own experience he knew the whole shameful situation in which art and artists find themselves, how a soulless or soulhardened society, which calls itself good but is in fact evil, counts art and artists as among its retinue of slaves whose task is to satisfy *its imaginary needs*.[25] Wagner is seeking the very soul of the German people. And what is it that has hardened their hearts? What is it that has dried up their souls? What is it that has turned them from life to death? Why, it is nothing less than the Christian religion. Judaeo-Christian morality is the morality of the herd which suppresses the passions, which fears life itself and which condemns those who are the disciples of Dionysos. Too late Nietzsche was forced to recognize that he had *bestowed* this whole analysis on Wagner: these ideas belonged only to Nietzsche *himself*. What he had heard 'in Wagnerian music had nothing at all to do with Wagner'.[26] As he fled from Bayreuth he knew he was on his own. And then there was one: he was 'the last disciple of the god Dionysos'.[27] Nietzsche did not need to set out from first principles. His criticism of morality is conveniently the advocacy of the opposite values. His criticism of the Christian religion becomes 'the anti-Christ'. His final views on aesthetics in the struggle of life emerge as the grounds for his rejection of Wagner.

In October 1888, only three months before his final collapse, at a frenetic time of his life, Nietzsche published *The Case of Wagner: A Musician's Problem*. The Preface opens with an amazing contrast: Nietzsche takes the side of Bizet – against Wagner! Without detracting in any way from the justified reputation of the French composer, he is hardly of the stature of Wagner. Nietzsche anticipates our incredulity. 'It is not solely out of sheer wickedness that I praise Bizet at the expense of Wagner in this work.'[28] Indeed a few weeks later in his last letter to Carl Fuchs he goes further: 'What I say about Bizet, you should not take seriously; the way I am, Bizet does not matter to me at all. But as an ironic antithesis to Wagner, it has a strong effect …'[29] Granted that Bizet is not of the stature of Wagner, why does Nietzsche make this choice? Indeed he advocates Bizet precisely because it is provocative. We must begin by saying, *given* that there is no comparison between them as musicians, what is it that raises the man of promise above the legend? For all Wagner's genius, far beyond the capacity of Bizet, what is it nevertheless that he lacks which Bizet possesses? In its everyday setting, without the physiological assault of Wagner's *son et lumière*, in its limited way, without Wagner's *Germanics* – 'obedience and long legs'[30] – in its focussing on but one thing, *Carmen* exhibits the very Dionysian values which Wagner in the end betrayed.

The two works, which on the *previous* grounds of aesthetics do not deserve to be mentioned in the same sentence, appeared a year apart. Bizet died prematurely in June 1875 at the age of thirty-six, only three months after the first performance of *Carmen*. Nietzsche first heard it in November 1881 and was to go on to hear it twenty times. As we have seen, Nietzsche's aesthetic judgment is that art should be life-enhancing and should affect the lives of those who hear (or see) it. A coded way of saying 'life-enhancing' might be the 'Dionysian affirmation of life'. Nietzsche was drawn to two intelligent and sensuous women in his life, but with all due respect to the talents of Cosima Wagner and Lou von Salomé, they were strictly amateurs when compared to *La Carmencita*. The gypsy factory-girl of Seville is the epitome of sensuousness and passion, indeed such a tart that the character had to be toned down in deference to the sensibilities of the first audiences. She lives her life to the full, a life of love, always haunted by the inevitability of tragedy. Nietzsche was drawn to the combination of the passionate living of life which in itself issued in premature tragic death. He claims that artists have mis-understood love – including Wagner! (Does a bear misunderstand honey?) 'Finally love – love retranslated into nature! Not the love of a "cultured maiden"! No Senta-mentality! But love as fate, as fatality, cynical, innocent, cruel – and thus true to nature.'[31] But as we have seen, for Nietzsche art is never simply the imitation of nature. It may have been nature which drew the dragoon corporal into the arms of the gypsy, but when Don José stabs her to death we are carried beyond nature, through tragedy, by the spirit of music.

> You can take me away:
> It's I who struck her dead!
> *(he throws himself on Carmen's body)*
> Ah, Carmen! My Carmen, my beloved.

The affirmation of the Dionysian passion, but also the enhance-ment of life. As we have seen, the artist becomes himself a work of art, but what of the listener? Nietzsche was clearly moved by the opera. 'One becomes a "masterpiece" one's self by its influence.'[32] And that is the criterion of the aesthetic, and the justification of art.

What was it then in Wagner's work which offended against this aesthetic criterion? There are three issues. The first is decadence: 'Wagner is the artist of decadence.'[33] As Peter Pütz describes him, 'for Nietzsche he is the type of the play-actor, the virtuoso of nuance and effect, overburdened with detail yet without any unifying creative power, brimming with knowledge but devoid of instinct'.[34] As we have seen, one of the areas of common ground between Nietzsche and Wagner was their appreciation of Schopenhauer. Nietzsche changed: Wagner did not. 'I am a child of this age, just like Wagner, *i.e. a decadent*; I am however conscious of it; I defend myself against it. My philosophic spirit defended itself against it.'[35] The conclusion of *The Ring* is Schopenhauerian: the new is no better than the old. The second issue is that Wagner's music satisfies religious needs.[36] 'There is nothing which Wagner has meditated on more profoundly than salvation: his opera is the opera of salvation.'[37] Indeed Nietzsche reviews all of Wagner's operas and finds this persistent theme: 'someone always wants to be saved in Wagner's works'.[38] Indeed for some, Wagner himself aspired to this role. At his funeral the Wagner Society of München laid a wreath at the tomb of their hero with the decadent sentiment: 'Salvation to the Saviour!' Others (Nietzsche exaggerates) expressed a rather different sentiment: 'Salvation *from* the Saviour.'[39]

There is, however, a third issue, which is a consequence of the first two. Wagner's work is decadent and includes the religious theme of salvation. If he is not after all committed to the Dionysian affirmation of life, his influence and that of his art cannot be to the enhancement of life. At the premier of *The Ring of the Nibelung* Nietzsche was shocked by the theatricality of the production. It was intended for effect: 'drama is the end, music is always but the means'.[40] Nietzsche recalls that Wagner's father was an actor – named Geyer. (Thus for devilment he implies that the family of the great anti-Semite was Jewish.) 'Was Wagner a musician at all?' Rather he was 'the most astonishing theatrical genius that the Germans have had ...'[41] Wagner, Wagner! Is this the name of a great musician? Surely it is not simply the name of an individual: it has come to symbolize so much more. For Nietzsche it is the symbol not of the overcoming of life, but of its decadence, not of art in the service of enhancing life but of degeneration. 'Is Wagner a man at all? Is he not rather a disease?'[42] Weeks away from his own collapse Dr Nietzsche, previously of Basel, the Francophile who chose Bizet, makes this diagnosis. '*Wagner est une névrose.*'[43]

How far had Nietzsche come from those, the happiest days of his life, at Tribschen. At what cost had he broken with this man who had been like a father to him – and an inspiration. It had been necessary for him to make the break, to criticize, to denounce and even – it was inevitable for a writer of such power – to ridicule, as the 'old artillerist' brought up his 'heavy guns against Wagner'.[44] Only when the break was made visible and irreversible did he lose his illusions and discover himself, as he made clear to Lou von Salomé. 'The renunciation that it required, the rediscovering of myself that eventually became necessary, was among the hardest and most melancholy things that have befallen me.'[45] Why were his greatest achievements always gained at such great personal cost, this disciple of the god Dionysos, the god of dance, gaiety and delight in life? The baton had not fallen from the maestro's hand: Nietzsche had wrested it from the grasp of 'the imposture of the grand style'.[46] Only *he* remained to carry on the task which he thought he might share with another. He, the very last disciple, noted to Overbeck with awe and no satisfaction at all, that 'what I long ago prophesied is now beginning – my becoming in some ways Wagner's heir'.[47]

As the inauguration of the Bayreuth Festival approached, Nietzsche, who had invested so much in it, began to have his doubts about Wagner: 'one day I came to myself in Bayreuth'.[48] When he absented himself from the second cycle did he ever have second thoughts? Did he wonder if he had been too hasty in his judgment of his friend and hero? But no, Wagner, who had helped him, unconsciously, in the development of his Dionysian philosophy, was to perform one final service for his supposed protégé: he would provide the proof which Nietzsche required. When they met in November 1876 in Sorrento for the last time Wagner laid before him in detail the Christian themes of his latest work, *Parsifal*. Nietzsche had already detected the turn to religion, not the religion of the old gods, but of the Crucified.

When Wagner returned to Germany, to play the anti-semitic card, he, 'the most triumphal, while in truth become a decayed, despairing *décadent*, sank down suddenly, helpless and disjointed, before the Christian cross'.[49] The alienation at Bayreuth spurred Nietzsche to begin a work which was to be entitled *Human All Too Human*. As a presentation copy – an intellectual and cultural anti-personnel time-bomb – winged its way to Wagner, so a beautiful copy of the text of *Parsifal* crossed in the post, dedicated humorously but significantly to 'his dear friend Friedrich Nietzsche, Richard Wagner, Ecclesiastical Counsellor'.[50] Confirmation: 'Wagner had become pious'.[51] As we have seen, however, if there was one thing more offensive to Nietzsche than being Christian, it was merely claiming to be Christian for the sake of public image. 'If Wagner was a Christian, then Liszt was perhaps a Church Father!'[52] Not that the maestro could ever become a humble Christian: 'he now became an oracle, a priest, or more than a priest – a kind of mouthpiece of the absolute, a telephone line of Transcendence. God's ventriloquist ...'[53] This personal abuse, so unusual for Nietzsche, gives some indication of just how damaged he had been by Wagner, whom he could never forgive.

It was not until Nietzsche made the break that he could find his own way, could find himself. He could then apply to aesthetics the materialism which had led him to such original conclusions about morality, and the anti-Kantianism which had featured in his epistemology. 'Aesthetics is indissolubly bound up with these biological presuppositions: there is decadence aesthetics, and there is *classical* aesthetics – the "beautiful in itself" is a chimera, like all idealism.'[54] He had begun his revaluation of ethics with chemistry, the move from psychology to physiology.[55] He can now do the same with aesthetics. 'My objections to Wagner's music are physiological objections: for what purpose is to be served by disguizing the same under aesthetic formulae? *Aesthetics is certainly nothing but applied physiology.*'[56]

6

Decadence

The death of God is the beginning for Nietzsche, or rather it is the middle. For this reason, unlike religion, which looks with anticipation to the end, his philosophy is of the great Noontide, the watershed.[1] The old world, the 'true' world is exposed, thereby bringing into view for the first time the real world. The old moral values of heteronomous ethics have lost their authority, yielding to the noble values. The aesthetics of *l'art pour l'art* give way to art in the service of life. Indeed the enhancing of life becomes the standard and criterion of each: truth, morality and aesthetics. Not 'life' in the sense of the continuation of the biological, but the turn from one mode of life to another. Nietzsche has several ways of describing these alternatives. As we have seen, the new life – which is presented as a return to an older mode of life – is now described as 'Dionysian'. The life which it replaces he describes pejoratively as 'degenerate' or *décadent*, a term which, as with *ressentiment*, is always used in the French form. Philosophy on his view should be exploring the Dionysian life and enabling people to realize it. But as already noted, he has little expectation of professional philosophy, which he accuses of 'Egyptianism'. 'All that philosophers have handled for millennia has been conceptual mummies; nothing actual has escaped from their hands alive.'[2] In the previous chapter, as far as art and the enhancement of life is concerned, Wagner is described as a *décadent*. At a first reading Nietzsche can seem to be outrageous in his comments: we need to pay attention to his very particular, even idiosyncratic, use of terms. In describing Wagner as *décadent* he is not referring to his moral life, which bourgeois society at that time might have condemned as degenerate. Indeed the maestro's life-style might seem closer to the Dionysian life. He is not even commenting on Wagner's dress sense: his hat could have served as a pup tent for three boy scouts. The most important symptom of *décadence* in Wagner was that his music served religious needs. It was art in the service of life, but a degenerate life. Decadence and religion go together: indeed this becomes Nietzsche's most consistent criticism of Christianity. With respect to the true world, moral values and the role of art, Christianity defines and promotes the decadent life. He is not implying that the Christian life is nothing but one orgy after another. If only. It makes sense only in the precise way in which Nietzsche defines his terms. In short, the life which he advocates as the last disciple of the god Dionysos casts him automatically in the role of the anti-Christ. This is the main focus in the revaluation of all values, as for example when he roundly declares Christianity to be a slave religion.

It was Nietzsche's delight to use his command of language, especially aphorism and metaphor, to shock, to dismay and hopefully to make people reflect on their lives. But the pronouncement that Judaism and Christianity are slave religions does not have this immediate effect: both religions have claimed as much themselves. One of the constant reiterations of Judaism is that God heard the cry of the Hebrew slaves in Egypt and rescued them in the Exodus. 'Thus says the Lord, the God of Israel: I made a covenant with your fathers when I brought them out of the land of Egypt, out of the house of bondage ...'³ A slave religion: yes, indeed and that is its sure historical foundation. As for Christianity, its foundation is the coming of God's only Son, not appearing as a ruler, a nobleman or a citizen of an imperial power, but in humility, 'taking the form of a slave (*doulos*)'.⁴ Paul describes the earliest Christian communities as constituted not of the educated or aristocratic in society. 'For consider your call, brethren; not many of you were wise according to worldly standards, not many were powerful, not many were of noble birth...'⁵ In reality the early church soon included members who were probably citizens, no doubt slave-owners and certainly middle-class, as Frend observes. 'The Pauline congregations may not have contained "many wise, mighty or noble", but there were plenty who had social pretensions and, more to the point, their own slaves, and houses large enough for congregations to meet.'[6] But whatever the reality, this is the abiding image: Christianity was originally a religion of and for slaves.

This theme has been revived in liberation theologies of the third world. Jon Sobrino is a Jesuit priest and theologian working in El Salvador. He claims that 'God's manifestation, at least in Latin America, is his scandalous and partisan love for the poor and his intention that these poor should receive life and inaugurate his kingdom'.[7] It is not that the churches include the poor: 'the poor evangelize the church'.[8] Julio de Santa Ana is a Methodist theologian from Uruguay who has produced a study on the subject for the World Council of Churches. The title of the first volume sets the scene: *Good News to the Poor: the Challenge of the Poor in the History of the Church.*[9] Nietzsche's revelation that Christianity is a slave religion is greeted in such quarters not with cries of denunciation and anger, but with agreement and affirmation. Amen!

The situation is intriguing, even convoluted. Nietzsche's words, designed to shock, might well be unsettling to that now well-established form of Christianity which is at ease with the ruling classes in Western society. No slaves they: slave owners in their time more likely. As early as the fourth century Constantine the Great chose Christianity to be the state religion of his newly unified empire. Its bishops, now civil servants, wore the royal purple, lived in palaces and were addressed by the aristocratic title, 'my Lord'. They took their place with the nobility and, in their commonality of interest, sought to deliver a subservient populace, accepting of the divine right of kings.[10] Slave religion indeed! What an insult, what a calculated slap in the face! It is for this reason that the situation is intriguing. Nietzsche is inadvertently recalling Christianity to its original form: the religion of and for the poor. His characterization of Christianity is in this respect at least close to some of the most authentic examples of Christian living in the modern world. In so far as Christianity for many centuries has been a religion organized for and by the rich and powerful, then ironically its values have been closer to those advocated by Nietzsche. But if the death of God means the end of authentic Christianity, it heralds the end of the values of the slaves. Unconsciously, though perhaps intuitively, Nietzsche has indeed set out in starkest contrast the gulf fixed between his 'noble' values and those of Christian faith. In accusing Christianity of being a religion of slaves, Nietzsche has not misrepresented it. That is not the end of his criticism, but rather its starting point. The death of God is a source of cheerfulness for him if it means the end of the values of the herd and the re-emergence of the values of the higher men. Thus Nietzsche the philosopher: whether it describes Nietzsche in his personal life we shall discuss in due course.

If the death of God is an event which has already occurred, but which takes a long time to be recognized, the emergence or re-emergence of the noble values among the higher men also has a history. The re-emergence in this respect is like a rebirth, a 'renaissance'. The fifteenth century saw the Renaissance in Europe, the rebirth of classical learning and the rebirth of the values of the ancient pre-Christian world. For Nietzsche it was 'the revaluation of Christian values; the attempt, undertaken with every expedient, with every instinct, with genius of every kind, to bring about the victory of the opposing values, the noble values'.[11] The Renaissance rediscovered the passions and affirmed life. In Olympia, 'an immoral roar of laughter – Cesare Borgia as Pope'.[12] Cesare Borgia (1475–1507) was duke of Valentinois, a criminal, a politician, the model for Machiavelli's treatise *The Prince*. As a man and as a pope he was the true son of his father, the Borgia pope Alexander VI. In his private life Nietzsche was a rather conventionally moral person, and we might doubt if he would have had any admiration for Cesare Borgia, but Nietzsche the philosopher could express admiration for such an egotistical, self-indulgent, wilful and cruel autocrat. As pope he carried into the

religious centre of Christendom a constellation of values fundamentally incompatible with those of Jesus and the early church. It
is this irony which delighted Nietzsche. The laughter in heaven –
the other heaven, the Dionysian heaven – is not that such a man
could exist against the church, outside the church, condemned by
the church, but that he could exist as its leader, a blood-stained
and corrupt pied piper, leading the herd to hell. To Nietzsche's
dismay this aspect at least of the Renaisssance was soon challenged, by an Augustinian monk who had taken vows of poverty,
chastity and obedience, a professor of theology, a biblical scholar,
a writer who was soon to make a contribution to the development
of the German language unrivalled in its history – till Nietzsche
himself. Martin Luther instituted a Reformation of all values, and
brought to an untimely demise the rebirth of pre-Christian values. 'Luther restored the Church ...'[13] Then there was Kant. 'If
we never get rid of Christianity, the Germans will be to blame.'[14]
This at least is Nietzsche's reading of history. Rather schematically he identifies these values with the Dionysian life-affirming
values which we have already discussed. It is a subject on which
Nietzsche had changed his position. In *The Birth of Tragedy from
the Spirit of Music* he praises the musical contribution of the
German Reformation. 'Luther's chorales, so inward, courageous,
spiritual, and tender, are like the first Dionysiac cry from the
thicket at the approach of spring.'[15] He includes Luther in the list
of 'our great predecessors'.[16] It is the Reformation which exhibits
the Dionysian rather than the 'Alexandrian-Roman revival of the
fifteenth century'.[17] He rejects the oft-repeated view that
Christianity triumphed because of the moral collapse of ancient
Rome. His reading of the transition is quite the opposite. 'As a
European movement, the Christian movement has been from the
very first a collective movement of outcast and refuse elements of
every kind (those who want to come to power through
Christianity).'[18] Of the two moralities previously discussed,
Christian morality is the morality of the slave class, literally, the
morality of the masses, of the herd. What is good for that class is
very different from the good of the ruling class:

here it is that pity, the kind and helping hand, the warm heart,
patience, industriousness, humili‚ , friendliness come into
⸻ qualities and virtually the
⸻ f existence. Slave morality
⸻ 'good' and 'evil'.[19]

⸻ ublimation and use of the
⸻ unciation, rejection, con-
⸻ by the 'moral mastur-
⸻ of this life in favour of
⸻ leemed guilty, so that in
⸻ here is the promise of 'a

⸻ origins of morality by
⸻ ry. So too his conclusion
⸻ ng therefore that he sees
⸻ the natural passions as a
⸻ 'a physiological regres-
⸻ themselves the good, and
⸻ being, losing all the life-

⸻ g life, when everything
⸻ ninated from the concept
⸻ to the symbol of a staff
⸻ who are downtrodden,
⸻ od, the sinner's God, the
⸻ the predicate 'saviour',
⸻ the predicate of divinity
⸻ ormation speak, such a

⸻ g we should be sensitive
⸻ k in this catalogue of
⸻ community, society or
⸻ herd over those of the
⸻ of the inadequate rather

than achievements of the competent, which seeks to fulfil the desires and aspiration of those who are so lacking in imagination and creativity, so ill-constituted in their lives that they can neither strive towards such goals nor even make the effort to attain them. But in this catalogue, which becomes familiar as his philosophy develops, Nietzsche adds another element which is seldom included in his books and often omitted by commentators. In addition to his complaint about what happens to the higher men in the midst of this degeneration, he is also complaining about what is happening to God. He is taking God's part, as if there is a 'higher God', just as there are 'higher men'. It is as if there is a higher God whose pleasure was to create the natural world, who looked upon his handiwork and 'saw that it was good', before proceeding to his greatest creation. 'Let us make man in our image ...'[25] The degenerates have rejected the natural, that which the higher God declared to be good. They have created a degenerate god in their own image. For Nietzsche this god is dead. Thank God! Thank the God who created man to be part of the natural world, to affirm life and manifest in that life the noble values. We cannot pursue this point now. Like the madman we come too soon. The noble God will be our subject in Chapter 11.

Returning to the main issue, Nietzsche characterizes Christianity as the religion of a decadent chosen people, chosen by a decadent God. At least this is how the reversal of values is now greeted. So often God is made over in the image of man, or rather in the image of the nation or tribe, reflecting their values and their needs. Christianity succeeded as the religion of the underclass of the Roman Empire, and the Christian God represented the decadent lives and values of this class. Just as Christianity is Platonism for the masses, so on the side of metaphysics, Platonism is the philosophy of *décadence*. As Deleuze points out, 'Socrates is the first genius of decadence.'[26] In *The Gay Science* there is a section on 'The Dying Socrates' in which Nietzsche comments on the last words of the philosopher as he drinks the hemlock. 'Crito, I owe Asclepius a rooster.' Given that this was the normal sacrifice to the god for those who sought recovery from illness, does this mean that life itself was an illness from which he had to be cured? Probably not, but it gives some indication of the distance Nietzsche had travelled from the days of his love affair with the Greek world.

> Socrates, Socrates suffered life! And then he still revenged himself – with this veiled, gruesome, pious, and blasphemous saying. Did Socrates need such revenge? Did his over-rich virtue lack an ounce of magnanimity? Alas, my friends, we must overcome even the Greeks.[27]

Both slave religion and the metaphysics of improvement are motivated by revenge. Deleuze comments on the reversing of good and bad which takes place in religion.

> No religious values are separable from this hatred and revenge from which they drew the consequences. The positivity of religions is only apparent; they conclude that the wretched, the poor, the weak, the slaves are good since the strong are 'evil' and 'damned'. They have invented the good wretch, the good weakling: there is no better revenge against the strong and happy.[28]

The reversal of values is required if there is to be a reversal of status. In slave religion there must be not only criminals, but sinners, as Deleuze observes: 'We can guess what the creature of *ressentiment* wants; he wants others to be evil, he needs others to be evil, in order to be able to consider himself good.'[29] The *ressentiment* which we meet in slave morality is now the fire which smoulders dangerously as righteous anger in slave religion.

This then is the basis of Nietzsche's rejection and criticism of Christianity. He is not repeating the well-worn atheist rejection of belief in the existence of God, nor does he join those self-congratulatory philosophers who have made a career out of the formulation of some rather precious criticisms of the traditional proofs intended to establish the existence of God. Still less is he rehearsing that moral criticism of Christianity which accuses

Christians of failing to live out the values to which they pay lip service, a criticism which in its existential cowardice and ethical conservatism first begins by accepting Christian moral values. No, this is a revaluation of all values, a rejection of Christian moral values altogether, a replacement of those traditional moral values not simply with another set of values, but with their opposites. Here is a very different criticism, that far from enabling mankind to rise above their animal ancestors, Christianity has been responsible for human degeneration. It has led not to life abundant, but to the impoverishment of life, to the endangering of the very species itself. It is not simply a criticism of Christianity, but an alternative to it, its antithesis: Christ and the anti-Christ, Dionysos against the Crucified. 'Christianity has taken the side of everything weak, base, ill-constituted, it has made an ideal out of *opposition* to the preservative instincts of strong life ...'[30]

As a rule of thumb what Christianity cherishes should be rejected. 'What a theologian feels to be true must be false: this provides almost a criterion of truth.'[31] Christianity therefore stands over against the wholesome, healthy life: 'hatred of the senses, of the joys of the senses, of joy in general is Christian'.[32] When we recall *that* photograph of Nietzsche, the glowering face, the fungus moustache, the sunken eyes – and all that before his breakdown – the accusation that Christians lack joy seems rather rich. The phrase 'a good night out with Nietzsche' springs to mind. However, we have already distinguished between Nietzsche in his private life and Nietzsche *qua* philosopher. This is the philosopher speaking, and he is making a serious point. Religion in Europe has a long tradition of condemning certain kinds of joy, the joys of the senses, sensuousness. The natural life is suspect.

> The Christian Church has left nothing untouched by its depravity, it has made of every value a disvalue, of every truth a lie, of every kind of integrity a vileness of soul. People still dare to talk to me of its 'humanitarian' blessings. To abolish

any state of distress whatever has been profoundly inexpedient to it; it has lived on states of distress, it has created states of distress in order to eternalize itself.[33]

It is not only Marx who can refer to religion as the opiate of the people,[34] Nietzsche can speak of 'an opiate Christianity'[35]:'those who know how to provide opiates and narcotic consolations', thus ensuring 'the continuation of real misery'.[36] On this view the whole sacramental structure depends on condemning human needs and replacing them with 'religious' needs which only the professionals can satisfy. A system which claims the sole authority for forgiving sins must be active in identifying sin and convincing ordinary men and women going about their natural lives that they are in danger for their eternal souls. No group of Christians can use his criticism against another group. As Nietzsche makes clear when writing to his devout mother, his criticism of Christianity is too fundamental 'to involve religious questions and shades of difference between confessions'.[37] With this Nietzsche's alienation from the Christian religion seems complete. It is to be distinguished from all hitherto existing criticisms of religion. He cannot be understood within that long line of philosophers who have doubted the existence of God. We have already seen that Nietzsche can defend the noble God against the god of decadence.

There is one final respect in which his position is to be distinguished from simple, ill-constituted and unreflective atheism.

> What sets us apart is not that we recognize no God, either in history or in nature or behind nature – but that we find that which has been reverenced as God not 'godlike' but pitiable, absurd, harmful, not merely an error but a crime against life. We deny God as God. If this God of the Christians were proved to us to exist, we should know even less how to believe in him.[38]

Atheism is the denial of God or gods. It has been taken to mean the denial of the *existence* of God or gods. But that is not its only meaning. As the early church moved out of Palestine into the Roman Empire proper, Christians were condemned as *atheoi*, as deniers of the gods. They, who believed in the true God, refused to show reverence to the gods who were unworthy of devotion. In the debate between theologians and atheistic philosophers the issue has been the existence of God. Nietzsche did not take part in this debate. He was alienated from the common assumption which united both sides, namely that this God is worthy of worship. Winner takes all. Either this worthy God exists or not. How much more devastating is Nietzsche's criticism. Even if this same God could be proved to exist – indeed, learned theologians, please do not even take the trouble to prove his existence – he is not worthy of our devotion. On ethical grounds we should resist him: his values are immoral. The early Christians suffered for their integrity: these gods are immoral. They are not the gods of life, but of degeneration and death. So for Nietzsche, the god of slave religion, if indeed he exists, is not divine. But fortunately for the future of mankind, he is dead, and with his demise so ends at last 'the Christian libel on life'.[39]

In a chapter dealing with decadence, with the libel on life, there are two further matters which must be raised, especially since once again they appear to involve Nietzsche in contradiction. The first is his view of the ascetic. Nietzsche touches on this subject as early at *Human All Too Human* when he turns his attention to Christian asceticism. Having come as far as we have, we can anticipate his analysis. Asceticism is unnatural: it represents a 'defiance of oneself', a tyrannizing of certain parts of our nature.[40] Certain appetites and needs are identified as the enemy within, inspiring disgust and self-contempt. Thus for example sexual desire can be easily satisfied (Nietzsche is speaking theoretically here), but if it is rejected and demonized it becomes unnatural and uncontrollable. Its relative importance, in a biological context, becomes unnaturally exaggerated, in a moral context. The ascetic ideal transforms a good into an evil, the life-enhancing into the life-destroying. The ascetic on this view is the decadent. Nietzsche returns to this subject in *The Genealogy of Morals,*

where he names the three factors which have had the most perni-
cious effects on European health: the ascetic ideal, alcoholism and
syphilis.⁴¹ (It is not difficult to see Nietzsche's biography herein
summarized.) But this is not Nietzsche's only view of asceticism,
or even his first. In 1887 he could actually advocate asceticism,
but as we should expect, he does so in his own terms. 'I also want
to make asceticism natural again: in place of the aim of denial, the
aim of strengthening …'⁴² It is not difficult to see how this would
work. Nietzsche is advocating self-discipline. An example of this
would be not the exercise of the passions but their sublimation.
But as we have seen, this means affirming the passions, using and
superseding them. It does not mean their rejection or self-
contempt. He can admire the single-mindedness, dedication and
determination of the ascetic, but the question is whether this
leads to the affirmation of life, to enhancement or to degeneration.
There is no real contradiction here in Nietzsche.

The second such issue is more complex, even profound, and it
concerns his view of suffering. Since he reaches back in morality
and in aesthetics to the physiological, it is not surprising that he
has some harsh aphorisms concerning those who are ill. Once
again, his unguarded language taken out of context can be used to
justify social and ethnic cleansing, which was no part of his
philosophy. For example, '"thou shalt not procreate"! Life itself
recognizes no solidarity, no "equal rights", between the healthy
and the degenerate parts of an organism …'⁴³ This is a very
ambiguous aphorism, since it mixes physiological and moral
judgments. 'Healthy' looks like a physiological category, while
'degenerate' in this chapter has been a moral category. There are
similar examples. 'The weak and ill-constituted shall perish: first
principle of *our* philanthropy. And one shall help them to do so.'⁴⁴
He realizes that his words seem cruel. 'That which is falling
should also be pushed.'⁴⁵ Indeed his words are strangely familiar,
whether spoken by governments of left or right. 'Beggars, however, should be entirely abolished!'⁴⁶ But if Nietzsche seems hard
on others, it is because of his attitude towards his own life. As we
have seen, he suffered from poor health throughout his life. In

part this was genetic: he got a Friday-afternoon body. In part it was due to bad luck: syphilis on a one-night stand. But it is his *attitude* to suffering, to sickness, to ill-health, to pain, which requires analysis. People whose health is damaged by their lifestyle may receive little sympathy, but in general illness attracts sympathy. It is regarded as unfortunate: indeed it constitutes a moral problem from a religious perspective. Nietzsche's view of his own suffering is very different.

> *Amor fati*: that is my innermost nature. And as regards my long sickness, do I not owe to it unutterably more than to my health? I owe to it a *higher* health, such a health as becomes stronger by everything that does not kill it. I owe to it also my philosophy.[47]

There is here the same switching between physiology and morality. Nietzsche is clearly using terminology in a precise and particular way – as usual. *Amor fati*: accept the hand you are dealt and play it positively, with belief and commitment, it is the means by which you can realize your life potential, not an obstacle to it. But there is still a mis-match, between the physiological and the existential. How can philosophy be facilitated by syphilis? Perhaps we should start at the other end. If the goal is the enhancement of life, then everything which detracts from this might be called 'sickness'. Pütz provides a list: 'sickness', like 'life',

> is not a biological concept drawn from the natural sciences. In its broadest physical and moral sense sickness connotes fragmentation of the totality of things. Its symptoms are overemphasis on the theoretical, the priority of analytical reason over instinct, and the predominance of knowledge over art. Nietzsche detects its further expression in the excessively high value put on learning, in democracy, equal rights for women, the religion of compassion and Wagner's *Parsifal*, and so on.[48]

This is an interesting list, and we have already encountered everything on it, but it seems too easy a solution to reduce Nietzsche's aphorisms to metaphor. Does sickness simply mean decadence? Someone who enjoys good health might use sickness or suffering as a metaphor, but hardly a man whose career was ruined by ill health, whose waking life was scarred by it and whose sleepless nights bore testimony to it. A great deal of unworthy theodicial nonsense has been written about the purifying value of suffering for the soul, presumably by those far removed from such experience. Nietzsche threads his way through this issue. 'I doubt whether such affliction "improves" us: but I know that it *deepens* us.'[49] It is as if Nietzsche is speaking of suffering in two ways, or rather that actual suffering has two effects. Yes, it is the pits, it is unnecessary, uncalled for, unjust – but it has a certain effect, or rather it can call forth two very different reactions. It can lead, understandably, to resignation, to resentment, to decline. In some cases it can bring perspective, evaluation, discrimination. The very loss of health, and consequently of control, makes us vulnerable: the closing of some doors opens up other possibilities. 'Profound suffering makes noble; it separates.'[50] No, it is not the suffering, but the attitude towards it, the coping with it, the seizing of a very different opportunity. Nietzsche returns to this theme of separation.

> Confidence in life is gone; life itself has become a *problem*. May it never be believed that one has thereby necessarily become a gloomy person, a moping owl. Even love to life is still possible – only one loves *differently*.[51]

When we are separated from life in its immediacy, we are related to it in a more subtle and indirect way, experiencing 'a second and more dangerous innocence in pleasure'.[52]

We cannot reduce illness to a metaphor of decadence. No one who has not suffered as Nietzsche suffered has the right to take this easy way out. But he clearly sees his illness as providing an opportunity that might not have occurred to him if his fate had been otherwise. For example, Hegel's famous aphorism offered a justification for life as it is: 'The real is rational: the rational is real.'[53] But Nietzsche could not find any comfort in the assurances of idealism. 'It was only *sickness* that brought me to reason.'[54] In a practical sense it released him from his duties as a philological drill-master. 'Sickness *liberated me slowly* ...'[55] At times his eyesight was so poor that he could not read for any length of time. But as can be seen from his lack of footnotes, his most creative writing came when he could refer to no other writer. 'At times when I am deeply sunk in work you will see no books around me: I would guard against letting anyone speak or even think in my vicinity.'[56]

Suffering therefore has at least two meanings for Nietzsche: physiological and existential. The former sufficiently dislocated him from the routine of life, perhaps the life of the ruminant, the life of the decadent, that he came to experience existential suffering. This latter was if anything the more disquieting. We have met this in the existential dismay, the 'logic of terror' which he experienced at the implications of the death of God. Nothing could be further from masochism, but Nietzsche associates suffering with life, with enhanced life. Zarathustra identifies himself as 'the advocate of life, the advocate of suffering'.[57] Nietzsche can designate art 'as the redemption of the sufferer – as the way to states in which suffering is willed, transfigured, deified, where suffering is a form of great delight'.[58] But in the end, it is not the pain but the occasion, not the suffering but the possibility- the potential which though human is far from being 'all too human'.

> Man, however, is the most courageous animal: with his courage he has overcome every animal. With a triumphant shout he has even overcome every pain; human pain, however, is the deepest pain.[59]

Amor fati is not fatalism. It is not the acceptance of fate, but the affirmation of life. It is not 'Russian fatalism', which at the last lies down in the snow and dies.[60] *Amor fati*, the love of fate, does not seek to explain suffering, to see it as unjust, as an obstacle to life, as the contradiction of life, as the enemy of all meaning in life. That way lies decadence. '*Amor fati*: let that be my love henceforth!'[61] This is the love of fate, the joyful affirmation of the specially and uniquely human life.

7

The Will to Power

One of the features of Nietzsche's work is his concern not with being, but with becoming. As he describes it, life is either development or decline, affirmation or degeneration. Mankind, the species, is either moving forward or falling back. His philosophy is dynamic, his subject is described with respect to the life power. There have been many attempts to provide a definition of human being. *Homo sapiens, homo faber – homo ludens.* The human being is a thinker, a doer, even a player. Human life has been understood in relation to a single experience: suffering, alienation, the pursuit of happiness or the search for a parking space. There have been attempts to identify a single factor which unifies human behaviour. For Freud it was the libido, the sexual or sensuous drive, or at least the drive towards self-preservation.[1] It is widely assumed that the mere preservation of life is the fundamental concern of all human beings. But Zarathustra teaches that 'the living creature values many things higher than life itself ...'[2] For human beings preservation would not be enough. The single, unifying experience for Nietzsche is the will to power. The meaning of the concept is not self-evident, but at least he is claiming that there is something more important than mere preservation of life. There is a drive which can lead people to risk their lives in order to achieve a higher or more fulfilled and satisfying life. 'Life is will to power.'[3] (Ironically there is little discussion of the will to power in the collection entitled *The Will to Power*.) The importance of the will to power for Nietzsche is two-fold. First, it provides a unifying perspective from which to understand human life and motivation. But secondly, it provides a criterion by which human actions can be evaluated. That is to say, the will to power is an expression of the natural life, and provides the natural basis for values. Turning away from the religious and metaphysical bases of moral and aesthetic judgments, Nietzsche finds in the will to power the new foundation which will save him from nihilism.

Some interpreters of Nietzsche have claimed that the will to power is a cosmological doctrine. Thus Maudemarie Clark explains that 'the idea is that the world consists not of things, but of quanta of force engaged in something on the order of "universal power-struggle", with each centre of force having or being a tendency to extend its influence and incorporate other such centres.'[4] The phrase she quotes comes from Richard Schacht's *Nietzsche*, but at that point Schacht is presenting Nietzsche's position as an empirical one. There is indeed a power struggle, and it is universal, but it is far from being simply Hobbes' *bellum omnium contra omnes*. He has in mind such passages in Nietzsche as the following. 'Granted finally that one succeeded in explaining our entire instinctual life as the development and ramification of *one* basic form of will – as will to power, as in *my* theory … One would have acquired the right to define *all* efficient force unequivocally as: *will to power*.'[5] Schacht is certainly not representing the concept as a cosmological doctrine. 'Here he has in mind everything from the processes of inorganic nature to "the organic functions" and even "the spiritual functions"…'[6] The will to power might be said to constitute a world view, indeed *The Will to Power* ends with the answer to the very question about the nature of this world. 'This world is the will to power – and nothing besides! And you yourselves are also this will to power – and nothing besides!'[7] While this provides a description of the world, it would be misleading to call it a cosmological doctrine, especially since Clark means by this a metaphysical doctrine.[8] It is Nietzsche's specific intention that the empirical observation of the will to power in all its 'ramifications' means the end of all metaphysical and religious systems. Whether he is correct, whether the concept is borne out in reality, whether it can perform the function he sets out for it, and whether it can provide the natural basis of evaluation – does not alter its anti-metaphysical, and in that sense anti-cosmological, character.

In the case of any other writer but Nietzsche, we might have added to this list the query 'whether it is true', but we have already noted that Nietzsche rejects the idea of truth, or rather some forms of truth, truth in its ontological context. Magnus has raised the question whether the will to truth is not itself an expression of the will to power. 'Knowledge, then, is a process of interpretation which is based upon vital needs and expresses the will to power as the will to master the otherwise unintelligible flux of becoming.'⁹ However, although certain kinds of knowledge might been seen as ingredients in the project of the will to power, Nietzsche has rejected the will to truth as an end in itself, as an expression of the religio-metaphysical worldview. Thus, in a passage on the subject 'Of Self-Overcoming' Zarathustra notes that for the wise men the will to truth is a will to power. However, he says this only to condemn them for their (possibly unconscious) religious desires. 'You want to create the world before which you can kneel ...'¹⁰

If the phrase 'will to power' is at first unclear, it subsequently seems inappropriate. The will to power is not a will, but then neither is it a will to power. As Heidegger points out, it is not will in the conventional sense. 'Will itself cannot be willed. We can never resolve to have a will ...'¹¹ And so he concludes that there is 'something more unified, more original, and even more fertile behind that single rude word, "will"...'¹² As usual with Heidegger his account of Nietzsche's position is but a stepping stone to reaffirming his own. 'Therefore we can say that will to power is always essentially will. Although Nietzsche does not formulate it expressly in this way, at bottom that is what he means.'¹³ Or rather it is precisely the opposite of what Nietzsche intended in his crusade to root out the dragon's teeth of essentialism. The will to power is not will. As Michel Haar points out, it is not a psychological observation about the subject, will, and its object, power. 'The Will that is Will to Power responds at its origins to its own internal imperative: *to be more*.' [14] Thus if the will to power is not *will*, neither is it a will to *power*. The goal is not power but fulfilment, which is then enjoyed as a sense of being empowered. As Magnus explains, the mastery is not mastery over others, but over the herd-type within us: 'self-mastery and self-overcoming primarily'.[15] It is never crudely a sense of power over others without reference to the transformation of the self. Deleuze is clear on the matter. 'In this way the will to power is essentially creative and giving: it does not aspire, it does not seek, it does not desire, above all it does not desire power.'[16]

As Nietzsche's values describe modes of existence, so the will to power describes not a will – and certainly not a will to overpower – but an authentic mode of existence. The concept is often misunderstood and carries connotations of the grasping and destructive exercise of power guided by no moral considerations, inspired by purely egoistic and hedonistic ends. Although it need not, the phrase "will to power" sounds ominous to us. Nor is this surprising: we stand within a culture formed by Christian moral values, and any revaluation of these values will sound ominous, alien, even threatening to us. For Nietzsche the will to power is that dynamic force which had led to the development of mankind as a species. It has been successful as a species over against others not by simply protecting itself, but by seizing opportunities, taking risks, by exploiting advantage. And of course some individuals and groups have done this more consistently, more effectively than others. We have already met them. They are the masters, the rulers, the aristocrats: they are the ones who have lived instinctively, who have employed their passions, have affirmed life. They have served themselves, but of course have benefited their communities and the species. As we have seen, this is not simply pushing others aside, not destroying everything that stands in their paths. No, through sublimation of the passions such individuals are able to control themselves and set themselves goals. In addition to every other way of describing them, they are for Nietzsche 'the higher men'. Such an individual who is able to sublimate the will to power, to exercise it to achieve a higher form of life, a life unimaginable and unachievable to the herd – such a one is the *Übermensch*, the Superman.

Nietzsche is here introducing a value judgment. This is not another life, but a higher life. He is making a value judgment, a moral judgment, on occasion an aesthetic judgement, based on this natural phenomenon, the will to power. Religion and metaphysical world views and values have been rejected, but the threat of nihilism has been overcome. And so *The Antichrist* begins with the revaluation of values. 'What is good? All that heightens the feeling of power, the will to power, power itself in man. What is bad? All that proceeds from weakness.'[17] The acceptance, the welcoming of this life force, this life-affirming attitude, is good. It begins with the biological and is sublimated into the higher life. There is a continuity between the two, and no rejection. However, the rejection of the will to power is a danger not only to the higher life, but to life itself. 'Wherever the will to power declines in any form there is every time also a physiological regression, a *décadence*.'[18] This is why Nietzsche is so violently critical of Christianity: it has undermined the will to power, declared it suspect – ominous. It has substituted other motivations, other forms of behaviour, other values and virtues. It 'has waged war to the death against this higher type of man, it has excommunicated all the fundamental instincts of this type, it has distilled evil, the Evil One, out of these instincts'.[19] For its own part, 'Christianity has taken the side of everything weak, ill-constituted, it has made an ideal out of opposition to the preservative instincts of strong life …'[20] Nietzsche has traced everything back to physiology: morality, ethics, ascending life and now the will to power. On this view Christianity is not guilty of anything so trivial as proposing an alternative set of values. It threatens life itself, the very continuation of the species. It may seem eccentric, but Nietzsche focusses on one of these alternative values, pity, returning to it again and again as an example of decadence, an attitude which opens the way to physiological decline.

As early as *Human All Too Human* he protests against the insensitive and thoughtless way that pity 'sets about quack-doctoring at the health and reputation of its patient'.[21] And what of the poor patient, who experiences it 'as a sign of contempt'?[22] If we recall Nietzsche's discussion of the original meaning of 'good', we can see why it is that pity 'thwarts the law of evolution, which is the law of selection'.[23] In Part Four of *Zarathustra*, the prophet has collected a motley group of higher men, although it becomes clear that they are not yet higher men, merely stepping stones on the path. He speaks to them in turn, including a man identified as the Last Pope.

> You served him to the last, asked Zarathustra thoughtfully, after a profound silence, do you know how he died? Is it true what they say, that pity choked him, that he saw how man hung on the Cross and could not endure it, that love for man became his hell and at last his death?[24]

Pity, being one of the Christian virtues, is opposed to the will to power. But the rejection of the will to power leads to degeneration and to death. Zarathustra soon encounters another figure on the path before him. It is The Ugliest Man, and at first Zarathustra is so embarrassed at the sight of this being that he turns to leave. Pity overcame him and he sank down. But with an effort 'he arose from the ground and his countenance grew stern'.[25] It transpires that the ugliest man has been persecuted and hounded by others. Yet that is not the worst of it. 'But it is their pity, it is their pity from which I flee and flee to you, O Zarathustra, my last refuge, protect me.'[26] This rejection of pity as dangerous to life must seem alien to us – a revaluation of values. But Nietzsche has in mind the effect which pity has on those who are its recipients: 'to offer pity is as good as to offer contempt'.[27]

The higher men arise when the other values, the noble values, are affirmed. This is the link between the death of God and the birth of the Superman. Nietzsche has nothing but contempt for democracy as a system by which the herd has gained control of society:[28] the lunatics have taken over the asylum. 'Residues of Christian value judgments are found everywhere in socialist and positivistic systems.'[29] Ironically, these Christian survivals are engraved on the founding documents of many movements which think of themselves as too critical and sophisticated to be taken in by the *ancien régime*. Liberty, Equality, Fraternity: everyone is equal. But behind this affirmation of worth stands the Christian belief that all are equal before God.

> Before God. But now God has died. You Higher Men, this God was your greatest danger. Only since he has lain in the grave have you again been resurrected. Only now does the great noontide come, only now does the Higher Man become – lord and master (*Herr*).[30]

After almost 2,000 years of Christian suppression of the higher men it would be too much to expect that they could immediately appear – but at least they can make a start. What was said about God, must now be said about the Superman.

> God is a supposition, but I want your supposing to reach no further than your creating will. Could you create a god? So be silent about all gods. But you could surely create the Superman. Perhaps not you yourselves, my brothers. But you could transform yourselves into forefathers and ancestors of the Superman, and let this be your finest creating.[31]

We can see here not simply the rejection of religion, but the emergence of an alternative to it. Nietzsche's project was to accept the end of religion and metaphysics – fully and without reserve or regret: to face nihilism and the end of all meaning, and finally to establish on a new and natural basis moral values, life values, to create a meaningful life and experience the joy of living that life. As we have seen, he detected everywhere continuing presuppositions that derive from religion and philosophy, presuppositions which must now be surrendered. He was particularly sensitive to teleology, the idea that the meaning of life is bestowed upon life from outside, especially from a religious purpose or metaphysical plan, that meaning comes to us from the end of history. This is a feature of the Judaeo-Christian tradition in its religious forms, but also in its philosophical, especially Hegelian form and even in its ideological, Marxist form. Hegel's understanding of the dialectical movement of history is a secularization of this religious view, just as Marx's philosophy represents a materialization of Hegel's philosophy of history.[32] Nietzsche considered Hegel's philosophy a 'disguised theology'.[33] It was one of the modes by which religious presuppositions were preserved even at a time when religious beliefs were in decline. As with all revaluations Nietzsche is exposing something which is so widely accepted in Western culture that it continues to be assumed even when its religious foundations have been removed. For example, the humanities do not simply include history, they make a value judgment about it. The ecclesiastical historian Gerhard Ebeling commented on the methodological significance of this fact. 'For King Midas, legend says, everything he touched turned to gold. For modern man everything, the whole of reality, turns to history.'[34] Nietzsche had anticipated the same point. 'To glorify the origin – this is the metaphysical aftershoot that breaks out when we meditate on history and makes us believe that what stands at the beginning of all things is also what is most valuable and essential.'[35] Today we could call the 'metaphysical aftershoot' simply 'ideology': it is the assumption that the value of the present is bestowed from the past. As Nietzsche observes, time is calculated from the first day of Christianity. 'Why not rather from its last? From today?'[36] What he is opposing is the idea that the moment has no inherent significance, no value as itself. In an early essay 'On the Uses and Disadvantages of History for Life' he conceives of the suprahistorical man, 'who sees no salvation in the process and for whom, rather, the world is complete and reaches its finality at each and every moment'.[37] He is concerned with the effects of this normative view of history, with its slogan 'let the dead bury the living'.[38] The value of life must not be bestowed from the past, nor from the future. We have seen that for Nietzsche the only reason for cheerfulness in face of the death of God is that 'our sea' lies open before us: 'we have become incapable of believing in a future determined for us'.[39] The Judaeo-Christian view is that history is moving in a providential direction: God is guiding it towards a moral goal – the Reign of God. In this context value is bestowed on life from the future. And this too has its secular forms. It is true that Hegel's philosophy was not so ambitious: 'the owl of Minerva spreads its wings only with the falling of the dusk'.[40] The reason of history can only be detected in retrospect. Marx by comparison intends to shape history to achieve a moral goal, a society of justice and fairness: the future of philosophy lies in the philosophy of the future. Historical materialism is clearly dependent on Christian eschatology. Those who stridently oppose religion are likely to be deeply influenced by its patterns of thought. As already noted, Nietzsche's philosophy is not of the past or the future, but of the present, not the origin or the end of the day, but the great Noontide.[41] In the same essay on history he therefore offers yet another revaluation of values. 'No, the goal of humanity cannot lie in its end but only in its highest specimens.'[42] There is a goal, but it comes from within human history: it is not bestowed from the future or from the past.

This is Nietzsche's view, not to be confused with Social Darwiniansm. In the nineteenth century this movement showed how biology influenced the social sciences. At least this is how it is often remembered, although in reality the influence might have been in quite the opposite direction. In our own time F.A. Hayek declared that Darwin made sense of a plethora of data by borrowing from the social sciences.[43] But Nietzsche knew this already: 'without Hegel there could have been no Darwin'.[44] In the midst of such diversity one thing is clear: the religious doctrine of providence, of divine plan and purpose, continued as a model for those who sought to give life a meaning apart from religion. Nietzsche saw in all this yet another example of the halting between two ways, the lack of imagination, the existential cowardice of those who knew of the death of God but would not embrace the new reality. 'Beware of superfluous teleological principles.'⁴⁵ Nietzsche therefore dashes any hope that it might be possible to re-establish theology through biology. He tells us that 'man as a species is not progressing. Higher types are indeed attained, but they do not last. The level of the species is not raised.'⁴⁶ Giants call to each other across the medium of history, indifferent to 'the excited chattering dwarfs who creep about beneath them...'⁴⁷

The goal of humanity therefore lies in the creation of 'its highest specimens'. While 'mankind as a whole has no goal',⁴⁸ it should encourage the conditions which lead to the appearance of the highest specimen. This is not Darwinian, it is once again the triumph of becoming over being. 'Man is something that must be overcome...'⁴⁹ It is with this thought that Zarathustra's Prologue begins. It is not possible for Nietzsche that the species as a whole could progress, could attain to the higher, enhanced and fulfilled life. That is not the goal. In this sense man is a bridge, not a goal. 'Man is a rope fastened between animal and superman – a rope over an abyss.'⁵⁰

> Behold I teach you the Superman. The Superman is the meaning of the earth. Let your will say: the Superman shall be the meaning of the earth! I entreat you, my brothers, remain true to the earth and do not believe those who speak to you of superterrestrial hopes. They are poisoners, whether they know it or not. They are despisers of life, atrophying and self-poisoned men, of whom the earth is weary; so let them be gone. Once blasphemy against God was the greatest blasphemy, but God died, and thereupon these blasphemers died too. To blaspheme the earth is now the most dreadful offence ...⁵¹

If life is to have meaning, it must be the meaning of life itself: for life to have a meaning which is bestowed from elsewhere is the same as admitting that life has no meaning. The meaning of life is life itself: but not all forms of life have such meaning. As we have seen, it must be that form which embraces the natural, sublimates the passions, sets its own goals, embraces the will to power and fulfils its potential. 'All gods are dead: now we want the Superman to live.'[52]

Such an affirmation is marked by integrity and courage, but is it enough? For all its intellectual power and purity, our hearts do not warm to it. Can such a life bring peace and joy to a species which is distinguished from all others by the awareness of time, and the consciousness of mortality? Nietzsche, remembered for his proclamation of the death of God, has yet to declare himself on the death of man. More to the point, he has yet to tell us how we can affirm life in the sure knowledge of our *own* death.

8

Eternal Recurrence

Nietzsche wished to be acknowledged, to be admired, to be influential, but not to be popular. And yet his name is known to the public beyond the confines of philosophy. The name itself has caught the popular imagination: at once alien and threatening, entirely appropriate when inscribed on *that* photograph. And the one book which goes with this image is the exotically named *Thus Spake Zarathustra*. Nietzsche might have been secretly charmed that his book, the one which he valued above all others, should have attracted the fascination of the masses, charmed yet reassured that nevertheless its message was still beyond their comprehension. This is nowhere better illustrated than in his characterization of the prophet's message as – eternal recurrence. No locksmith's art, no security company's technology ever barred entry to a property more effectively than this concept. By asserting that this is the key to his whole system of thought and life, Nietzsche guaranteed that the herd would be excluded from the inner court of his philosophy, from that enlightenment which might lead them to the higher life itself. He was more unyielding than the Galilean teacher he claimed to oppose, in refusing to cast pearls before swine. (However, Nietzsche pointed out that 'the sacrificial animal does not share the spectators' ideas about sacrifice',[1] and we might speculate that swine might be justified in taking the view that in the great scheme of things pearls have no real value.)

The meaning of eternal recurrence is at the outset obscure, and the more it is studied, the more ambiguous it becomes. In the whole of Nietzsche's philosophy this concept, which Heidegger could describe as 'bewildering',[2] has generated most debate both as to its meaning and its viability. Is it fish, fowl or red meat: science, cosmology or metaphysics? These are interesting alternatives, to which we shall presently turn, but for the most part they omit a prior and more profound question. This question concerns the nature of the obscurity surrounding the concept of eternal recurrence. It is not simply the obscurity of the way the concept is used, but rather the circumstances in which it comes to be used. In Europe since the Enlightenment there has hardly been a sharper mind, a more incisive thinker and certainly no philosopher with a greater command of language than Nietzsche. How is it then that he has chosen as the key to his whole philosophy a concept so obscure and ambiguous? Certainly not through any lack of ability to clarify the meaning to himself, or to express it to his readers. Is it in order deliberately to confuse, to warn away the innocent? But no, the obscurity lies at a deeper level. Of course what he is saying is a revaluation of European culture, and consequently he has to struggle against the assumptions and prejudices which are not only deep-seated in the modern mind, but also embedded in the structure of received language. In such circumstances, what Nietzsche strives to express will seem unfamiliar and obscure. But even this does not quite describe the situation. The obscurity lies not in the reality it seeks to express, but in itself. As a boy growing up on Clydeside I recall skilled tradesmen saying, 'If you don't have the tools, don't attempt the job.' It is as if Nietzsche has chosen the wrong tool for the job, perhaps one which is incompatible with the job, a tool which would finally prevent him from achieving the end he has set for himself of expounding the true nature of things and the path to the higher life. Worse than that, it is possible that Nietzsche suspected it was a concept ill-fitted for its task, but by a *tour de force* he pressed it into service, made it serve his ends – though imperfectly. The same Clydeside platers would say, 'The bigger the problem, the bigger the hammer.' And as we know, Nietzsche wrote a book on precisely this subject, *How to Philosophize with a Hammer*.[3] But why would such a linguistic craftsman make use of an unsuitable tool? Therein lies the final obscurity: it is as if Nietzsche had been *given* the tool. It came to him already formed and it was not open to him to do with it as he might have wished. The obscurity lies in the origins and not in the outcome. But with this gnomic utterance we must put to one side this line of thought, at least till we have, like master chefs turned master sleuths, determined the true nature of this fish, which is so unlike fish that it could easily be mistaken for fowl or red meat.

If the concept of eternal recurrence is so obscure, so ambiguous in its meaning, so opaque in its origins, where on earth should we begin our understanding of it? Inevitably there have been attempts to find its origins in Greek philosophy, but Nietzsche was not consciously developing a theme from any predecessor, least of all – though most appropriately characterized – the melancholic philosopher known as 'Heraclitus the Obscure'.[4] Reflecting on the writing of his first book, *The Birth of Tragedy*, Nietzsche was later to concede that eternal return might have been taught by Heraclitus,[5] but Deleuze is correct in claiming that 'Nietzsche does not recognize his idea of eternal return in his predecessors of antiquity'.[6] In passing we might note that although Nietzsche mentions a relatively small number of writers, normally to criticize them, he rarely suggests that his own position derives from something he read. We have noted that with his failing eyesight there were periods when he could not read. This was no limitation, as we have already observed. 'At times when I am deeply sunk in work you will see no books around me: I would guard against letting anyone speak or even think in my vicinity.'[7] This reflects not his intellectual isolation, but his confidence in his own originality. He was not a collector or summarizer: 'my ambition is to say in ten sentences what everyone else says in a book – what everyone else does not say in a book.'[8] But if the idea of eternal recurrence does not come from the intellectual tradition, where on earth are we to begin?

If there is one thing we have learned about Nietzsche's philosophy, it is that we always begin at the same place. Where *on earth* to begin, where else than with theology, or the lack of it, with religion or the loss of it, in other words with the death of God. And so indeed it transpires. Book Three of *The Gay Science* begins with Nietzsche's first reference to the death of God.[9] With the death of God, with the end of the religious view of the universe, what is left to the perceptive observer? If we reject the notion that the world is a single organism (no Gaia for this misogynist) or even a machine (*pace* Paley), we must reject all anthropomorphic projections. Although there are laws of nature, there is no plan, no direction, no goal: 'and the whole musical box repeats eternally its tune which may never be called a melody ...'[10] The penultimate section of *The Will to Power* deals with 'the new world conception'. The idea that the world has a beginning and an end is not scientific, or at least is bad science. It arises not from observation, but 'with an ulterior theological motive'.[11] We have here the same position as above, laws without purpose, processes without progress, chance without mechanical regularity:

> it follows that, in the great dice game of existence, [the world] must pass through a calculable number of combinations. In infinite time, every possible combination would at some time or another be realized; more, it would be realized an infinite number of times.[12]

Zarathustra's animals are part of nature, and recognize the cycle of birth, development, decline and death, and rebirth.[13] The cyclical view of (infinite) time relates more nearly to our experience and to scientific observation than a linear view of time, a creationism which is unrelated to life or to modern astrophysics. In ringing the changes on the implications of this alternative world-view Nietzsche takes a further step, which is mathematically unsound.

> And since between every combination and its next recurrence all other possible combinations would have to take place, and each of these combinations conditions the entire sequence of combinations in the same series, a circular movement of

absolutely identical series is thus demonstrated: the world as a circular movement that has already repeated itself infinitely often and plays its game *in finitum*.[14]

This last point is far from being 'demonstrated', but fortunately for Nietzsche it can be set aside without undermining the motion which he is describing as eternal recurrence of the same: it must be affirmed as a consequence of the death of God.

It is necessary to stress the relationship between eternal recurrence and the death of God. As Jaspers explains, Nietzsche emphasized the concept because '*it finalizes the "death of God"* and, in addition, amounts to an overcoming of nothingness'.[15] There has been a great deal of discussion of the viability of eternal recurrence considered as a scientific theory, but such discussion is confusing and frustrating when taken out of the context of the death of God. Nietzsche was no scientist and certainly could not be expected to provide the kind of evidence upon which scientists might revise their positions on the nature of the physical universe. It was at that time when Nietzsche was preparing to launch the concept of eternal recurrence that, according to Lou von Salomé, he planned to spend the next ten years in the study of natural science, in order to provide a firm foundation for his philosophy.[16] His enthusiasm for science waned, and in any case, as we shall see, the foundation for belief in eternal recurrence was not scientific evidence. Even Maudemarie Clark in her excellent review of the literature on eternal recurrence[17] breaks the link between eternal recurrence and the context in which it arose, the death of God. Thus she quotes Nietzsche's claim that eternal recurrence 'is the most *scientific* of all possible hypotheses'.[18] However, this sentence occurs within a discussion of 'European Nihilism'. After the death of God there is no meaning in life, 'as if everything were in vain'. 'Let us think this thought in its most terrible form: existence as it is, without meaning or aim, yet recurring inevitably without any finale of nothingness: "*the eternal recurrence*".'[19] As we shall see, this was not to be Nietzsche's reading of the

situation, since he has overcome European nihilism. 'The
European form of Buddhism: the energy of knowledge and
strength compels this belief. It is the most scientific of all possible
hypotheses. We deny end goals: if existence had one it would
have to have been reached.'[20] Eternal recurrence is the most
reasonable world-view, and in that sense the most scientific – for
those who have experienced the death of the Western, Christian
God. Clark, as others sympathetic to Nietzsche, is disappointed
that eternal recurrence, fundamental to his whole philosophy – by
his own admission, his own insistence – should be supported by
no 'proofs', but as we have previously noted, Nietzsche held that
the foundation of Western science, like those of Western metaphysics and morality, are unacknowledged religious premises,
one of which is that the universe is not eternal. Eternal recurrence
does not arise from within science, but from without, not as its
consequence but as its premise. It is for this reason that Nietzsche
is competent to formulate this teaching – but only when it is
linked to the death of God.

Since Nietzsche is not speaking here of anything so
insignificant or transient as the world (planet Earth), eternal
recurrence might also be described as a cosmological theory. That
is, according to Magnus, 'Nietzsche has attempted to provide a
true theory of the universe.'[21] Although the concept deliberately
eschews any thought of meaning in the cosmos, yet it presents
us with a model which describes the pattern of universal and
rhythmic development and decline. However, Nietzsche had no
interest in science for science's sake. Eternal recurrence might be
described as science or cosmology, but we know that these things
could not be of interest to Nietzsche unless they had implications
for his main project, the higher life. It is not surprising therefore
that in further references to eternal recurrence other elements
appear, human and existential elements. Clearly he was driven by
the implied question: if the universe is characterized by the
eternal recurrence of the same, what are the implications for
living? But this is not at all the same thing as saying
that Nietzsche was indifferent to the truth or falsity of eternal

recurrence as a cosmological doctrine. Magnus, in his *Nietzsche's Existential Imperative*, advocates a 'normative' understanding of the concept. 'Recurrence (and its real or possible truth) is a visual and conceptual representation of a particular attitude toward life.'[22] But as with all existentialist reductions, we should have to ask whether there is no external, non-subjective dimension. Who would choose to adopt and advocate 'a particular attitude toward life' by means of such an obscure concept if it were possible to do without it as a mere metaphor?

At the beginning of Part Three of this 'book for everyone and no one', Zarathustra becomes a wanderer, and a teacher – addressing sailors on board ship, telling them 'Of the Vision and the Riddle'. Nietzsche is the philosopher of becoming, not of being. Indeed, as Deleuze sums it up: 'Recurring is the being of what becomes.'[23] He is the philosopher of the moment. But the moment is a moment in time, a gateway which the path from the past has just reached, the very same gateway through which stretches out the future all in a straight line. Zarathustra's interlocutor of the moment, the dwarf, knows better. '"Everything straight lies," murmured the dwarf disdainfully. "All truth is crooked, time itself is a circle."'[24] This is new: it is not simply that the path runs back for all eternity, and runs forward for the same. If time is a circle, then the moment stands at a point which already has been the past, and which will be reached yet again in the future. Heidegger cannot resist seeing in this 'the concealed essence of Time'. 'Thinking Being, will to power, as eternal return, thinking the most difficult thought of philosophy means thinking Being and Time.'[25] As though embarrassed by this conclusion, he denies that this means assessing Nietzsche against the criterion of 'a book entitled *Being and Time*'![26] But we return to Zarathustra's question, 'Must not all things than *can* run have already run along this lane? Must not all things that *can* happen *have* already happened, been done, run past?'[27] All this in theory, all this in the great generality of things, yes, but also in their particularity.

And this slow spider that creeps in the moonlight, and this moonlight itself, and I and you at this gateway whispering together, whispering of eternal things – must we not also have been here before? And must we not return and run down that other lane out before us, down that long, terrible lane – must we not return eternally?[28]

The same particularity may have been found in Pythagoras. Magnus quotes Eudemus of Rhodes who claims that Pythagoras taught that 'everything will eventually return in this self-same numerical order, and I shall converse with you, staff in hand, and you will sit as you are sitting now, and so it will be in everything else, and it is reasonable to assume that time too will be the same'.[29]

Nietzsche has begun with the scientific, even cosmological theory of eternal recurrence, but he is now presenting us with a human response to the theory, its consequences, its lessons. What is that response? Nietzsche the psychologist, or perhaps we should simply say Nietzsche the most sensitive observer of human moods and feelings, indicates that our response to the eternal recurrence is very different from the view which might be taken by a scientist, whether mathematician or astrophysicist. Earlier we recalled from *The Gay Science* the passage in which after the death of God we quit the land, and sail out on to a sea without the old landmarks and navigation stars. 'But there will be times when you will realize that it is infinite and that there is nothing more dreadful than infinity.' Here we have the same response. For the cosmologist it might be a path, but anyone who internalizes eternal recurrence views 'that long, terrible lane' with apprehension and awe. More than that, in discussing the section in *The Gay Science* entitled 'The Meaning of Our Cheerfulness' we saw Nietzsche shoulder the heavy burden of announcing the consequences of the death of God, as he played the role of 'the teacher and advance proclaimer of this monstrous logic of terror ...'

Eternal recurrence is intriguing, debatable, the substance of academic controversy where reputations can be enhanced or destroyed. But does Nietzsche not deserve better than this fate? He has done us the service of offering us not something so inconsequential as an argument or a concept: for our sake he offers something of himself. Such is his command of language, the power of the pictures he conjures up before us; surely we also experience at least for a moment, the terror, the existential panic which engulfed him at the thought of eternal recurrence. In the secondary literature there are many discussions of eternal recurrence, but few if any refer to this point of existential terror. Eternal recurrence is reduced from a vital life issue to an intriguing little intellectual puzzle. Nietzsche's public life was tragically short. Perhaps it is as well that he did not survive to witness the adoption towards *his* work of an attitude which he had condemned as 'Egyptianism' – the mummification of his work – and of himself. If we truly wish to understand the significance of eternal recurrence for Nietzsche then we must extend our examination of it beyond the criteria of mathematics and even logic. Eternal recurrence is in transition: what began as a theory for understanding is becoming a doctrine for living. At one level, if eternal recurrence describes the nature of the universe it may be interesting, even fascinating as a theory, but ultimately irrelevant to our brief lives. But at another level, and this is the genius of Nietzsche, even if we cannot influence eternal recurrence, the attitude we adopt towards it may influence us.

For Nietzsche, Zarathustra is the prophet of eternal recurrence, and he considered the first exposition of its implications to be found at the end of Book Four of *The Gay Science*. Indeed in *Ecce Homo* it is this theme, which extends knowledge to life, which produces the combination he admired in the Provençal knights, *gaya scienza*, the combination of laughter and wisdom.[30] As we have seen, Dr Nietzsche diagnosed a modern malaise and prescribed a cure. After the death of God modern life lacks meaning and significance, or rather, the loss of any perspective from which life could have value is the very condition which is described metaphorically as the death of God. And as if this were not enough bad news for one day, Dr Nietzsche now adds terror to chill the blood, vertigo to make the most stable mind dizzy. As we emerge reeling from the surgery, this is the prognosis which lies before us. Is this life vain and intolerable? Then be prepared to live it again and again, eternally. What is to be done? Should we change our doctor, or at least ask for a second opinion? But we have not come out empty-handed. With the diagnosis we have also been given a prescription. Our hopes rise, but only to be dashed when we read that the good doctor recommends the poison itself as the cure.

To recap: most people go on happily with their lives, ignorant of the death of God, spared from its logic of terror. The ruminant life is not worth living, but at least it is not threatened with existential despair. Only a few experience their lives as lacking in meaning, value, significance. They are not content with lives which are lightweight, lacking in substance. Should they turn back and join the herd, or should they take courage, acknowledge the death of God, stare eternity in the eye – and discover to their delight the new substance, the new weight to their lives: *gaya scienza*! So it is fitting that the terror which could be good news is first expounded in *The Gay Science*, in a section entitled 'The Greatest Weight'. It is so important that we should have the text before us.

What if some day or night a demon were to steal after you into your loneliest loneliness and say to you, 'This life as you now live it and have lived it, you will have to live once more and innumerable times more; and there will be nothing new in it, but every pain and every joy and every thought and sigh and everything unutterably small or great in your life will have to return to you, all in the same success and sequence – even this spider and this moonlight between the trees, and even this moment and I myself. The eternal hourglass of existence is turned upside down again and again and you with it, speck of dust.' Would you not throw yourself down and gnash your teeth and curse the demon who spoke thus? Or have you experienced a tremendous moment when you would have answered him, 'You are a god and never have I heard anything more divine.' If this thought gain possession of you, it would change you as you are or perhaps crush you. The question in each and everything, 'Do you desire this once more and innumerable times more?' would lie upon your actions as the greatest weight. Or how well disposed would you have to become to yourself and to life to crave nothing more fervently than this ultimate eternal confirmation and seal?[31]

A few pages on, Book Five begins with the section 'The Meaning of Our Cheerfulness' which we discussed earlier, and here we see the same dialectical movement. We can either turn away from the terror and live in what Sartre called 'bad faith',[32] hiding from ourselves the truth which we know in our hearts, lying to ourselves about our situation, betraying ourselves about our real condition – and potential – or we can take heart, lift up our spirits and attain a higher life than is possible for browsing ruminants and self-deceivers.

Nietzsche is generalizing about the human condition in the modern world, but the particular from which the analysis arises is his own painful, destructive experience. It is fitting therefore that having experienced sympathy for him in time of crisis (though God forbid we should show him pity), we can now rejoice with him. Behind him lies the no-saying, the decadence, the libel on life. By his courage he has won through to this, the highest affirmation of life. Not an ideal life, not another kind of life in another sphere, but the affirmation of this life. As Löwith points out, Nietzsche refuses the alternatives of the determinism of the natural and the freedom of idealism: he unites 'the willing of the individual with the cosmic imperative'.[33] The great 'immoralist' has established, in the view of Deleuze, 'a rule as rigorous as the Kantian imperative', a rule which Deleuze summarises thus: 'Whatever you will, will it in such a way that you also will its Eternal Return.'[34] Magnus sees in Nietzsche's pluralism a further distinction from Kantian ethics. The affirmation of life is just that: Nietzsche does not prescribe any particular actions.[35]

It would be good to pause at this point, to recover from the existential stress and strain of this extraordinary journey to life, to enjoy the moment and the exuberance of the *gaya scienza* – but here come the Egyptians again. A typical question concerns how this understanding of eternal recurrence is related to the scientific theory with which we began. If there is no continuity of memory or consciousness, can it actually be this life which recurs? Alternatively, Clark contrasts the demon's question with the more familiar human (female) enquiry: 'If you had it to do all over, would you marry me again?'[36] But is this really such a different question? Is it an innocent enquiry about a matter of fact, which as it transpires is no matter of fact at all, or is it not in its own way simply a cry for affirmation? Another question is whether if we do indeed, in recognition of eternal recurrence, affirm life and achieve a higher state, does that have any bearing on what kind of life it is that recurs? If Nietzsche were simply presenting us with a cosmo-mathematical theory, then of course everything recurs: the good, the bad and the cor blimey. Of course if an individual achieved a higher form of life, then that life would recur – as would the 'lower' form. But even if eternal recurrence is presented in such objective forms, Nietzsche's own interest in it has to do with its existential impact. This gives the impression – which I believe to be false – that he is claiming that to achieve the higher life now is to ensure that it is the higher life which recurs. This might be a form of *samsara*, but it cannot be supported from Nietzsche's presentation of eternal recurrence. However, several commentators have taken the view that Nietzsche teaches the selective view, that is, that by choosing a particular life now the individual ensures that it is this life which recurs and *not its alternatives*. Heidegger understands Nietzsche in this sense,[37] which is the more strange since in his analytic of *Dasein*, Heidegger had insisted that the inauthentic is as *real* as the authentic. Deleuze takes the same line. 'Why should affirmation be better than negation? We will see that the solution can only be given by the test of the eternal return: what is better and better absolutely is that which returns, that which can bear returning, that which wills its return.'³⁸ But whether what should return does return must depend on a moral fabric undeclared, which owes nothing to eternal recurrence. Magnus also finds selectivity in the doctrine, a transition from the categorical imperative to an existential imperative, but he has lost interest in the empirical basis of the doctrine and regards it simply as a 'countermyth'. It is viewed exclusively as an existential imperative: 'eternal recurrence intensifies the dynamics of choice, because whatever I choose to be, that I shall be for infinite recurrences'.³⁹ The doctrine is now the basis of evaluation. 'That which possesses value is that which can be willed unto eternity. With the loss of an absolute instrument of judgment of conduct, the "that" which can be willed is no longer a single act, but a mode of being; a life. Whether or not life is worthy of infinite repetition becomes Nietzsche's principle of selection and redemption.'⁴⁰ But is redemption the effect of eternal recurrence, or the existential use to which it is put? To this point we shall return in the next chapter.

On the question of selectivity Nietzsche is perfectly clear. Zarathustra teaches that he will return 'not to a new life or a better life or a similar life. I shall return eternally to this identical self-same life ...'⁴¹ But Nietzsche goes out of his way to emphasise this point in a typically dramatic way. In the section 'Of the Vision and the Riddle' Zarathustra recounts a dream, which is also a riddle. On the wild desolate cliffs he suddenly detected by the light of the moon, 'a young shepherd writhing, choking, convulsed, his face distorted; and a heavy, black snake was hanging out of his mouth. Had I ever seen so much disgust and pallid horror on a face?'⁴² I apologize to any reader who has felt nausea at having to read this account without warning, but the feeling of disgust, of nausea is precisely the point of the story. The prophet calls to the young man to bite! Bite! Finally he does bite through the snake and recovers. Who can answer the riddle? The answer emerges in a later section entitled 'The Convalescent', in which the animals rehearse his teaching on eternal recurrence. Zarathustra recalls 'how that monster crept into my throat and choked me!'⁴³ Eternal recurrence means the return of the great men of society, which pleases Zarathustra. However, it also means the return of the small. 'I had seen them both naked, the greatest man and the smallest man: all too similar to one another, even the greatest all too human. The greatest all too small. That was my disgust at man. And eternal recurrence even for the smallest. That was my disgust at all existence. Ah, disgust. Disgust! Disgust!'[44]

If the open sea is not bright, not all that returns is Dionysian.

By this time Nietzsche has entirely lost interest in the scientific theory, the cosmological model. He has set in place the last piece of his great project – not a world–view, but a prescription for life itself. Who would be able to rejoice in eternal recurrence? Only the higher men, only those who live the post-religious, post-metaphysical life, who have overcome the morality of good and evil, who have rejected the ascetic ideal; those who live instinct-ively, who rejoice in the passions and sublimate them; those who create the meaning and value of their lives. Only such as these could rejoice in eternal recurrence, or rather we should say that since eternal recurrence simply as a theory is of no interest to Nietzsche, affirmation of eternal recurrence is the test of whether they are indeed higher men or not. Negatively the acceptance of eternal recurrence closes the door to the old religio-metaphysical life. Positively it opens up the way to that new life of meaning, of value, of weight, for which Nietzsche longed. 'Was that life? Well then. Once more!'[45]

On this happy note perhaps we can take our leave of this complex matter. But no, we have still to take up again that cryptic assertion, that gnomic utterance about the obscurity of the concept of eternal recurrence, with which this chapter began. The obscurity is inherent, because of the circumstances of its origins. The concept was *given* to Nietzsche and therefore he had to work with it within certain constraints. Nor does this mis-represent Nietzsche – neither was it the only experience of its kind. Two instances occur within the very same section of *Ecce Homo*, within the chapter dealing with the origins of *Thus Spoke Zarathustra*. He tells us that during a stay in Italy, near Genoa,

while out walking he conceived of Zarathustra. Or rather, he tells
us no such thing. 'It was on these two walks that the whole of the
first Zarathustra came to me, above all Zarathustra himself, as a
type: more accurately, *he stole up on me* ...'[46] Soon Nietzsche is
musing on the nature of inspiration.

> If one had the slightest residue of superstition left in one, one
> would hardly be able to set aside the idea that one is merely
> incarnation, merely mouthpiece, merely medium of over-
> whelming forces. The concept of revelation, in the sense that
> something suddenly, with unspeakable certainty and subtlety,
> becomes visible, audible, simply describes the fact. One hears,
> one does not seek; one takes, one does not ask who gives; a
> thought flashes up like lightning, with necessity, unfalteringly
> formed – I have never had any choice. An ecstasy whose
> tremendous tension sometimes discharges itself in a flood of
> tears, while one's steps now involuntarily rush along, now
> involuntarily lag; a complete being outside oneself with the
> distinct consciousness of a multitude of subtle shudders and
> trickling down to one's toes ... Everything is in the highest
> degree involuntary but takes place as in a tempest of a feeling
> of freedom, of absoluteness, of power, of divinity.[47]

Nietzsche did not conceive of Zarathustra, did not dream up a
strange work in a classical style, did not decide from wheeze or
whimsy to adapt for his own purposes the founder of the ancient
Persian religion, a religion, ironically, of good and evil.
Uninvited, his Zarathustra came to him, by inspiration.
Inspiration is yet another word which has been degraded in
modern times. Like native islanders who find instruments and
garments in a shipwreck which refer to things they know not of,
so in modern culture words which were once necessary to witness
to the depth of existence, to the mystery of being, are debased and
used for commercial purposes: a sextant used as a hammer. But
Nietzsche knew better: indeed it was part of his struggle against
what he saw as the philistinism of German society. Inspiration.
There is no other or better word; he knows of none, but he will

not deny or misdescribe his experience just because it is a religious term. Nor should we be taken in by his opening bluster, as if for amusement he dons the fancy costume of another age, as if he is merely adopting the mind-set of one who has 'the slightest residue of superstition'. He describes this experience accurately in the most orthodox religious terms. It is the constant theme of the mystics of many cultures, the feeling of being the temporary home 'of power, of divinity', without any loss of individuality or personal freedom.

It is a most unexpected and extraordinary passage, which raises doubts – if we ever had such doubts – about Nietzsche's description of himself as an entirely irreligious man. Inevitably we shall pursue this point in the following chapters. Nietzsche is not entertaining himself by analysing the use of the word 'inspiration' among mystical writers. He is relating to us a kind of experience which was previously called religious, and which he cannot describe in any other terms. It is like the self-professed atheist who, when spotted at the annual carol service, shrugs, smiles sheepishly (did I mention that he was sitting near the manger), as if to say, well … Quite, well what? The experience is real and there are no other words to describe it and no other more appropriate place in which the story can be told. More to the point, Nietzsche is not describing one isolated occasion. Zarathustra was not the only experience of inspiration which had come to him, uninvited, unsought – disturbingly unwelcome. Two pages before the reference to Zarathustra, another religious experience is detailed for us. Indeed in *Ecce Homo* this other incident is the subject of the very opening paragraph of the chapter on *Thus Spoke Zarathustra*. Nietzsche clearly feels that we must know about this matter if we are to understand the origins of his greatest work and the focal point of its message – the eternal recurrence of the same. If the passage on inspiration comes as a surprise, the following is something of a puzzle.

I shall now tell the story of Zarathustra. The basic conception of the work, the idea of eternal recurrence, the highest formula of affirmation that can possibly be attained – belong to the August of the year 1881: it was jotted down on a piece of paper with the inscription: '6,000 feet beyond man and time'. I was that day walking through the woods beside the lake of Silvaplana; I stopped beside a mighty pyramidal block of stone which reared itself up not far from Surlei. Then this idea came to me.[48]

Nietzsche chooses to tell us something about the experience, but keeps a tight control on it. Indeed it is more an incident than an experience: of the experience he tell us almost nothing, but he is in no doubt as to its reality. A few weeks before that, he had undergone experiences which seemed to pave the way for this particular revelation. In *Ecce Homo* he refers to a parallel experience of his friend Peter Gast, 'who was likewise "reborn" ...'[49] And in a letter to Gast written in August 1881 he describes the elation of the time, and its tears. 'Not sentimental tears, mind you, but tears of joy, to the accompaniment of which I sang and talked nonsense, filled with a new vision far superior to that of other men.'[50] This was not simply a nice feeling, but what Birault calls 'Dionysian beatititude',[51] and it should be read in parallel with the 'coming' of Zarathustra. It is an experience of inspiration, of what he called 'divinity', the content of which is eternal recurrence, 'the highest affirmation that can possibly be attained'. As Heidegger notes, 'the thought of eternal return was not discovered in or calculated from other doctrines. It simply came.'[52] Or as Pierre Klossowski puts it, 'the idea itself emerges as a specific doctrine; nonetheless it preserves its character as a revelation'.[53] But we must bear in mind that the account was written eight years later and, more importantly, after Nietzsche had worked out the implications of eternal recurrence as affirmation, as *gaya scienza*. Thus he is running together the original experience and his later more elaborated view of its significance – a common phenomenon in those recalling defining moments in their lives. It is notoriously difficult to separate an experience from its interpretation,[54] but here I am distinguishing the experience from an elaboration which concerns not so much an interpretation as its implications. The description of the rock, 'a mighty pyramidal block of stone which reared itself up', suggests that Nietzsche had what would now be described, following Rudolf Otto, as a 'numinous' experience.[55] It sounds like a mystical experience in the sense of seeing into the heart of reality. There have been those who have 'explained' the experience as the first symptoms of Nietzsche's final illness. How convenient! How reductionist! And does that mean that we should discount all of his works written after *Daybreak*? On Nietzsche's own view *everything* human arises from physiological conditions: how we evaluate it relates to the enhancement of life.

Nietzsche himself therefore relates eternal recurrence to particular experiences, which have revealed the true nature of things. For this reason alone I should not wish to follow Clark when she attempts to extricate the great man from the folly of this doctrine. She claims that it would be possible to find in Nietzsche's works an argument 'for accepting the ideal of affirming eternal recurrence that depends on neither cosmology nor metaphysics'.[56] But this fails to address the question of why Nietzsche was constrained to use a concept which cannot simply be demythologized and reduced to a metaphor. Even Jaspers strikes a strange note on this subject. 'Nietzsche's idea of eternal recurrence is philosophically as essential as it is questionable: to him it was most overpowering, while probably no one since then has taken it seriously.'[57] It is the more strange that this existentialist philosopher, psychologist *manqué*, should fail to ask what it is that overpowered Nietzsche to the extent that he should espouse such an unfashionable and unlikely construction. To raise this question, rather than to believe the concept is how we should take it 'seriously'. When Furness calls eternal recurrence 'a metaphysical nonsense, a desperate remedy, an attempt at substitution'[58] he is dividing the empirical basis of the concept from the use to which it is put, as if the doctrine were a mere device which Nietzsche could decide to use or not.

Two things might strike us about the incident of the pyramidal rock at Surlei. The first concerns which is more surprising: that Nietzsche should tell us so little about the incident or that he should mention it at all; that he should describe it as a religious experience or that he should make it the basis of his message about the end of religion? It is certainly a tribute to Nietzsche's intellectual integrity that he should tell us that his greatest creation, Zarathustra, and his ultimate teaching, eternal recurrence, both come from experiences which Nietzsche himself encourages us to think of as broadly religious. This leads to the second point which might strike us about the passage. Earlier I claimed that the obscurity of the concept lies not in the reality it seeks to describe, but in the term itself. This relates in particular to the use of the word 'eternal'. Nietzsche's belief in recurrence may be right or wrong, but it makes sense in mathematics, in astrophysics and in cosmology – except that we should have expected him to use the phrase 'infinite recurrence'. 'Infinite' (*unendlich*) is a mathematical term, 'eternal' (*ewig*) is a religious or metaphysical term. But are they not synonyms? In this case not.

This in turn leads to a final point. In our earlier discussion in this chapter, we followed the convention of describing eternal recurrence as in turn a scientific theory, a cosmological view and a metaphysical doctrine. That convention is based on the *false* assumption that physics leads on to metaphysics. It is a false assumption, and one which Nietzsche himself specifically rejected. As I recalled earlier in this chapter, Nietzsche held that Western science as much as anything else is based on religious and metaphysical foundations. The significance of the incident at Surlei is that the idea of eternal recurrence came to Nietzsche as a religious or metaphysical revelation, not as a scientific hypothesis. It represents yet another revaluation of values, the replacing of a Western Christian linear view of history with a cyclical view of history more akin to that found in Taoism, Hinduism or Buddhism. However, it still comes as a revelation, as a numinous experience. Nietzsche is touched by the eternal, not by the infinite. Eternal is a qualitative term, infinite is quantitative. The obscurity of the concept of eternal recurrence arises from the fact that Nietzsche uses it in two different contexts, neither appropriate. In the first he extends it into the sphere of natural science, in which eternal is inappropriate. In the second he uses it in his attempt to counter religion (or at least one specific and dominant form of religion), which by definition it cannot do. By his own insistence that eternal recurrence is the foundation of his work, he preserves religion at the heart of his own philosophy. His loyalty is therefore to the necessity of the eternal, even if it compromises his position on religion. Thus in his earliest book his quest had begun. 'It may be claimed that a nation, like an individual, is valuable only insofar as it is able *to give quotidian experience the stamp of the eternal.* Only by so doing can it express its profound, if unconsciousness, conviction of the relativity of time and the metaphysical meaning of life.'[59] Magnus comments on the necessity of the eternal. 'A world without eternity, Nietzsche must have thought, was unfit for human habitation: but eternity "beyond" or "behind" the transitory was worse still.'[60]

We should have to conclude that eternal recurrence is a fundamentally religious concept, arising from a numinous experience which came to Nietzsche. Thus, notwithstanding his irreligious writings, his actual relationship to religion bears further examination. Does the quality 'eternal' belong to the infinity of the sequence of recurrence, or to the quality of the higher life which its affirmation yields? If in reality it is the latter, then there is a close parallel between Zarathustra's message to the higher men, and the teaching of the Hellenized Christ of the Gospel of St John. In both eternal life begins now, in this world. 'My sheep hear my voice, and I know them, and they follow me; and I give them eternal life, and they shall never perish ...'[61] Nietzsche's word to those who followed him sounds like a parallel message rather than an alternative, 'Let us imprint the emblem of eternity on *our* life!'[62]

9

Nietzsche's Faith

Again and again in the course of this study we have noted that Nietzsche's philosophy begins with the death of God. It is described as a quasi-historical fact, certainly a cultural event, but beyond that Nietzsche welcomes it as the end of the old and the beginning of the new. Or more accurately it is precisely the reverse. If we were to draw a parallel with Hayek's history of political economy, it is the return to 'the abandoned road',[1] what Nietzsche regarded as the natural life of mankind forsaken because of religious bewitchment. There is, however, an important difference between the two. Hayek is describing an economic order which emerged dramatically in eighteenth-century Europe, only to be deserted in the early part of the twentieth century. In calling for a return to 'the abandoned road' of free enterprise he was espousing a system which was identified relatively recently in human history, in the work of the Scottish moralists. Nietzsche too is calling for a return to the abandoned road, or rather advocating that mankind now abandon its short-lived and disastrous experiment with religion. However, we must not think that the abolition of religion is an end in itself, as if with its disappearance all would be well. Nietzsche's concern is not with religion but with life, with the struggle of life and above all with the affirmation of life, the ascending, enhancing life. His condemnation of religion relates to its suspicion about life, the natural life of instinct and passion, to the condemnation of life, to the judgment of good and evil, to sin and guilt. His condemnation of religion relates to the libel on life, to the call for improvement.

Stated thus, Nietzsche does not attack all forms of religion, but the higher religions, the improvement religions of good and evil and of course and especially Christianity.

When Nietzsche calls for a return to the abandoned road it is not to recall mankind to a period before religion. It would seem from anthropological and archaeological evidence that for *homo sapiens* there is no such period. Rather he recalls us to the natural life, to the communities of good and bad which he described earlier. He is not concerned if that life includes religion, so long as it is natural religion, what he is pleased to call pagan religion. Natural religion was part of the fabric of good and bad. And a particular feature of it was to encourage and enable people to live the natural life, the life in harmony with their environment, both social and material. These religions do not seek to change or to improve people. Their taboos are intended to erect a fence against any disastrous straying from the communal path. It might be surprising, but it is entirely consistent that Nietzsche can therefore present himself as an essentially religious man, a disciple of the god Dionysos. He can condemn the Christian religion not simply by rejecting religion, but rather by comparing it to another form of religion. 'Dionysos versus the Crucified.'

> Is the pagan cult not a form of thanksgiving and affirmation of life? Must its highest representative not be an apology for and deification of life? The type of a well–constituted and ecstatically overflowing spirit! The type of a spirit that takes into itself and *redeems* the contradictions and questionable aspects of existence.[2]

Of course it is not possible for anyone in the modern world to be a devotee of that ancient god, but we can see that Nietzsche's enemy is not religion, but a form of religion which has a particular and debilitating effect upon human life. There can be other religions or other aspects and forms of religion which have a more positive and wholesome effect. It should therefore come as no surprise to find that Nietzsche has always been viewed as a religious figure. As Jung observes, 'Nietzsche was no atheist, but his God was dead.'[3] Bernard Zelechow observes that 'although Nietzsche disavowed Christianity and atheism he is a religious thinker'.[4] And Erich Heller in his incisive and insightful essays on Nietzsche, 'the renegade *homo religiosus*', also detects the character of the man behind the slogans. 'He is, by the very texture of his soul and mind, one of the most radically religious natures that the nineteenth-century brought forth …'[5] And in his Rectoral Address, Heidegger could describe Nietzsche as 'the last German philosopher who was passionately in search of God'.[6] Nor is this a modern fad. Anthony Ludovici was one of the earliest writers to recognize the permanent significance of Nietzsche's work, but in a biography published only a few years after the great atheist's death he was not taken in by the superficial bluster. 'No careful reader of his works can doubt that Nietzsche was a deeply religious man.'[7] Only those who have been and continue to be religious can experience the death of God.

If Nietzsche is regarded as a religious figure, it is certainly not a device to incorporate him and therefore silence his uncomfortable criticisms. Rather it is necessary so to describe him if we are to do justice to his concerns and his philosophy taken as a whole. As I pointed out at the beginning of this study, Nietzsche's philosophy cannot be adequately presented by those who censor his interests by treating only their own. Deleuze compiles an impressive list of passages in which Nietzsche is prepared to make positive assessments of religion. He then draws his conclusion. 'Commentators who want to make Nietzsche's atheism into a temperate atheism, or even want to reconcile Nietzsche with God, rely on all these texts.'[8] It would seem by implication that those who ignore such texts are somehow more objective. But in the midst of this workshop where the air is filled with the sparks of axes being ground is there not another category of scholar, those who simply take Nietzsche at his word?

A religious critic of religion, the apparent contradiction turns out to be an example of a familiar pattern. The whale is not the enemy of the elephant, as Eric Cantona might have observed. They inhabit completely unrelated environments: they live in worlds which do not intersect. Conflict presupposes that individuals or groups confront each other on common ground. *They* may scoff at the suggestion that they have anything in common, *they* may deride the view that they share anything important, but of course to the outside observer they display a whole range of family resemblances. The Young Hegelians were resolute in their rejection of the Master, and yet Hegel was the only thinker worthy of their criticism. We are familiar with the deficiencies of the spectrum model of political opposition. On a circular model, the more extreme the positions adopted by two parties, the closer their features come to resemble one another. It is the moderates at the centre who are the odd ones out. The relevance of all this should be clear if we were to describe the moderate position as 'Egyptianism'. Nietzsche does not belong with those who have a purely objective or academic interest in philosophy, but rather with those for whom life itself is an issue. Georg Brandes, the only scholar to lecture on Nietzsche's works during his lifetime, wrote to him in 1888 concerning a series of lectures given in Copenhagen before an audience of some three hundred. A young painter commented: 'What makes this so interesting is that it has nothing to do with books, *but with life*.'[9] It is not at all surprising that one of the great and enduring studies of Nietzsche's work was undertaken by Karl Jaspers, who in his own philosophy wished to transcend objectifying thinking and contribute to the great questions of existence. Professional philosophers for the most part have declined to follow the example of Jaspers, 'to testify before the students to philosophy proper'.[10] But testimony is precisely what we find in Nietzsche. For all his historical expertise and erudition his subject matter is – himself. Sometimes with immodesty, frequently with lack of balance, always with alarming honesty, it is the courage and integrity of his exploration that is so gripping, so devastating, so challenging. 'You know these things by way of thinking, yet your thought is not your experience but the reverberation of the experience of others; as your room trembles when a carriage passes. I am sitting in that carriage, and often am the carriage itself.'[11] Philosophy for

Jaspers 'is the thinking that transforms my consciousness of being as it awakens me and brings me to myself in the original impulses whose pursuit makes me what I am'.[12] At the heart of Nietzsche's philosophy is a project to transform his own life and the lives of any who read, appreciate and value his writings. Jaspers too was alienated from religion, at least in its objectifying tendencies,[13] but he saw a necessary relationship between religion and his own position. 'Philosophy appears to need religious soil to grow in.'[14] It is significant that he described his position as 'philosophical faith'.[15] To do justice to the project at the centre of his work it would be appropriate to speak also of Nietzsche's philosophical faith. Indeed on the opening page of one of his early books Nietzsche describes himself as a writer. 'Does it not seem as though some faith were leading him on, some consolation offering him compensation?'[16] In this chapter we shall draw attention to its main elements, and their relationship to religion.

As we have seen, Nietzsche presents us with more than a critique of religion: he provides us with an alternative to it. This in itself distinguishes him from many contemporary philosophers. His criticism is not dismissive, as if religion could be pushed aside by name-calling. Religion identifies important issues, and as its critic Nietzsche affirms their importance. It is the fact that he formulates his own answers to the questions of religion that gives his philosophical faith family resemblances with religion. Feuerbach, the first of the Young Hegelians to mount a criticism of Hegel's system, could view philosophical faith and religious faith as synonymous.

> He who has an aim, an aim which is in itself true and essential, has, *eo ipso*, a religion, if not in the narrow sense of common pietism, yet – and this is the only point to be considered – in the sense of reason, in the sense of the universal, the only true love.[17]

We need not follow him down this Romantic route to recognize the family resemblances. Faith is not in itself a religious category. There are religious, philosophical and ideological faiths. But they have this in common: those who hold a certain faith live their very lives within its context. It determines their self-understanding. It provides a picture – of the world, of society, of the individual. Curiously the position defined by faith does not emerge cumulatively, step by step, as a conclusion to an argument. That is to say it cannot be demonstrated objectively to the casual observer. Kierkegaard described it as being finally achieved by a leap: 'the leap is the category of decision',[18] a point echoed by Heidegger in his lectures on Nietzsche. 'We come to being as a whole always and only by means of a leap that executes our very projection of it, assisting and accomplishing that projection in its process.'[19] The truth of the position is confirmed in the lives of those who come to affirm the picture. Those who are not troubled about such issues find themselves outside the debate. It is for this reason, as noted, that Nietzsche despised mummification in philosophy. As Kierkegaard implied, only two kinds of people can understand these issues, those who are passionately for them and those who passionately against them.[20] It is not surprising that so many studies have been undertaken comparing Kierkegaard and Nietzsche: their writings are characterized by testimony and passion. Kierkegaard wrote as a Christian, but Nietzsche did not mistake the continuity between his position and those who had gone before. Disgusted at the direction of the new *Reich*, he declared himself to be a 'good European', and heir of the rich European spirit. He may have outgrown his Christian ancestors, but not their commitment to their faith:

> for their faith they willingly sacrificed possessions and position, blood and fatherland. We – do the same. For what? For our unbelief? For every kind of unbelief? No, you know better than that, friends. The hidden Yes in you is stronger than all Nos and Maybes that afflict you and your age like a disease; and when you have to embark on the sea, you emigrants, you, too, are compelled to this by – a *faith*![21]

Nietzsche's position is a faith and not a system. Its worthy adversaries are other faiths, not other philosophical systems. It is not difficult to identify some of the elements in Nietzsche's philosophy which give it the character and substance of a faith.

1. A faith makes a judgment against the contemporary world. Something has gone fundamentally wrong. Things are not as they should be. No preacher ever mounted the pulpit to greet his congregation with a contented smile and the reassuring words that everything is just fine. No more does Nietzsche. Things are far from just fine and something better be done about it. In his case it is not improvement, but restoration. There is nothing objectively wrong: only to the eyes of faith.

2. Faith therefore comes as bad news: it exposes the taken for granted as flawed. What was previously accepted, even cherished, is now pilloried. By its moral and aesthetic values faith condemns and sets aside.

3. Faith is met with resistance. People do not wish to be alienated from their nearest and dearest, from everything that has been precious to them. Nietzsche was all too aware that many who knew of the death of God declined to acknowledge it in public. We referred to this previously as bad faith: the refusal to keep faith with themselves. Faith in this sense is far from wish-fulfilment: it can be threatening, it can be the 'logic of terror'.

4. But if faith comes as bad news it could not be justified at all unless consequent on the acceptance of the bad news, there was the possibility of good news. I have referred to this as a dialectical movement in Nietzsche's philosophy, for example in the 'Our Cheerfulness' passage. The good news (the 'gospel') is the consolation of faith from the logic of terror. Whether it brings happiness to the heart, it brings peace to the mind.

5. To those who accept the logic of terror, the destruction in the dialectic, there is at last hope. Hope is a feature of faith and Nietzsche's message is one of hope – at least to the few. Indeed faith is often for the few, too demanding for the many, requiring dedication and single-mindedness beyond the masses.

6. Faith brings a new understanding – of the self, of the world – what the New Testament calls 'repentance' (*metanoia* = a change of mind).[22] It can feel like a rebirth. We recall Nietzsche's

own experience of this kind in 1881, which he associates with that of his friend Peter Gast, 'who was likewise "reborn"'.[23]

7. Faith is the affirmation of life, the new life. This is Nietzsche's message, but since the two go together, those who are not roused to put their lives to the test will not experience the empirical evidence upon which the faith is confirmed. 'Egyptians' need not enquire further.

The list could be extended much further with general features, but four further elements will now be considered which are more particular to Nietzsche's own position.

8. The life of faith – religious, philosophical or ideological – is a life which requires change. It presupposes that at the outset we have made wrong choices. When an alternative is presented to us we can change our minds (repent). How naïve! Yes, we can resolve to change, but anyone who has made and broken New Year resolutions knows that it takes more than an act of will to change our lives. And resolve fares no better in philosophy. Heidegger's analytic of *Dasein* is one of the great achievements of phenomenology, but his conclusion is as weak and lacking credibility as it is disappointing, that death consciousness can lead to authentic life by an act of resolve.[24] Nor does Nietzsche fall into this trap. Earlier I referred to the secularization (and trivialization) of religious terms. When I lived in New York a number of years ago the building where shoppers could change their trading stamps for coveted goods was called 'The Redemption Centre'. Redemption seems a peculiarly religious concept, but the Greek term *apolutrosis* was originally a secular concept, describing for example how a benefactor might buy the freedom of a slave. The slave, who might have been a freeman who by some poor decision had fallen into bondage, could not free himself, could not undo the consequences of his own life. But the benefactor would bear the cost of his freedom. This was a very powerful metaphor to describe the action of God. Christ the Redeemer delivered people from the consequences of their sins, bearing the cost himself. Over the centuries a familiar transition took place: the term ceased to be used in secular society and

therefore by default came to be a technical religious term. The question, however, lingers, as to whether secular society might some day experience a reality for which it no longer has a term. Will any secular thinker be both sensitive to the issue and courageous enough to reappropriate the term from religion? This is precisely what has happened, but redemption now looks to be such a peculiarly religious concept that it comes as something of a shock to see it used in a non-religious context. Elsewhere I have discussed its use by Marx in the *Economic and Philosophical Manuscripts* (1844). In anticipating the character of the new sphere in society Marx describes both its character and its task:

> ... a sphere, finally, which cannot emancipate itself without emancipating itself from all the other spheres of society, which is, in short, a total loss of humanity and which can only redeem itself by the total redemption of humanity. This dissolution of society, as a particular class, is the proletariat.[25]

This is how Tom Bottomore translates the famous though cryptic passage in which Marx seems to transfer the work and the self-sacrifice of Christ to the proletariat. Apparently even in its ideological form, faith sees that we are not always able to free ourselves from our past lives. Or again, as I was writing this book news came that the body of El Che was at last to be returned to Cuba. The commander of the Second Column in the Cuban Revolutionary War of 1959, Che Guevara later went to Bolivia to support revolution in that country. There he was captured and shot. In a tribute to his dead comrade Fidel Castro said quite simply: 'His blood was shed in Bolivia, for the redemption of the exploited and the oppressed.'[26] Once again, here is the recognition, in ideological faith, that there are circumstances in which a redeemer must come if people are to be empowered to change their lives.

Redemption is a central concept of Christian faith. We may be surprised to find that it recurs in Marxism, which through its indebtedness to Hegel inherited many religious insights. Redemption in religious faith, in ideological faith – but surely not in philosophical faith, surely not in the work of the master critic of religion, surely not in the thought of the man who shocked all Europe by claiming to be the Anti-Christ. Alas, I regret to inform those who expected more of Nietzsche: redemption is an important element in Nietzsche's philosophy. Worse than that, he even looks with longing for the coming of the Redeemer.

9. As early as the *Untimely Meditations* Nietzsche tells us that a species which has developed to its upper limits can transcend these limits, not through the mass of people, but through a small number of individuals whom fortuitous circumstances have enabled to emerge: 'mankind ought to seek out and create the favourable conditions under which those great redemptive men can come into existence'.[27] But although redemption continues at the heart of his philosophy, its causes and its occasion change. Zarathustra addresses the matter in a section entitled 'Of Redemption'. The rabble who form his audience might well wonder who is Zarathustra. Is he a liberator? 'Will – that is what the liberator and bringer of joy is called: thus I have taught you, my friends! But now learn this as well: the will itself is still a prisoner.'[28] The will is a prisoner because the future is closed off. Account must be taken of the past: revenge must be taken. And yet the will is unable to change the past. 'The will that is the will to power must will something higher than any reconciliation – but how is that to happen?'[29] The prophet breaks off at this point, leaving his hearers in disarray – but not of course his readers. We are better equipped than they. There are two inescapable elements in the teaching of Zarathustra which gives us the clue. First there is 'the spirit of revenge', which has been till now 'mankind's chief concern', the call for punishment. Secondly there is 'that law of time, that time must devour her children'.[30] But Zarathustra accepts neither proposition. There must be redemption, but now on the basis of his teaching – the death of God, the end of the spirit of revenge, and eternal return, the end of the law of time. Earlier in this section he already gave his answer, but so cryptically that his hearers did not hear. 'To redeem the past and to transform every "It was" into an "I

wanted it thus!" – that alone do I call redemption!'[31] In *Ecce Homo* Nietzsche identifies himself with the message of the prophet. 'On one occasion Zarathustra strictly defines his task – it is also mine – the *meaning* of which cannot be misunderstood: he is *affirmation* to the point of justifying, of redeeming even the entire past.'[32]

10. It is now clear why we had such difficulty in the previous chapter with the concept of eternal recurrence. Is it fish, fowl or red meat: science, cosmology or metaphysics? It now transpires that it is faith, a philosophical faith which is difficult to distinguish from religious faith. The death of God marks the end of the belief in linear time, the future judgment, the goal of history. With the passing of the old faith, a new faith arises. It is epitomized by the belief in eternal recurrence: everything follows from this, beginning with redemption itself. As Jaspers observes, eternal recurrence is for Nietzsche 'a means to salvation'.[33] I have already indicated that the similarity between the two faiths is more than functional: it extends to the structure and content. For this reason many commentators have approached Nietzsche's faith as an exercise in comparative religion. As Paul Valadier observes, 'the thought of eternal recurrence, itself so difficult to clarify, now makes sense if we see it as replacing the Christian centre of gravity. Then we can understand it as a reflection on the most profound nature of reality (and, thus as a kind of "religious" thought) and not as a cosmology or scientific pretension.'[34] Karl Löwith describes the theory of eternal recurrence as 'an avowed substitute for religion …'[35] For Michel Haar the doctrine of eternal recurrence presents us with a familiar pattern. 'But how will this doctrine come to take hold? In the same way a religion does, the elect being those who have faith in their own lives as lives worthy of being repeated innumerable times. A religion diametrically opposed to all religions that only promise a better life, happiness in a world beyond, this doctrine offers happiness on earth to all those who are capable of this faith.'[36] As Haar points out, there will certainly be no talk of judgment or punishment. 'It is a religion without sin and without error, for everything that repeats itself infinitely is neither good nor bad, it is

innocent; it simply *is*.'[37] And finally, he adds, 'the eternal return
must be understood as a religion of pure possibility; just as the
simple thought of eternal damnation was able to modify the
actions of men, so the faith in each instant of life as being worthy
of returning should raise humanity far beyond itself.'[38] For Hans
Küng eternal recurrence is a myth, 'and in practice it was useful
to Nietzsche as a substitute for religion after he had lost all
religion: to use his own words, as "religion of religions"'.[39] A faith
above all faith? Rather a religion beyond all religions. For
Nietzsche the thought of eternal recurrence should come slowly.
'It is to be a religion of the freest, most serene, and most sublime
souls – a lovely meadow-land between gilded ice and pure sky!'[40]
Small wonder that Jaspers considers that eternal recurrence,
'with its consequences for our awareness of being, our conduct
and our experience, has taken the place of belief in God'.[41]

11. To recap: in addition to the general features which
Nietzsche's position shares with other forms of faith, there are
certain characteristic elements. We began with the conditions
which lead to the men of redemption. In his later writings three
things happen. The first is that the category of redemptive men is
reduced to a single being. It is difficult to exaggerate the
significance of this movement. A redemptive class (which is a
Marxist concept) gives way to a Redeemer. This brings the
concept directly into line with its religious origins. '... the true
Redeemer will come'.[42] The second change in the concept is
longing, which also recalls the situation of the early church. In the
weeks and months after the Ascension of Jesus the early
Christians fervently anticipated his return. In his Second Coming
he would appear, not as a humble servant of God, but as the
Judge of the world, not in weakness but in power. As the years
passed, as the imperial persecutions recurred, as the situation
became more desperate, Christian faith was marked by eschatological longing. It was eschatological longing, longing for the end
of time, the consummation of history. It is with these words that
the whole of the Bible ends. 'Amen. Come, Lord Jesus.'[43] It is a
longing located in the sequence of time, and yes, this longing is

also a feature of the philosophical faith of Nietzsche. Indeed Heller can even go so far (too far, I believe) as to see eternal recurrence as an alternative to the Second Coming.[44] Nietzsche anticipates one who will come at 'this great and decisive stroke of midday, who will make the will free once more and restore to the earth its aim, and to man his hope; this anti-Christ and anti-nihilist, conqueror of God and Unbeing – one day he must come'.[45] This is a longing also located in the sequence of time, but of course in Nietzsche it is midday and not midnight, a moment at the centre and not at the end. But as in the case of the persecuted Christians of the *Apocalypse*, we can hear the desperate note enter Nietzsche's words. He will come: no, he *must* come. But the third development in this doctrine is that the redemptive men are not reduced to a redemptive man. The Redeemer is not a man, not even a higher man, and he has never yet appeared on earth. Well, perhaps he has never yet materialized on earth, but Nietzsche has already had experience of him. In *The Gay Science*, the first book written after his mystical religious experience at Surlei, he writes as if he has already encountered the Redeemer. 'No, life has not disappointed me. On the contrary, I find it truer, more desirable and mysterious every year – ever since the day when the great liberator came to me ...'[46] It is as if his experience of inspiration revealed to him not an idea – but a person, a Redeemer. Following on the comment by Deleuze, no doubt there are those who will see this as metaphor, as a manner of speaking, a symptom of illness. They must answer to Nietzsche, but this is what *he says*.

If all this is surprising, it is not without its difficulties. What is the relationship between the great Liberator, the Superman and redemption? For Nietzsche Zarathustra is the teacher of eternal recurrence, and as we have seen, it is faith in eternal recurrence which liberates, which redeems. Even if Nietzsche is redeemed by Zarathustra, it is in fact the acceptance of eternal recurrence which redeems, which transforms every 'It was' into 'I wanted it so'. It is tempting to identify the Superman as the Redeemer, but this can hardly be. If Zarathustra eventually teaches eternal recurrence, he begins with the nature and the coming of the Superman. The message of the Prologue is this: 'I teach you the Superman. Man is something that should be overcome. What have you done to overcome him? All creatures hitherto have created something beyond themselves: and do you want to be the ebb of this great tide, and return to the animals rather than overcome man?'[47] But this has nothing to do with eternal recurrence, it is a return to the earlier discussion about human life and the animal instincts, about the sublimation and transcending of the passions. 'Behold, I teach you the Superman. The Superman is the meaning of the earth. Let your will say: The Superman shall be the meaning of the earth! I entreat you, my brothers, remain true to the earth and do not believe those who speak to you of superterrestrial hopes. They are poisoners, whether they know it or not.' [48] The Superman does not come as Redeemer: he is the outcome of the affirmation of life. 'Man is a rope, fastened between animal and Superman ...',[49] 'a bridge and not a goal'.[50] Mankind is not saved by the Superman: the Superman is created by mankind. Once again the death of God is the starting point. Zarathustra points out that mankind cannot create gods (*pace* Feuerbach). 'But you could surely create the Superman. Perhaps not you yourselves, my brothers. But you could transform yourselves into forefathers and ancestors of the Superman: and let this be your finest creating.'[51] Nietzsche is clearly excited at this prospect. I believe that Clark misinterprets the sequence when she claims that 'the value of human life therefore derives completely from its status as a means to the [Superman], the negation or overcoming of the merely human'.[52] But the process concerns not the negation but the supersession of the human, and it is not the 'merely human' which is superseded, but specifically that higher human mode which affirms life.

The Superman is not an individual, but an ideal. Indeed Haar sees in the Superman as an ideal 'a subtle restoration of metaphysics and ethics'.[53] We can agree to this in the sense that Nietzsche is certainly a metaphysical thinker, but the formation of an ideal does not demonstrate that he is restoring an idealist form of metaphysics – which together with Christianity is his main subject of attack. The Superman is an ideal, an aspiration which under certain circumstances could be materialized. This mode of being is indeed the meaning of the world, but not its redeemer.

12. While there are rational elements in the leap of faith, there are also affective elements, and we must examine the place of joy in Nietzsche's faith. The sequence of faith, as I have described it, begins with anxiety, depression, even in Nietzsche's case terror, but must end in a sense of peace, well-being, happiness. The faithful should be wreathed in smiles! This was one of Nietzsche's criticisms of religion: 'hatred of the senses, of the joys of the senses, of joy in general is Christian'.[54] But joy is not the first thing that springs to mind at the mention of the name of glowering Nietzsche. His school friend Paul Deussen recalls, 'I have heard him utter many an ingenious remark, but I have seldom heard him tell a good joke.'[55] We have already recalled the incident over the new suit, on the occasion of his visit to the home of Ottilie Brockhaus to meet her brother the maestro. It was quite amusing, and no doubt he regaled his friends Richard and Cosima with the story some years afterwards in Tribschen, but it hardly prepares us for the excessive claim by Gilles Deleuze. 'Those who read Nietzsche without laughing – without laughing often, richly, even hilariously – have, in a sense, not read Nietzsche at all.'[56] Perhaps he should get out more.

However, the issue of the joy that comes with faith is more subtle than all of this, and it relates to Nietzsche's history of ill-health. Most people would sympathize with the wistful observation of an invalid that if you lose your health, you have lost everything. Alternatively we admire those who grin and bear it, who refuse to let their illness determine their lives. Nietzsche, who raised introspection to a philosophical method, declined both of these options. As with the sublimation of the passions, Nietzsche accepted, affirmed and transcended his poor health. He enlisted it in the outworking of his faith. He bent it to his will, until without the least hint of masochism it contributed to the joy of life. 'Art as the redemption of the sufferer – as the way to states in which suffering is willed, transfigured, deified, where suffering is a form of great delight.'[57] Indeed Michael Tanner, who scarcely mentions Nietzsche and religion at all, sees his approach to suffering as the key to his thought. 'Nietzsche's fundamental concern throughout his life was to plot the relationship between suffering and culture, or cultures. He categorizes and grades cultures by the way in which they have coped with the omnipresence of suffering, and assesses moralities by the same criterion.'[58] He claims that Nietzsche was therefore concerned with greatness rather than with goodness. 'Greatness, one might say, to anticipate, involves putting pain to work; goodness involves attempting to eliminate it.'[59] The main problem with Nietzsche's observations about suffering is similar to the problem of his treatment of evil. Evil is not one thing, and it surely cannot be set aside as simply an expression of the interests of the underclass, dressed up in ethical terms. There is evil, such as child abuse, which brings genuinely moral condemnation and revulsion from across the class and interest spectrum of society. In a similar way we should want to distinguish between suffering arising from a genetically caused illness and the suffering which is caused by the child abuser. Nietzsche clearly coped positively and courageously with his wretched health. Only his friends had any idea of the extent of his suffering. Indeed the shrewd Lou von Salomé could see one obvious conclusion to be drawn. 'He suffered in fact so deeply from life that the certainty of the eternal recurrence of life must have held something terrible for him.'[60] The condition was not constant. In *Ecce Homo* he described the period immediately after his mystical experience. 'I could often have been seen dancing ... I laughed a lot ...'[61] I earlier quoted the sentence from *The Gay Science* concerning the coming of the great liberator. It begins, 'No, life has not disappointed me. On the contrary, I find it truer, more desirable and mysterious every year ...'[62] This alone would justify Hollingdale's observation: 'No, Nietzsche's life was singularly devoid of what would normally be called pleasure, but it was emphatically not devoid of happiness.'[63] This is the paradox of faith: it can bestow meaning and significance even on pain and suffering.

13. There is one final element which is characteristic of faith. It can be described in several ways, but it is the attitude of devotion. The individual whose life is characterized by faith acknowledges something greater than his or her life, of more value and enduring worth. Indeed it is the object of faith which bestows worth and makes life worth living. This is obvious enough in religious faith, where the individual is consecrated to God, but it is just as obvious in ideological faith, where individuals are prepared to die for the cause. In faith even death has a meaning. Faith overcomes the terror of the finality of death. Or to reverse the matter, the loss of religious faith or any other kind of faith can expose the individual to the terror of meaninglessness. This was the experience of Nietzsche. The death of God and the logic of terror he experienced as terror in face of his own death.

In the fourth of his *Untimely Meditations*, 'Richard Wagner in Bayreuth', Nietzsche muses on these matters.

> Art exists so that the bow shall not break. The individual must be consecrated to something higher than himself – that is the meaning of tragedy; he must be free of the terrible anxiety which death and time evoke in the individual: for at any moment, in the briefest atom of his life's course, he may encounter something holy, that endlessly outweighs all his struggle and all his distress ...[64]

Two things might strike us about this passage. The first is the language of devotion, indeed it is the language of religious devotion. The individual must be consecrated to something higher than himself. Only in this way can he overcome the terror of death. But at this stage Nietzsche did not yet have a philosophical faith. He could identify the need, but of course he could not simply invent a faith to fulfil that need. Faith arises often mysteriously and normally unsought. It would be misleading to say that faith can perform this function of bestowing meaning in face of death. Rather it is faith in something higher than oneself.

Of course people consecrate themselves to things that are not higher, that are not worthy, that are illusory. This way lies eventual destruction and despair, but Nietzsche is more discerning, and this leads to the second point which might strike us about the above quotation. What is this something to which the individual might quite rightly and justifiably consecrate himself? Certainly not an idea or a theory. No, the individual should be consecrated to the holy, the holy which can be experienced at any moment, probably unsought.

What are we to make of all this? We know that as a student Nietzsche lost religious faith. It is therefore assumed that he became irreligious, that he thought there was nothing to it. An alternative scenario seems to be emerging. Rudolf Otto identified the experience of the holy as the foundation of all religion. 'There is no religion in which it does not live as the real innermost core, and without it no religion would be worthy of the name.'[65] The process by which the original experience is schematized into beliefs and doctrines is another matter. Nietzsche was clearly alienated from religion in its institutionalized form; that is to say, for him it no longer preserved within it the original experience of the holy. What emerges here is his continuing consecration to the holy as that which gives meaning to life and frees him from the anxiety of death. If he is fortunate, then he will at some point come to a new faith, a faith in something higher than himself, worthy of his devotion, a faith based on his experience of the holy.

With hindsight we know that he came to such a faith, and it brought him great joy. Its doctrinal form is eternal recurrence, but it is now clear why he called it 'eternal' and not 'infinite'. Eternal is a religious category which expresses the nature of the holy, qualitatively different from the infinite. It is the character of the eternal that Nietzsche advises us to stamp upon our lives, but not as in the Christian religion or Platonic idealism. As we have already noted, Magnus is right to say that 'a world without eternity, Nietzsche must have thought, was unfit for human habitation; but eternity "beyond" or "behind" the transitory was worse still'.[66] Nietzsche expounds a philosophical faith by which to live; it has family resemblances with religion and we now see that it has a common origin in the experience of the holy. It is no doubt also present in the mystical experience at Surlei. Not surprisingly Nietzsche did not want his faith to be absorbed into the mass of religions. In the last chapter of *Ecce Homo* he writes of himself as 'a destiny'. 'And with all that there is nothing in me of a founder of a religion.'[67] Given his view of the rabble Nietzsche declares: 'I do not want "believers" … I have a terrible fear I shall one day be pronounced holy …'[68] Yet at a more subtle level it is true that those who consecrate their lives to the holy are a testimony to it before others. As Nietzsche's body was being lowered into the grave, Peter Gast, his closest friend, bade him farewell with these words: 'May your name be holy to all future generations!'[69] And why is it that Nietzsche comes and comes again, to ever new generations, to young people who are not attracted to religion which resents life and philosophy which avoids it? Is it because he speaks to them of life, that he has consecrated himself to life, that to encounter Nietzsche is to be in the presence of the holy, and it is awesome? 'A wholly pious man must be an object of reverence to us: but so must a man wholly permeated with a sincere impiety.'[70]

In all this we are not putting words into Nietzsche's mouth. To the contrary, we can hardly believe our ears. This is not an attempt to make Nietzsche out to be something he was not. To the contrary, that has already been done by those who for whatever reason ignore or suppress the evidence of his philosophical faith. Indeed now that we have this evidence before us the distinction between religious faith and philosophical faith seems less clear. Nietzsche's faith is both imbued with and influenced by the insights of religion. As I noted at the outset, Nietzsche the man of faith saw himself in continuity with those 'who died for their faith'. He proceeds with faith.

> We do not yet know the 'whither' towards which we are driven once we have detached ourselves from our old soil. But it was from this same soil that we acquired the force which now

drives us forth into the distance, into adventures, thrusting us into the boundless, the untried, the undiscovered ...[71]

It is for this reason that perceptive scholars have not hesitated to call him a deeply religious soul. It is also becoming clear that his rejection of religion – in its institutional forms – may have been out of his consecration to the holy itself. A truly irreligious man would not have thought the project worthwhile. Again and again this philosopher who in life never ventured from dry land turns to the metaphor of the sea.

And whither then would we go? Would we cross the sea? Whither does this mighty longing draw us, this longing that is worth more to us than any pleasures? Why just in this direction, thither where all the suns of humanity have hitherto gone down? Will it perhaps be said of us one day that we too, steering westward, hoped to reach an India – but that it was our fate to be wrecked against infinity?[72]

10

Jesus of Nazareth

'Dionysos against the Crucified.' So end the writings of Friedrich Nietzsche. In so far as Christ Crucified is the basis of Christian doctrine and morality, then Nietzsche is indeed the anti-Christ. He was critical of the Christian religion in a more profound and consistent way than any other writer before or since. It is perhaps surprising therefore to discover in his writings many lengthy passages in which he makes a very positive evaluation of Jesus of Nazareth in contrast to the Christ symbol of religious faith and belief. It is as if doctrine is his enemy rather than the person of Jesus, Jesus the man – Jesus the Jew.

We might begin by noting that Nietzsche dissociated himself from anti-semitism. He was well aware that it was all-pervasive in Germany, and proposed that it should be rooted out.[1] He did not follow his early mentors in this matter, Wagner and Schopenhauer. Anti-semitism was fostered by 'a diet composed entirely of newspapers, politics, beer, and Wagner's music'.[2] When we consider Nietzsche's reputation during his public life the situation is not without irony, even tragedy. On the one hand he identified himself with the intellectual and cultured classes, but from them he did not receive the acclaim for which he so longed. On the other hand he was something of a cult figure amongst extreme groups, including anti-semites, whom he despised. Even so, recognition is recognition and in spite of himself he was intrigued by this development, as we can see from a letter to Overbeck in 1887.

Among all the radical parties (Socialists, Nihilists, Anti-semitists, Christian-Orthodox, Wagnerians) I enjoy an amazing and almost mysterious esteem. In the *Anti-semitische Korrespondenz* (which is only sent privately, only to 'trusted party members'), my name appears in almost every issue. Zarathustra, the divine human being, has bewitched the anti-Semites; they have their own anti-semitic interpretation of him, which has given me a good laugh.[3]

Overbeck might have been rather confused by the thought of Nietzsche having a good laugh, but Nietzsche himself should have pondered why it was so easy for anti-semites to develop their own interpretation of Zarathustra – or rather why it was so easy for them to find in Zarathustra a philosophical exposition of their most heartfelt prejudices. His elitist disdain for the masses made him indifferent to the populist uses to which his work was increasingly put, so that while he detested anti-semitism, somehow in the twentieth century his name is associated with it. For example, National Socialism declared Jesus to be an Aryan, so that they might separate Jesus from the Jews. They were then able to denounce the Jews without alienating the Christians; indeed by this route they made it possible for many Christians to join in the denunciation. But Nietzsche scorned such 'Christian-Aryan worthies'.[4] Thus although he finds disgusting what he calls 'the youthful stock-exchange Jew', he praises the Jewish people 'whom we have to thank for the noblest human being (Christ), the purest sage (Spinoza), the mightiest book and the most efficacious moral code in the world'.[5] In Nietzsche's early writings we therefore find two very different types of saying about the Jews. Positively, European Jews are 'the strongest, toughest and purest race',[6] they could take over Europe if they so willed – but do not,[7] they have purified the intellectual life and brought people 'to listen to reason',[8] and they can produce art such as no one else can.[9] Indeed as if to scandalize German anti-semitism he can speak of the fulfilment of the Jewish destiny in the next (twentieth) century: 'then there will again arrive that seventh day on which the ancient Jewish God may *rejoice* in himself, his creation and his chosen people – and let us all, all of us, rejoice with him!'[10] Indeed in a Christian country he can provocatively prefer the Old Testament to the New. In the former he finds 'great men, a heroic landscape ... a people'.[11] By comparison, in the New Testament he finds people obsessed with sin, who persistently address God with a familiarity (*Auf-du-und-du*) which is in the worst possible taste.[12] To have glued the New Testament to this superior work is a 'sin against the spirit',[13] not least because the philologist in him finds the Greek so appalling.

On the other hand he has harsh words to say about the Jews. It was they who invented sin as an experience;[14] they have 'a more profound contempt' for human being than anyone else;[15] they have inverted the values of life and have turned the expression 'the world' into 'a term of infamy'.[16] And when all this is said and done, from 'the tree trunk of Jewish vengeance and hatred' has grown the unique branch, 'a new love, the deepest and sublimest love'.[17] What looks like another contradiction is removed if we see that there is nothing of anti-semitism here. He is praising and condemning two sets of values, in the light of his previous revaluation.

All early Christians were Jews, but they certainly did not repudiate their Jewish faith in the process. For them the new faith was but the next step in the development of the old. Some were sectarian Jews for whom the events of the life and death of Jesus fulfilled their exotic apocalyptic speculations. A few were Sadducees, for whom Jesus was the perfect high priest who fulfilled and transcended the temple cult – which was as well, when in AD 70 the Romans razed the Second Temple to the ground. From then on the future of Judaism lay with synagogues, the rabbis and the teaching of the Law. It is not surprising that the most influential Jew within the early church was a Pharisee, Saul of Tarsus, reinvented as Paul.

If any individual is responsible for the development of the Christian church and its doctrine that individual is Paul. For this alone we might assume his place in heaven is assured. Yet in modern times there has been a particular kind of criticism focussed on Paul. Those who have wished to retain the Christian faith but to reform it in some radical way have set Paul over against Jesus. Jesus is praised – of course – but Paul is blamed: blamed for the institutionalization of the new faith, blamed for the complexity of doctrine, blamed for quietism towards the state or slavery, blamed for misogynism. Curiously we have the same division here in Nietzsche. As early as *Daybreak* (1881) he had some disparaging things to write about 'the first Christian', i.e. Paul, whom he describes as ambitious, superstitious and cunning.[18] Nietzsche, as we shall see, has some admiration for the actual figure of Jesus, and correctly observes that Paul virtually ignores the life of Jesus in favour of a doctrine about his life. Or rather a doctrine which is not about the life of Jesus at all, but about the efficacy of his violent death and life after death.[19] We see the contrast again when he refers to Paul as 'that disastrous wrong-headed fellow' and accuses him of having 'resurrected on a grand scale precisely that which Christ had annulled through his way of living'.[20] Nietzsche is on good grounds when he implies that the early church created a religion which catered for the expectations and religious needs of the 'pagans' of the Hellenistic world: temple, mystery, priesthood, altar, sacrifice, dying and rising god, virgin mother goddess. However, he was almost a century too soon in attributing it to Paul.[21]

As indicated, this is a common move among groups who wish to associate Jesus with their own understanding of Christian faith. But why should *Nietzsche* make the point? Jesus was a Jew, and his religion was sectarian Judaism: why should this self-appointed anti-Christ be concerned if Paul develops a religion which is substantially different from that of Jesus? What does it have to do with him? This religion, that religion – it is all the same thing surely. Apparently not. What is at stake here is the same distinction that we find in Nietzsche's examination of moral values. He sees two ways of being religious. It is the distinction between the religion *of* Jesus and the religion *about* Jesus. The religion *of* Jesus, the religion which Jesus practised, is about embodying certain values, about affirming life, being prepared to die rather than betray these values. As Nietzsche reads it, the religion *about* Jesus is none of these things. It is a religion which pins its faith and hopes on what Jesus has done, what the life and especially the death of Jesus have achieved. Faith represents a weakness of will, just as conviction represents a weakness of mind. This contrast seems very familiar. On this view Jesus is something of a higher man, and his followers are the herd: the shepherd and his sheep. It transpires that Nietzsche is not against Christianity, *tout court.* He may no longer be drawn to it personally, but apparently it is important for him to distinguish between two forms of the religion: the Christianity of Jesus and the Christianity of Paul. It is something of an anachronism to speak of the Christianity of Jesus, since Christian faith arose only at Pentecost, but it is clear that Nietzsche means to contrast the religion of Jesus (by whatever name) and the religion which has been constructed about him.

> Christianity is still possible at any time. It is not tied to any of the impudent dogmas that have adorned themselves with its name; it requires neither the doctrine of a personal God, not that of sin, nor that of immortality, nor that of redemption, nor that of faith; it has absolutely no need of metaphysics, and even less of asceticism, even less of a Christian 'natural science'. Christianity is a way of life, not a system of beliefs. It tells us how to act, not what we ought to believe.[22]

Apparently religion is not all of a piece: he can actually advocate a particular form of Christianity, for those who like that kind of thing. The terminology is confusing, but the point is clear enough. 'What did Christ deny? Everything that is today called Christian.'[23] What a strange alliance! It is as if Jesus too is the Anti-Christ. He stands over against this new Golden Calf, this destructive demonic figure which the ruminants have constructed in their own image. Shoulder to shoulder, not one but two Anti-Christs, standing proud and firm against the church's Christ. But with this we come to an even more surprizing development in Nietzsche's thought. It is an important point, and must be approached by a brief digression.

Those who are familiar with historical-critical studies of the New Testament will already recognize the scenario, the distinction between the historical Jesus and the Christ of faith. This distinction first appeared in an essay written by the philologist (yes, another philologist) H.S. Reimarus, entitled 'Concerning the Intention of Jesus and his Teaching'. Reimarus died in 1769 and the essay was published posthumously by G.E. Lessing in his series of *Contributions to Literature and History from the Ducal Library at Wolfenbüttel*. Reimarus was influenced by the English Deists, John Toland, Anthony Collins and Matthew Tindal. His intention was to undermine Christianity as a revealed religion, but unlike his predecessors, who had pointed to historical inconsistencies in the Gospels, Reimarus pointed to the disparity between the assertions of the creed and their historical basis – or lack of it. The picture he paints of the historical Jesus was viewed as offensive, even blasphemous at that time. He presents Jesus as an opportunist Messiah, whose bid for power failed. The disciples of Jesus had spent several years with him, enjoying an interesting and leisurely time, living in the reflected glory of the pretender: they did not want to return to the hard life of fishermen. They therefore made up a story about Jesus having risen from the dead, and appointing them as his successors. Reimarus concludes that 'the new system of a suffering spiritual saviour, which no one had ever known or thought of before, was invented after the death of Jesus, and invented only because the first hopes had failed'.[24] With promises of material rewards for those who believed their message, 'they saw that the game was not yet lost'.[25] Like precursors of the American prosperity gospel, they found that money came pouring in. 'This was a savings bank in which everyone with whatever little fortune he possessed strove to buy shares in the speedily expected kingdom of heaven …'[26] Small wonder Reimarus did not publish this piece during his lifetime. It is not only scurrilous, but without value as a historical study of Jesus. Its significance, however, was that it could only be answered by a better, a more accurate historical study. As Albert Schweitzer noted, 'before Reimarus, no one had attempted to form a historical conception of the life of Jesus'.[27] For the first time it raised the question of the relationship between what can be said about Jesus based on our limited historical sources, and what is confessed in the creeds about Christ. This project was to surface periodically and inconclusively for the next two hundred years. It still lies like a time bomb, ticking away in the basement of dogmatic theology.

The most famous attempt to evaluate the historical material of the Gospels was that of the young Hegelian, David Strauss, in his work *The Life of Jesus Critically Examined*, published in 1835. As Horton Harris says, 'it split the century into two theological eras – before and after 1835'.[28] This amazing work of scholarship examined the Gospels verse by verse and at the end the Bible seemed to many to have 'been almost reduced to a heap of rubble'.[29] There were those who claimed that the numerical value of Strauss's name in Hebrew was 666! In his vain attempt at a reply, Eschenmayer, author of *The Ischariotism of our Days*, conceived of a competition in hell for those who had done most damage to the Christian faith. H.E.G. Paulus, the much-esteemed rationalist New Testament critic, was to be pipped at the post by the twenty-seven-year-old. 'And now the youth receives the prize and the old man the "highly-commended".'[30] Nietzsche had read Strauss's work at school. *The Life of Jesus Critically Examined* had a profound effect on him. As J.P. Stern observes, 'the young Nietzsche's reading of it as a student of theology at Bonn (1864–5) completed a process begun during his last year at Schulpforta; it led to his rejection of the Christian faith and his refusal, at Easter, to take Communion'.[31] As we have seen, the situation was more complex than that. It frequently happens in mathematics that a brilliant young scholar makes an original contribution in his twenties, and is appointed to a prestigious chair. He becomes an administrator and only occasionally returns to his discipline. Sadly his mental powers are depleted, his creative imagination diminished: sad, even embarrassing. So it was when Nietzsche finally came to write on the hero of his youth, 'the incomparable Strauss'.[32] In 1873 he published 'David Strauss the Confessor and the Writer', the first of the *Untimely Meditations*. Nietzsche was almost the same age as the precocious author of *The Life of Jesus*, but in the intervening years the searing intellect, the moral courage had diminished. Nietzsche discusses not the young lion, but the author of *The Old Faith and the New* (1872), who cannot conceive of 'a model code for life but the *bellum omnium contra omnes* and the privileges of the strong ...'[33] The young Strauss was a committed Christian, whose epic work was intended to save Christianity from the rationalism of Paulus *et hoc genus omne*. The old Strauss had long since departed from the faith. It is therefore ironic that the young, Christian Strauss was of more significance to Nietzsche than the no-longer Christian Strauss, the darling of the culture philistines. Once again, the labels are less important than the values which are exhibited. The young Strauss was influential on Nietzsche, but for our present purposes we must turn to the French writer, Ernst Renan, whose *Life of Jesus* was published in 1863. It is his work that provides us finally with the clue to this further development in Nietzsche's relationship to Jesus. Not that Nietzsche would welcome any comparison with 'that buffoon' Renan.[34]

Strauss had studied at Blaubeuren and Tübingen intending to enter the Lutheran ministry. Renan trained as a Catholic priest at St Sulpice in Paris. Strauss was appointed to a chair in Zürich, but was never allowed to teach there because of his views. Renan was appointed to the chair of Semitic Languages at the Collège de France, but immediately removed the next year on the publication of his book. The book, the first part of a multi-volume work, was made possible by a grant from Napoleon III enabling him to travel to the Middle East in 1860. The significance of this journey was that it enabled him (so he claimed) to cross the historical divide between the time of Jesus and middle of the nineteenth century. Renan had his own agenda, namely, to show that the religion of Jesus was substantially the same as Renan's romantic natural religion. His description of the life and ministry of Jesus is replete with Romantic terminology. Luke's Gospel contains 'some circumstances full of tender feeling, and certain

words of Jesus of delightful beauty ...' Physically standing in
Palestine provided him, so he claimed, with a 'fifth gospel', in
which he saw 'living and moving an admirable human figure'.
The scenes in Palestine, he thought, differed little from the time
of Jesus. In the evening beautiful young women still go down to
the 'muddy stream'. Jesus 'always clung close to nature'. He had
no liking for the city, official religion or the political events of his
time. The life in Galilee was 'charming and idyllic'. His teaching
is the 'delightful theology of love'. His religion is 'a religion
without priests and external observance, resting entirely on the
feelings of the heart', and 'human brotherhood'. Young Galilean
women accompanied him, 'and disputed the pleasure of listening
to and tending him in turn'. He rode on a mule: 'the large black
eyes of the animal, shaded by long eyelashes, gave it an expression
of gentleness'.[35]

Perhaps only those of a strong constitution can continue to the
end of *The Life of Jesus*. It tells us a great deal about its subject –
Ernst Renan. It provides us with the classic paradigm of the quest
of the historical Jesus:

(*a*) A rejection of the historical forms of Christian belief and
practice.

(*b*) An attempt to rescue Jesus from the distortions of this
system which misrepresent him.

(*c*) An alternative form of religion, in this case romantic, but
normally non-metaphysical and essentially moral. Two further
features characterize the quest of the historical Jesus.

(*d*) Amazingly, it transpires the Jesus actually held the same
views as the author.

(*e*) Consequently, Jesus legitimizes the religious beliefs of the
author. Thus the religion of Jesus had nothing to do with Judaism
or Christianity: it is identical with the romanticism of Ernst
Renan.

(*f*) Finally, therefore, the author and those like him actually
understand Jesus better than do the Christians. Jesus belongs
with Renan and the Romantics. They liberate him from the
constraints and distortions of orthodoxy.

I have spent some time on the issue, because it will now be clear that Nietzsche has added one more portrait to the gallery of the historical Jesus. (The gallery of course continues to receive new acquisitions to this day.) In the best traditions of Renan Nietzsche presents us with a picture of Jesus which looks remarkably like his own ideal. 'One could, with some freedom of expression, call Jesus a "free spirit" ...',[36] a term which Nietzsche uses to describe himself and those who share his views and values. Which is more surprising: that he makes this claim about Jesus, or that he thinks it *worth* making? Renan wished to advocate his own romantic view of natural religion, but Nietzsche surely does not advocate any kind of religion. Renan saw no contradiction in using the authority of Jesus to legitimize his own position, but surely this is no way for Nietzsche to proceed. What authority could Jesus have for him? Or was it an *argumentum ad hominem*? Was it that he would prefer people not to be religious, but given that many are, then they should practise a non-metaphysical form of religion? Possibly, but this does not in fact account for the position which Nietzsche develops. Yes, he claims that the religion of Jesus was of this moral, non-metaphysical kind. Clearly it was not, but in this he uses the authority of Jesus to legitimize a way of living rather than a way of believing. Thus the concepts of atonement, redemption, penance are all set aside in favour of evangelical practice.[37] The Kingdom of God is an experience of the heart, it does not 'come' chronologically.[38] Sin, repentance, forgiveness[39] are no substitute for the new inward life, set out in Christ's example.

> The exemplary life consists of love and humility; in a fullness of heart that does not exclude even the lowliest; in a formal repudiation of maintaining one's rights, of self-defence, of victory in the sense of personal triumph; in faith in blessedness here on earth, in spite of distress, opposition and death; in reconciliation; in the absence of anger; the completest spiritual–intellectual independence; a very proud life beneath the will to a life of poverty and service.[40]

In the tradition of Renan, he is sure that he can understand
Jesus better than those who approach him from the perspective of
Pauline faith. 'Only we, we emancipated spirits, possess the pre-
requisite for understanding something nineteen centuries have
misunderstood.'⁴¹ The religious mode might not be Nietzsche's
first preference, but it is possible to exemplify the noble values
even in this medium. When the historical Jesus can be divided
from the Christ of Christian faith it is possible for Nietzsche to
express admiration for him – even although the terminology
becomes inconsistent: '… in reality there has only been one
Christian, and he died on the cross'.⁴² He finds it scandalous that
many who entirely ignore the example of the historical Jesus
should call themselves by his name – and dare to take com-
munion.⁴³ This specific reference must recall his own refusal to
take communion in 1865. Did this decision arise simply from his
loss of faith, or was there in addition a sense of outrage at the sight
of those who *did* communicate? It would be a tragedy to rival that
of King Lear, whose most sensitive and loving daughter would
not say the words which only she could truly say, because those
who were unworthy of them had already pronounced the words
so brazenly.⁴⁴ The brash young student who had lost his faith
might well decide to assert his manhood over against his gentle,
swarming female relatives by absenting himself from
Communion – and all that rubbish. In the event his position is
quite the reverse. He who can no longer accept the bread and take
the cup has such continuing reverence for the holy that he is
offended by those who do. This Cordelia of the sacrament, this
'defiant prodigal',⁴⁵ still cares.

> We are no longer Christians: we have grown out of
> Christianity, not because we dwelled too far from it, but
> because we dwelled too near it, even more, because we have
> grown *from* it – it is our more rigorous and fastidious piety
> itself that forbids us today to be Christians.⁴⁶

And now when it comes to his designated opponent the anti-
Christ leaps to the defence of 'the noblest human being'. It is not

that Nietzsche could make such a distinction between the noble Christ and Christ of the herd, it is that he seems to *care*. 'The church is the barbarization of Christianity.'[47] His more familiar criticism is that Christianity has led to the degeneration of those whom it has influenced. Now the accusation is that it has led to the degeneration of that for which the noblest human being stood. Previously Christianity was all of a piece and could be denounced without proviso. Now it is possible to advocate the Christianity of Christ over against the Christianity of the Christians. Indeed, he can on occasion acknowledge that even within the Christian church, within that tradition which has barbarized what Christ originally exemplified and taught, even in this unlikely, unpromising and hostile environment, it is possible to detect what we might call noble Christians, Christians who have some-how been loyal to their noble exemplar.

From this spirit, and in concert with the power and very often the deepest conviction and honesty of devotion, it has chiselled out perhaps the most refined figures in human society that have even yet existed; the figures of the higher and highest Catholic priesthood, especially when they have descended from a noble race and brought with them an inborn grace of gesture, the eye of command, and beautiful hands and feet.[48]

A curious mixture of elitism and romanticism, but what is entirely absent from this observation is the familiar swingeing criticism of religion and the derogatory remarks about priests who feed off the misery of men and women. In a letter to Overbeck he comments on his own relationship to Christianity. 'As far as Christianity is concerned, I hope you will believe this much: in my heart I have never held it in contempt and, since childhood, have often struggled with myself on behalf of its ideals.'[49] If only one line is drawn, then clearly these 'serious' Christians are on the same side as Nietzsche: they espouse and exemplify the noble values. Only one issue remains: need their commitment to the noble values be through the medium of religion, or could they discover that these values could be embodied outwith religious faith?

> These serious, excellent, upright, deeply sensitive people who are still Christian from the very heart; they owe it to themselves to try for once the experiment of living for some length of time without Christianity; they owe it to their faith in this way for once to sojourn 'in the wilderness' – if only to win for themselves the right to a voice on the question whether Christianity is necessary.[50]

Nietzsche is remarkably tolerant and open towards such people. They display some of the qualities of affirmation which he admires, and none of the qualities of the herd, which he despises. He has an affinity with such people, not in spite of the fact that they are religious, but because he once was as they are. 'Do not underestimate the value of having been religious ...'[51] He can have no relationship to the herd, but he is drawn towards these serious Christians: 'the most serious Christians have always been well disposed towards me'.[52] The serious Christians intuitively understand the first and only Christian, follow his example, affirm life and embody the noble values.

If only one line is allowed, then Nietzsche can take his place alongside the first and only Christian, the 'holy anarchist'.[53] But what if this noblest human being declines to be on the same team? Many inconsistencies in Nietzsche have proved to be a misunderstanding of his terminology. But we are here confronted by a glaring inconsistency. The values of Jesus are not in fact the noble values of Nietzsche. Nietzsche, this man who was no man but in turn 'dynamite', a 'battlefield', who denounced every halting between two ways, now seems to be proceeding confidently in two directions at once. On the one hand he censors the life, religion and teaching of the historical Jesus, omitting those elements which are decadent. On the other hand, he denounces the Christian herd for not adhering to the (actual) teaching of Jesus. By the first route he performs the traditional move of legitimizing his position by claiming that Jesus exemplified the noble values. By the second route he defends Jesus against the church which has forsaken its Lord's teaching – even although this teaching is in important respects decadent – in Nietzsche's terms. Three examples must suffice.

First, although Nietzsche advocated the noble values in the present time, his original description of those who embody such values looks more like a Viking than a victualer, more like a Norseman than a nurseryman. What would such a noble Viking figure do to those who, like the disciple Judas, conspired against him behind his back, who were paid to spy on and betray him? And what would such a horn-helmeted worthy do to those who came at dusk to attempt to lay hands on him? Yes, he would kick ass, and a few more anatomical features beside. By comparison Nietzsche challenges Christians with the practice of Jesus. Look at his behaviour, not beyond the event to some theological interpretation of the event that loses sight of the actions of Jesus. 'He does not resist, he does not defend his rights, he takes no steps to avert the worst that can happen to him – more, he provokes it. And he entreats, he suffers, he loves with those, in those who are doing evil to him.'⁵⁴ If his father had heard 'the little pastor' preach on this theme, how proud he would have been. But surely Nietzsche has simply discerned the values of the historical Jesus, frequently ignored in favour of theological evaluation. The fact that these values are those of 'the helping hand' ethic which he previous denounced as decadent does not now disturb him. Secondly, Jesus 'fights against hierarchy within the community'.⁵⁵ Since Jesus recognized the authority of the priests of the temple and specifically that of the high priest, Nietzsche may well be wrong here. But the important point is that he, who had preferred aristocracy and rank against democracy, is praising an anti-hierarchical protest. There is a way in which we could make sense of this in Nietzsche's own terms. As we noted in Chapter 4, his admiration, strictly speaking, is for the values of the rulers, not for the rulers, who might at any time betray the noble values. Nietzsche could well have taken the view that the Jewish leaders represented such a betrayal. In such a case the hero of faith might arise, the solitary figure could stand over against the betrayers, representing the values they had forsaken. Given his sympathy for Jesus, especially in the last events of his life, this might well be Nietzsche's picture of the situation. Except for one detail. Nietzsche scoffs at Renan's characterization of Jesus as a hero. The hero of the ancient world is quick to defend himself and asserts his rights. Nietzsche chooses another category to describe Jesus, one which at first hearing is offensive, namely 'idiot'. By this he certainly does not mean someone who is mentally defective. It is more likely that he is guided by etymology. In classical Greek *idios* meant 'private' as opposed to 'public'.[56] Jesus would therefore appeal to him as a man who goes his own way, by his actions and demeanour exposing and thereby judging the unworthy judges. And thirdly, Nietzsche lists behaviour among Christians specifically prohibited in the early Church. 'Whoever says today: "I will not be a soldier", "I care nothing for the courts", "I shall not claim the services of the police", "I will do nothing that may disturb the peace within me: and if I must suffer on that account, nothing will serve better to maintain my peace than suffering" – he would be a Christian.'[57] This certainly constitutes a moral challenge to contemporary Christianity – but what does it have to do with the noble values? Nietzsche frequently idealizes war and the discipline of military service. What would have happened to a Viking who declared himself a pacifist?

It is an unsatisfactory outcome. Previously we noted that Nietzsche in his revaluation of all values goes beyond the traditional 'Christian' criticism of Christianity, the criticism that Christians are not living up to their own standards, the standards of Jesus. The importance of his new criticism is that he rejects as decadent the Christian values which are found in Jesus – and which to its shame are seldom found in the church. But now he is defending these decadent values. Yet he has already prepared us for as much. 'I am one thing, my writings are another.'[58] Nietzsche's philosophy describes a life, the life of the embodiment of noble values. It is exemplified in the Vikings: the life of affirmation and of passion. But this is not the life of Nietzsche, who admits that he is a decadent. Indeed there could hardly be a greater contrast between the life he advocated and the life he himself led. In *Who's Who in Philosophy* he could hardly have put his leisure time activities down as 'ravaging and carousing'. He seems to have had no sexual activities in his adult life, and he frequently tells us that he and alcohol are incompatible.[59] Not a candidate for Viking of the year. He clearly halts between two ways, or rather he would dearly wish to see a combination of the noble values and the noblest human being, or as he describes such a one: 'the Roman Caesar with Christ's soul'.[60]

11

The Noble God

It was a matter of distress and frustration to Nietzsche that his work attracted no attention in Germany. In fact there was interest in his philosophy elsewhere. The tragedy was that his public life was over before extensive discussions began. During the years of his illness he was not aware of the growing debate. For example Alexander Tille, of the University of Glasgow, was impressed by Nietzsche's naturalism. 'Why should we not look at [man] as being above all physiological, and measure first of all the value of his art, civilization and religion by their effect upon his species, by the standard of physiology?'[1] This is a very perceptive reading of Nietzsche, and Tille advocated this position against Spencer, Fiske, Balfour and Huxley. On the other hand, Nietzsche attracted interest in eastern Europe. Georg Brandes lectured on him in Warsaw and St Petersburg. His work was attracting attention in the Slavic lands, attracting the attention of the police as well as scholars: his books were banned in Russia. As the final darkness closed in upon him, Nietzsche sent a parcel of his books to Princess Demitrievna Tenicheff, for dissemination. What must she have thought when the sender's name was prominently displayed as *The Antichrist*![2] An eccentric title, as it seems to us today, and not a little neurotic. But in the nineteenth-century it was not a title which one could claim without dispute. As we have seen, when it came to damaging the Christian religion, David Strauss was deemed a world-class contender. But Strauss himself deferred to Ludwig Feuerbach, the first critic of Hegel from within the Young Hegelians. 'If the end of the world were to come in the nineteenth-century, then, of course, he would have to be called the Antichrist.'³ Not all contenders were worthy of the title and, as we have seen, Nietzsche, who seemed an admirable candidate, rather compromised himself in his admiration for the historical Jesus, the noble Christ, the first and only Christian. Nietzsche's claim to fame rests in part on his assumption of the title "the Antichrist". If this is in dispute, then at least there is one phrase which sets him apart from all other critics of religion, 'God is dead'. If only it were so. In the event this fierce critic of religion only criticizes some kinds of religion, but is willing to make a positive evaluation of other kinds. Surely he will not yield on this premise that God is dead! After all, I have argued that the death of God is the starting point of his philosophy: the criticism of religion is the foundation of his entire philosophy. Alas, even here Nietzsche's position is not quite so clear cut as we might suppose. At the outset it seemed that all forms of religion were dead, deadly, a libel on life itself, degenerate and unworthy. In the event it is not so, not quite so. We must steel ourselves for the possibility that the same is true of the death of God. Yes, some forms of God, some religious constructs are dead, deadly, un-worthy of belief, destructive of human life. But to our surprise, amazement – and no doubt to the disappointment of some – this is not Nietzsche's last word on the matter. But once we have come to terms with this possibility, it is not surprising after all. If Nietzsche is such an admirer of Jesus, who believed in God the Father and called him *Abba*; if Nietzsche was such an admirer of serious Christians, noble Christians with beautiful feet, then it follows that the God in whom they all believed must be a very different God from the god of the herd, the idol, the god of death, the Golden Calf of the ruminants. And so indeed it transpires.

As we have seen, in the tradition of the historical Jesus move-ment, Nietzsche declares that it is possible to be a (noble) Christian without 'the doctrine of a personal God'. If he espouses the noble values without belief in God, that is how he would like others to live. But because of his admiration for Jesus and noble Christians he also reflects on what kind of God would be worthy of belief. This is an interesting and significant project, and Nietzsche reverses the terms of the sterile debate. The issue is not whether God exists or not, but what is it that is reverenced as God.

> What sets us apart is not that we recognize no god, either in history or in nature or behind nature – but that we find that which has been reverenced as God not 'godlike' but pitiable, absurd, harmful, not merely an error but a crime against life. We deny god as God. If this God of the Christians were proved to us to exist, we should know even less how to believe in him.[4]

In the old ineffectual debate the outcome was winner take all. Either God exists or not. Nietzsche makes a much more devastating point. What if the God who exists is unworthy of being God? More fundamental than the mere existence of God is the moral question of what is it that is reverenced as divine. Nietzsche is therefore free to speculate about God: not whether God exists or not, but what would the noble God be like, a God who would be as different from the god of the herd as the higher men are different from the ruminants. This sounds very much like a case for Ludwig Feuerbach. According to his projection theory, the attributes of God are the projected aspirations and values of those who worship Him.[5] It would seem that Nietzsche exhibits the same projection: the God whom he would consider to be worthy of worship would be the God whose attributes reflect the noble values. However, while this was Feuerbach's criticism of those who practised projection, it loses its force in the case of Nietzsche, who is only concerned with which values are deified, not whether such a God exists or not. He can therefore entertain himself by speculating about what kind of God could be reverenced, how such a God would act and how this noble God might appear on earth. Previously he was not offended by the man Jesus, but by the degenerate Christ as constructed by the herd. Here he is not alienated by the possibility of theism, but by 'monoto-theism', that deadly boring God who is worshipped by those who themselves have never affirmed life.

Nietzsche's alienation from biblical moral values and virtues has been dealt with earlier in some detail. We might assume that he was equally alienated from the God of the Bible, but this is not necessarily so. He welcomes the death of God, the death of the God of pity, the God who is to be loved as one loves one's neighbour, but this is not the only God in the Bible, not the only picture of God. There is a parallel in *Moses and Monotheism* when Freud makes a distinction between the God whom the Hebrews encountered in Egypt and the storm God of the Sinai. God in Egypt is the God who rules even the pharaoh, an imperial eirenic God. The storm God, Yahweh, is alarming, dangerous, out of control, the God required for the conquest of Canaan and the genocide of the resident population. Now there is a God who might appeal to Nietzsche! This is the new God revealed to Moses at the burning bush.[6] He is characterized by only one feature: He is holy. The holy and the profane are qualitatively different. A 'holy man' suggests to us a person with two characteristics. He is a man of a certain spiritual presence, and a man of the highest moral integrity in a fallen world. But Rudolf Otto, in his classic examination of the holy to which we have already referred, maintains that the second feature represents a 'clear overplus of meaning'.[7] We tend to use 'holy' and 'moral' as synonyms, but 'the holy' is not a moral category. Nietzsche anticipates Otto by some forty years, but goes beyond him in one important respect. If the holy is not a moral category, neither is it an aesthetic category. In *Human All Too Human* he makes some subtle points about religious architecture.

> Everything in a Greek or Christian building originally signified something, and indeed something of a higher order of things: this feeling of inexhaustible significance lay about the building like a magical veil. Beauty entered this system only incidental-ly, without essentially encroaching upon the fundamental sense of the uncanny and exalted, of consecration by magic and

the proximity of the divine; at most beauty mitigated the dread
– but this dread was everywhere the presupposition.[8]

It is of significance that the terms 'uncanny' and 'dread' are
precisely those which Otto later uses in characterizing the holy.
Das Grauen, 'dread', carries with it associations of horror and
shuddering. It is the experience of fear, fear not of the known but
of the *un*known. The holy is the basis of religion, and it lies prior
to morality and aesthetics, as yet untouched by the categories of
good and evil. Thus at Jericho the Israelites 'utterly destroyed all
in the city, both men and women, young and old, oxen, sheep,
and asses, with the edge of the sword'.[9] This was genocide,
carried out in the name of the holy God. The holy is not a moral
category, and a holy war has nothing to do with morality.

But there is another aspect of the holy to which Nietzsche
draws attention – its danger to human beings. Otto wrote of the
numen, the numinous, that sense of awe in the presence of the
divine. Nietzsche sees in religious art a necessary concealment of
the divine. In discussing Greek art and literature he says that no
one ever thought the god was identical with the image: 'the image
is supposed to be the visible evidence that the *numen* of the
divinity is, in some mysterious, not fully comprehensible way,
active in this place and bound to it. The oldest image of the god
is supposed to *harbour and at the same time conceal* the god – to
intimate his presence but not expose it to view.'[10] The statues of
the gods do not accurately represent them, not through in-
competence, but 'to *fend off* any association of them with anything
human'.[11] The holy is awesome and dreadful, but too close con-
tact with it is dangerous, fatal. When King David captured the
Philistine city of Jerusalem and wished to make it into his capital,
he arranged for the ark of the covenant to be taken up into the
city. Fresh oxen and a new cart were used to carry the holy chest
up the steep, rocky path. The joyful occasion soon turned to
tragedy in the most dramatic manner.

And when they came to the threshing floor of Nacon, Uzzah
put out his hand to the ark of God and took hold of it, for the

oxen stumbled. And the anger of the Lord was kindled against Uzzah; and God smote him there because he put forth his hand to the ark; and he died there beside the ark of God.[12]

David was angry at this action, the striking down of an innocent young man who only intended to serve God in a humble and helpful way. But God's anger is not as David's anger. Holy anger is not righteous anger. Uzzah died not as a punishment for sin but because of the mis-match between the holy nature of God and the human nature of man, because it is necessary 'to fend off any association' between the two. He died because of the holiness of God, which overrides the morality of good and evil. Yes! This is the kind of God Nietzsche could acknowledge, affirm. Zarathustra exclaimed, 'I should believe only in a God who understood how to dance.'[13] Such a God would respond to the Dionysian spontaneity of the dance, the affirmation of life in forgetfulness of order – rational order, moral order. Well, only a few verses further on from the tragic incident concerning Uzzah, we have such an outburst as the king celebrated the bringing of the holy ark into Jerusalem: 'and David danced before the Lord with all his might ...'[14] No line dancing here, but Zarathustra (and Nietzsche on a good day) would have joined in. Any disciple of the God Dionysos would have understood this abandoned celebration.

Of course life in a covenant with such a holy God would be intolerable: things have to be ironed out, made more orderly, predictable, manageable. And so the religion of Israel was put under modern management, that is, a priestly class emerged. It is at this point that morality supervenes, in particular the morality of 'Thou shalt not!' It is worth making the point that Nietzsche has nothing to say against the holy God, the uncontrolled and uncontrollable God, the holy God who is beyond good and evil. It is the system of moral values attributed to God to which he objects. As we have seen, his enemy was Christian morality, especially as it continued in its various metamorphoses of science and socialism. 'A critique of Christian morality is still lacking.'[15] But his enemy is not the holy, noble God. 'At bottom it is only the moral god that has been overcome. Does it make sense to conceive a god "beyond good and evil"?'[16] Just as Nietzsche took the side of Jesus against his inadequate followers, so now he takes the side of the noble God against the priestly caste. It is they who are concerned about good and evil, it is they who wish life to be controlled by tables of laws, it is they who make a living out of sin. 'Think of the tremendous fuss these pious little people make over their trespasses! Who cares? God least of all.'[17] The noble God with imagination and creative power beyond anything conceivable to human beings created the universe: was His grand plan to culminate in a balance sheet of petty trespasses? At the outset Nietzsche exposed and opposed the influence of religion on the life of mankind, the narrowing down, the distortion, the degeneration. But now religion is viewed as a tendency of inadequate people, an institution quite separate from the noble God. Indeed worse than that, the noble God is now made – religious! It is as if of all the things which God created for His grand purpose, He certainly did not create religion. The noble God has no interest in religion: it is not His scene. By all means respond in worship to the numinous, to the dread, to the awesomeness of the holy God. But for this holiness has been substituted moral goodness.

Nietzsche carries this criticism into 'a critical examination of the Christian concept of God'. Once again the contrast is between God the moral accountant and the God who is beyond the categories of good and evil.

> Such a God must be able to be both useful and harmful, both friend and foe – he is admired in good and bad alike. The anti-natural castration of a God into a God of the merely good would be totally undesirable here. One has as much need of the evil god as the good god ... Of what consequence would a god be who knew nothing of anger, revengefulness, envy, mockery, cunning, acts of violence?[18]

For all feminist talk about the male image of God, it is left to the misogynist Nietzsche to pursue the metaphor in a powerful way. The holy God is awesome, dreadful, uncontrollable. How much more alarming is the castration of such a powerful being, like some Samson caught defenceless under the knife. Surely the foundations of the universe would be shaken. And yet they have done it. That was the message of the Madman concerning the death of God, so here the death of the holy God, the noble God.[19]

The *Will to Power* ends with an affirmation. 'This world is the will to power – and nothing besides! And you yourselves are also this will to power – and nothing besides!' And what more natural and logical that this should be Nietzsche's understanding of the noble God. 'There is in fact no alternative for Gods: either they are the will to power – so long as they are that they will be national Gods – or else the impotence for power – and then they necessarily become *good*.'[20] God is dead, or at least the moral God is dead. But the noble God is not dead. It is the religious transformation of the doctrine of God, the image of God, which has in its projection produced an unworthy God who thankfully now is dead or dying. The danger is that religion will fatally wound the God beyond good and evil. He, who pervades His marvellous creation, enjoying it, revelling in it, He is now being reduced to a cosmic snoop who observes us in everything we do. Nietzsche sees this with the freshness of the child. '"Is it true that God is everywhere present?" asked a little girl of her mother. "That is indecent, I think."'[21] Yes, indecent for human life, but Nietzsche is more concerned that it is indecent for God. Is this God's work? Is this how it has all turned out?

> When the prerequisites of *ascending* life, when everything strong, brave, masterful, proud is eliminated from the concept of God; when he declines step by step to the symbol of a staff for the weary, a sheet-anchor for all who are drowning; when he becomes the poor people's God, the sinner's God, the God of the sick par excellence, and the predicate 'saviour', 'redeemer' as it were remains *over* as the predicate of divinity as such: of what does such a transformation speak, such a *reduction* of the divine?[22]

It is significant that this passage occurs in *The Antichrist*. We saw in the last chapter that Nietzsche is not against Christ, the noble Christ. Indeed he defends the noble Christ against the distortions of those who wish to make him serve their religious needs. And now he is not against the noble God. Indeed he defends the noble God against those who would seek to remake God in their own image. If Israel were not prepared to allow the noble God free rein, they should have been done with him once and for all. To redefine him was unworthy. 'The old God could no longer do what he formerly could. One should have to let him go. What happened? One altered the conception of him: at this price one retained him.'[23] The God of affirmation and spontaneity, committed to the well-being of the nation through the warrior king, becomes a God who rewards and punishes the nation because of sin. The defeat of the nation is interpreted as a punishment. Through defeat and restoration Israel conceives of its God as a universal omnipotent God, and as Neumann observes, 'an omnipotent god valued humility and meekness over manly pride. The priests who interpreted that deity's will naturally were preferred to the now defeated warriors.'[24] And soon an enslaved Israel, filled with *ressentiment* against the noble rulers, interprets the actions of their captors as evil. The priestly caste now rewrites history, as if the moral order were revealed to Moses: as Kofman says, it 'triumphed over the world by devaluing it'.[25] Every natural relationship is now viewed as having no value in itself: its value is bestowed through religion, through the world moral order, the will of God – and (in a thought which could have come from Marx) the *interests* of the priestly class.[26] 'As far as man has thought, he has introduced a bacillus of revenge into things. He has made even God ill with it, he has *deprived existence* in general *of its innocence* ...'[27] Nietzsche might not believe in the God of ancient Israel, but this God, the original God, the noble God, is a God *worthy* of belief.

Along these lines we detect two different attitudes of Nietzsche towards the Jews. On the one hand he can express admiration for a nation exhibiting self-confidence, affirmation, creativity,

courage, determination. They are a people whose delight is the
holy God of Israel. But he has no such admiration for a subdued
and subject people, filled now with *ressentiment*, who believe in a
moral world order which declares the aristocratic life – and their
own previous life – evil. They are the people of a God of punishment and revenge – or at least this is how they now perceive God.
Nietzsche can express everything he wishes to say on this subject
without a trace of anti-semitism. However, those who read his
words superficially may mistake his abrupt and abrasive aphorisms for anti-semitism, and some may be eager to read him in this
way.

As we have seen, the death of God is a metaphor, a colourful
way of announcing the death of religion, the birth of a culture in
which religion will no longer be credible. We can ring the changes
on the meaning of this dramatic metaphor, but ironically the one
thing it does not mean is that God is dead. Since Nietzsche by
this time did not believe in the existence of God, he was not
entering this familiar debate. He did not believe in the existence
of God, the old God or the noble God. But this does not prevent
him from making some original observations about the nature of
God. There are 'those timeless moments that fall into one's life as
if from the moon ...'[28] At such times he can reflect on the
different possibilities, the different profiles of the divine.

> And how many new gods are still possible! As for myself, in
> whom the religious, that is to say god-forming, instinct
> occasionally becomes active at impossible times – how
> differently, how variously the divine has revealed itself to me
> each time![29]

He has declared that the old God, the God of pity – the pitiable
God – is dead and should have no place in human affairs. He does
not believe in the existence of the noble God, or does he? Why
does he not simply say that he has speculated about the divine,
what is worthy to be called divine? Why does he say more
specifically that 'the divine has revealed itself to me ...' Is this a
reference to his mystical experience at Surlei, the moment in

which he experienced the holy, the awesome and the truth of the eternal recurrence? However that may be, he now feels free to make some observations about how a noble God would and should act, were He to exist.

Serious Christians, the ones Nietzsche says 'have always been well disposed towards me', might be challenged by these thoughts. Have they misrepresented God? Have they too easily accepted a non-biblical tradition in which God has been alienated from the very world both human and natural – which He created and declared unequivocally to be 'good'? Nietzsche's works are full of intriguing aphorisms, precisely because he has freed himself of the common assumptions and presuppositions which found our views on a wide variety of subjects, from natural science to theology. Biblical scholars have emphasized the significance of creation in six days – as represented in the priestly narrative with which the whole Bible opens. A job well done and the Almighty, even the Almighty, deserves to put the divine feet up. But what would be the reaction of a child? 'What shall we do now?' Who has not taken a child on a long walk, a shopping expedition, to attend an international match, or involved them in preparing a meal for the whole family, a day ending with fatigue but satisfaction – only to hear a fresh little voice pipe up: 'What shall we do now?' What a busy week for God! Starting from scratch (or nothing to scratch) on the Saturday evening, by the Sunday evening the whole system of light and darkness is up and running. By the evening of day four the sun and moon are functioning efficiently. By the fifth day the sea monsters inhabit the oceans and the birds swarm in the skies. No panic: everything is still on schedule, and a delivery has been promised for Friday, without fail. By close of business on day six the plants have arrived for the now abundant cattle – and mankind is taking possession of the planet earth. Our attention turns to the subsequent account of creation, featuring Adam, Eve, the serpent and the Fall. But Nietzsche is still back there at chapter 1 with the child's question. 'Only the most acute and active animals are capable of boredom.'[30] If this is true of the higher species, what of the

Creator Himself, especially a noble God whose energy and creative imagination are undiminished even after such exertions. Nietzsche can even envisage a theme for a great poet: 'God's boredom on the seventh day of creation.'[31] Some years later Nietzsche returned to this thought. After creating the world God was bored. When Adam was created into the world (the second creation account), *he* became bored. But the Creator was well able to deal with this situation. 'Consequently God created woman. And then indeed there was an end to boredom ...'[32] We might note that there exists in the Garden of Eden a special tree, 'the tree of the knowledge of good and evil'.[33] Through Eve there comes into the human world not evil, but the knowledge of good and evil. In consequence the noble God, the God of spontaneity and unrestrained creative imagination and power, is transformed by Adam and Eve into a Judge, who metes out punishment.[34]

It would be tempting for Nietzsche to present a noble God, a God of the noble values, as a God who goes His own way, caring nothing for mankind. But the fact of creation acts as a constraint. The God who creates the world must have some purpose for it. The God who creates mankind with such propensity for degeneration must be prepared to take the initiative in redeeming the work of His hands. Nietzsche does not hesitate to oppose the noble God to the degenerate God, nor does he hesitate to enter the field of doctrine.

> For in itself the opposite would be possible; and there are indications of this. God conceived as an emancipation from morality, taking into himself the whole fullness of life's antitheses and, in a divine torment, redeeming and justifying them: God as the beyond and above of the wretched loafers' morality of 'good and evil'.[35]

There is still a need for redemption. In his first book Nietzsche had conceived of 'God as the supreme artist, amoral, recklessly creating and destroying ...' and went to the theme of redemption. 'Thus the world was made to appear, at every instant, as a successful solution of God's own tensions, as an ever new vision projected by that grand sufferer for whom illusion is the only possible mode of redemption.'[36] There is still a desperate need for atonement – but these doctrines look very different in this new scenario, the world created and ruled by the noble God. Atheists and critics of religion have dismissed such matters as irrelevant metaphysical, mythological transactions which do not reach to the real world of human relations. Not so Nietzsche. Such matters are profoundly significant, for they reflect the assumptions and values of the society which holds these beliefs. He is conceiving of a God who is not predictable, manageable because constrained by the laws of morality, but 'one who at any rate is not humanitarian'.[37] Here is the same opposition as before. As scepticism spread in the nineteenth-century, people no longer believed that the world was of such a nature that it supported belief in the humanitarian God, the God of pity. Perhaps Nietzsche should have kept silent at this point: the traditional argument from design is breaking down. However, he boldly wrests the initiative. If the world as we conceive it turns out to be an imagined world, which does not support belief in the old God, then the conclusion is not that there is no God. He rehearses their argument: 'The Christian moral God is not tenable: hence "atheism" – as if there could be no other kinds of god.'[38] Rather, let us conceive of a God who *is* supported by the new world-view (Nietzsche's world-view). 'You are all afraid of the conclusion: "from the world we know, a very different god would be demonstrable, one who at any rate is not humanitarian" – and, in short, you hold fast to your God and devise for him a world we do not know.'[39]

God has been reduced to a supremely human, humanitarian being, having the supreme attributes of goodness and knowledge. This is not simply an anthropomorphic view of God, but a God who mirrors the interests, ethos, the sense of order and gentility of a social class. 'Is it necessary to elaborate that a god prefers to stay beyond everything bourgeois and rational? And, between ourselves, also beyond good and evil?'[40] Nietzsche, who at the level of morality is promoting the noble values, at the level of affirmation the will to power, invites us at least to conceive of a God whose attributes are not the projections of the middle class.

> Let us remove supreme goodness from the concept of God: it is unworthy of a god. Let us also remove supreme wisdom: it is the vanity of philosophers that is to be blamed for this mad notion of God as a monster of wisdom: he had to be as like them as possible. No! God the *supreme power* – that suffices! Everything follows from it, 'the world' follows from it![41]

If God had after all to redeem the world, then it would not be by some rational calculation, but from His passionate and all-consuming nature. And if He had to enter human society in order to do this, He would not be able to do this as Himself. Here Nietzsche is revising the doctrine of incarnation. When Paul ('that disastrously wrong-headed fellow') describes it, he says that God 'emptied himself, taking the form of a servant, being born in the likeness of men'.[42] Now it is unlikely that Nietzsche would think of God appearing as a slave! No, he begins at another point. In answer to his own question, 'What is noble?,' he gives a long list of the qualities of the higher men. The higher men, who embody and exhibit the noble values, would not be higher if they appeared as themselves. This provides Nietzsche with the clue to the incarnation.

> Always disguised: the higher the type, the more a man requires an incognito. If God existed, he would, merely on grounds of decency, be obliged to show himself to the world only as a man.[43]

God would be incarnate in a man who exhibited the noble values: the noble God would be revealed (and concealed) in the higher man. Would such a Son of God lead, as recommend by the Pauline tradition, 'a quiet and peaceable life, godly and respectful in every way'?[44] He most certainly would not, but then nor did the original Son of God, the noble Christ. Nietzsche takes his lead from Sophocles, who claimed that 'a man who is truly noble is incapable of sin …'[45] What then is the nature of the incarnation of

the noble God? 'A god come to earth ought to do nothing whatever but wrong; to take upon himself, not the punishment, but
the guilt – only that would be godlike.'[46]

If this is the will of the noble God for life on earth, what then
would life in heaven be like? Nietzsche does not speculate on this
prospect. From what we have already said, heaven will certainly
not be a religious place. It will not be eternal singing hymns and
opening doors for people. No, if this is the heaven of a God who
still has His balls, then it will be full of precisely those men whom
the confidant custodians of the tables of the law have long since
consigned to hell. Or as Nietzsche chips in, not denying himself
the pleasure of a chauvinistic observation, 'has it been noticed
that in heaven all interesting men are missing? Just a hint to the
girls as to where they can best find their salvation.'[47] The noble
God the Creator, the noble Son the Redeemer. To speak ill
against the world made by such a holy God, to condemn the
values incarnate in His Son, this would be the true sin against the
Holy Spirit.[48]

Is all of this neatly and comprehensively summed up in the
motto: 'Dionysos against the Crucified'? Who could possibly
think so? Even Irigaray's mermaid knows better.

> But were Dionysos and the Crucified One really different? Did
> they not, secretly, have the same birth within your universe? If
> so, you would have engaged and sought to overcome only a
> sham, phony contradiction – one created by a subjective error.
> The game would stop for lack of contestants. Upon the
> discovery that the two actors were the same gender and types,
> perhaps? You would have failed to search far enough or deep
> enough to find the source of your antagonisms, and the origin
> of your resentment.[49]

Five times in the last few pages of *Ecce Homo* he asks the same
question: 'Have I been understood?' And this from the greatest
master of the German language to date. Why at the end of his
public life, when his philosophical system had been set out at last
in a frenetic flurry of publications, why this insistent, anxious,

even poignant question? His public writings end with this question, a question so lacking in confidence that it is clearly rhetorical. 'Have I been understood? *Dionysos against the Crucified*.' This, the last disciple of the god Dionysos, is the first apostle of the noble God, the Unknown God of his youth.[50]

12

Nietszche Contra Lyotard

With the passage of time most writers become dated: we are conscious that they inhabit a very different world from our own. Their assumptions about society and the natural order of things are factors which must first be understood and then taken into account before we can begin to assess the value of their work. They speak, but they do not address us. By comparison there are a smaller number of writers for whom the passing of the decades seems to mean nothing. David Hume and Karl Marx speak to us directly; they insert themselves uninvited into contemporary debates, writers to whom we return again and again. A century or even two centuries make no difference: they are modern men regardless. In this notable list we might also count Nietzsche, who comes again and again, uninvited to challenge and disturb us, a spectre at the feasts of the culturally assured and the intellectually secure. However, we might well hesitate about according him the accolade of being for ever a 'modern' thinker. Is it not Nietzsche himself who has brought the word into disrepute? He is hailed as the father of postmodernism – and he has no equal. We know that secretly he would be delighted to have such a following, while at the same time with a mixture of bluster and abuse he would drive these acolytes from the outer court of his temple: 'I do not want "believers" ...'[1] Those who have acknowledged his genius have therefore done so indirectly, through dialogue, through a dialectical process of clarifying their ideas as they discuss his views, advancing their arguments as they respond to his position. This is clear for various titles. Luce Irigaray, *Marine Lover of Friedrich*

Nietzsche; Jacques Derrida, *Spurs*; Giles Deleuze, 'Nomad Thought'; Jean Granier, 'Thinking with and Against Nietzsche'; Lars Gustafsson, 'Dr Nietzsche's Office Hours are Between 10 am and 12 noon'. Yes, Nietzsche is the father of postmodernism. In a world of uncertainty at least this is true beyond question. His protest notwithstanding, this argumentative and ungrateful fellow must accept the gold award of International Association of Trend-setters, Bandwagon-boarders and Culture-gurus. Nietzsche is the father of postmodernism, of that there can be no doubt. Really? It must be all too clear what is going to happen next. Many are the boxes into which people have tried to place Nietzsche: none has been capable of holding him. It transpires that Nietzsche, this most destructive of all critics of Christianity, affirmed that Christianity is still possible, and admired Christians with beautiful feet. This fearless foe, who flourished the title of Anti-Christ like a banner to embarrass his family, disconcert his colleagues and alarm a Russian gentle-woman was warm in his praise of Jesus, for him the greatest human being. This prophet of a period of gloom and eclipse, who could dine out on his proclamation of the death of the moral God could without the slightest hesitation go on to conceive of the Noble God. This customer who has wearied the postal services of all Europe by returning to sender so many titles, surely he cannot decline this great honour of paternity of postmodernists everywhere. Knowing Nietzsche – oh yes, he can. A moment's reflection indicates that Nietzsche's periodization of European history is fundamentally different from that of the postmodern analysis. But beyond that, the whole point of his philosophy, the very reason for his writing, represents a fundamental rejection of everything that postmodernism stands for – or fails to stand for.

The word 'modern' derives from the Latin *modernus*, that which is 'of the present time'. After Constantine established Christianity as the religion of the Empire, in the fourth century, the term was used to contrast the Christian present and the pagan, Roman past. The Christian world was the modern world. Ironically but appropriately, the reverse position was taken at the time of the Renaissance. The modern world is often dated from 1450, when the rebirth of classical learning provided a perspective from which the Christian world could be judged. A further development came in the eighteenth century. The secular nature of the modern world was established at the Enlightenment: the religious world was the world of the past, while the world 'of the present time' was the new social, culture and intellectual world of the age of reason. The concept of 'modern' is itself modern: it is a term of evaluation. It is a way of referring to that which belongs to the present, as contrasted with the past, but beyond that it carries a value judgment. Modern medicine is preferred to what passed for medical treatment in previous times. A modern bathroom is preferred to a shed at the bottom of the garden. To modernize means out with the old and in with the new. For New Labour the whole country needs to be modernized. Industry must be modernized, that is, reorganized according to modern management principles. The National Health Service must be modernized according to principles of efficiency. Not that everything in the modern world is morally superior to what belongs to the past. Modern chemical warfare is lethally efficient and morally repugnant. The modern ecological crisis is largely man-made, the outcome of the self-indulgent life-style of the northern hemisphere. Modern is a term of evaluation, but not of moral evaluation. It has a good image. Or rather it has had a good image. In the most recent times the term modern seems strangely dated. *The Modern Homes Exhibition* has an image of what was current in the 1950s and 1960s. For the first time the term is being used with dismissive connotations. To describe a building now as 'modern' is to place it in a period of the recent past. We are living in a time of transition. Schematically the modern world has been described as that period of history, 1789–1989, from the fall of the Bastille to the fall of the Berlin Wall. When we speak now of 'modernity' we are looking back to our recent past, to a period from which we are increasingly alienated. It is claimed that we now live in a post-modern world. Given the flood of books which have appeared on the subject, and the number of careers launched on its rising tide – it must be true. Or rather, should we not pause for at least a moment to ask whether it is an appropriate term at all? As we have seen, the term modern has no content. It refers to the present time. Its content is whatever constitutes the experience of this period. So in the Byzantine period modern meant Christian as opposed to pagan. In the Renaissance it meant classical as opposed to Christian. In the Enlightenment it meant secular as opposed to religious. Whatever is, is modern. How we define modern depends on the characteristic features of the age. We need not be fixated on etymology to observe that it is not possible to be postmodern: we can only be post that which was previously called modern, that which deserves the title no more, that which reluctantly yields up the crown to a new age. However this is not a Lewis Carroll text: we cannot make terms mean what no one else takes them to mean. New modern, postmodern – the more important question concerns the characteristics of current experience which mark a transition from the previous age to our own.

By definition postmodernity takes up a position with respect to modernity. Its self-definition, indeed its necessity emerges from that which is lost. Modernity had certain features, but these have gone: postmodernity has about it the air of bereavement. We can characterize the experience in terms which are all too familiar from our study of Nietzsche.

(*a*) Loss of truth. People do not seek anything as ambitious or pretentious as the truth. They do not attempt to establish the facts. The object of their striving now is for information which can be used, for data which can be efficiently processed. The motivation is functional. The achievement of ends is the value in use. There is no religious or metaphysical perspective by which truth could be established or evaluated.

(*b*) Loss of consensus. Remnants of a moral consensus are assumed, but the reality is otherwise. On TV panel programmes there is no agreement on matters such as justice, equity, penal policy, foreign aid, organ transplantation, euthanasia. But the lack of agreement is simply the outworking of a more disturbing underlying reality. There is no consensus on where to begin or how to proceed: there are no moral starting points and no moral criteria.

(*c*) Loss of vision. There is no agreement on aesthetics. Taste is in the mouth of the beholder. 'I don't know anything about physics but I do know what I like.' Everyone's likes and dislikes constitute the final arbiter of beauty. Previously a dead sheep was a matter for the Department of Agriculture; now it is the concern of the National Gallery of Art.

There are many ways of describing postmodernity, and it will be clear that I have chosen to illustrate it by using the three categories which were the subject of Chapters 3, 4 and 5 above. These categories, central to Nietzsche's philosophy, are the loss of the foundations of truth, moral values and aesthetic judgments. It is not difficult to see why Nietzsche is pronounced father of postmodernism. No, he did not cause this crisis, but he did foresee it and proclaim it. There is, however, one detail – a mere detail – to which we should draw attention, out of deference to Nietzsche himself. In his work, these features characterize not the postmodern but the *modern* world. It is for this reason, not etymological fetishism, that I pointed out the redundant nature of the term 'postmodern'. In these three features Nietzsche describes *the present age*.

Elsewhere I have written at some length about the philosophy of Karl Marx.[2] In the course of this study of Nietzsche I have resisted the temptation to draw parallels with Marx. The danger in such a comparative approach would have been to fail to follow Nietzsche's thought to the very end. However, it is appropriate here to draw attention to a passage from *The Communist Manifesto*, not because it is in any sense a parallel text to Nietzsche, but because it is sometimes quoted by the exponents of postmodernism. The fact that in all other respects they ignore Marx – as if he could have been profoundly observant in this and utterly mistaken in everything else – has its own significance. It will be clear that I am casting doubt on the coherence and integrity of the term 'postmodern' and the necessity and usefulness of employing it. One danger is that its use suggests a scheme of periodization which returns us to the very idealism which it purports to eschew. It reinstates the rather dated view that the course of cultural history can be characterized by romantic ideas. We have already examined Nietzsche's materialism: he would certainly have repudiated such fable construction. It is all the more surprising that postmodernists, so dismissive of Marx, should quote this writer who made the materialization of Hegelian idealism the foundation of his reinterpretation of history. The postmodern romantic idealists begin with 1789 and the fall of the Bastille. This event does not belong in the calendar of socialism, but marks the establishment of the bourgeois era in French society. A more significant date would be 1776, not the creation of the even more bourgeois state across the sea, but the publication of *An Inquiry into the Nature and Causes of the Wealth of Nations*. In this work Adam Smith laid the foundations for the new discipline of political economy. Marx, who read it in Paris in a French translation, pays tribute to its influence on his own work.[3] It enabled him to characterize the effects of capitalism not simply in the transformation of the economic base of society, but in the consequent changes in the cultural superstructure. In *The Communist Manifesto* (1848) he describes the new social reality which this mode of production has produced.

> Constant revolutionizing of production, uninterrupted disturbance of all social conditions, everlasting uncertainty and agitation distinguish the bourgeois epoch from all earlier ones. All fixed, fast-frozen relations, with their train of ancient and venerable prejudices and opinions, are swept away, all new-formed ones become antiquated before they can ossify. All that is solid melts into air, all that is holy is profaned ...[4]

The world before capitalism was a world of traditional political and economic structures, typically for Marx the world of feudalism. The premodern world was characterized by inherited social, familial and personal relations: hierarchy and patriarchy. This premodern world was swept away by the modernizing revolution of capitalism which brought about new political and economic institutions, and revolutionized social relations at the same time. Everything that was familiar, comforting, secure (from the perspective of the ruling class) was dissolved. Marx borrows a telling phrase from *The Tempest*, 'All that is solid melts into air ...'⁵ This describes the effect of the modern world on the remnants of the pre-modern world. It had dissolving and corrosive effects on the previously assumed and taken for granted. But just as Marx claimed that capitalism produced its own gravediggers, so it is now claimed that the modern world produced the conditions under which its own new and confident certainties have begun to dissolve. 'All that is solid melts into air, all that is holy is profaned.' Two things might strike us at this point.

(*a*) The first is that those who use the quotation from Marx normally use only the first half: 'All that is solid melts into air ...' It is typical of Marx – Marx the atheist, Marx the opponent of religion (it is all so reminiscent of Nietzsche) – that he should think it important to add this important effect of the capitalist revolution: 'all that is holy is profaned'. He is not simply speaking of the fate of the churches, but more importantly of the effect of capitalism on the things most precious to the human and humane life.

(*b*) The second is the new reality of change. That which was solid and trustworthy in the pre-modern world was dissolved, but it is not being replaced by a new permanence. Or rather impermanence is the new permanence.

There is an interesting consensus here. For Marx the death of feudalism is marked by the experience that 'all that is solid melts in the air'. It is an experience of the *modern* world. For Nietzsche the death of God, the loss of foundation, is marked by the passage from being to becoming. This too is the experience of the *present* age. Nietzsche and Marx are both called as witnesses to the legitimacy of postmodernism, but both decline paternity. This last point demonstrates even more clearly that Nietzsche cannot be drawn into the postmodern analysis. Above I noted three features which might be taken to characterize the postmodern age. To these can be added a fourth. Taken together they bear witness to the loss of the meaning of life, indeed loss of the idea of that life could or should have a meaning. There is the loss of the conception of what would count as the meaning of life. The experience of the modern world involves the loss of the foundations of truth, moral values and aesthetic judgments, but what is that common foundation? The answer in a word is, God. In Chapter 2 we dealt with this matter at some length. The death of God is the metaphorical mode in which Nietzsche describes the loss of the foundation of the world. Truth, morality and aesthetics have all been based on religious premises. When the foundation is removed the life of meaning and significance is rendered impossible. To see the relevance of this issue for our present discussion we must set out two rather different tables of periodization:

Nietzsche	*Romantic neo-idealism*
1. The natural life of mankind	
2. Christian life	(*a*) Premodern period
	(*b*) Modern
3. Post-*mortem dei*	(*c*) Postmodern
4. Empowerment	

For Nietzsche, period 1. is the natural life of mankind, including, as we have seen, natural religion. It is above all a life without interference. It knows neither Socrates nor Paul: it is a world without moral improvers. Period 2. is characterized by idealist metaphysics and above all the biblical religion of good and evil. This is the period of foundationalism, when truth, morality and aesthetics are all secured by God. It is also the period when meaning and value are bestowed on human life by teleological reference, the purpose of God. Period 3. is characterized by the death of God, the dismantling of the unified system, the experience of the 'logic of terror'. It is a life lived without truth, morality or aesthetics, a life without meaning or purpose. Nietzsche's term for this period is 'nihilism'. Much of Nietzsche's energies go into calling on people to be honest, to recognize that they are now living in period 3. after the death of God. In both the *Cheerfulness* and the *Madman* passages – earlier quoted in full – he challenges those who know better to face up to the reality of their new situation.

Comparing this sequence to the other table, it is clear that the Romantic neo-idealist periodization does not correspond to Nietzsche's. Here the first period (*a*), the premodern, is the history of the human race up till 1450 or even 1789. (Does this not in itself seem unlikely?) The division made by Nietzsche between periods 1. and 2. is here of no consequence. Period (*b*), the modern age, is characterized by the emergence of man as 'the measure of all things' (Protagoras). The essential difference between the premodern and the modern on this count is the emergence of natural science. This is not the decisive division for Nietzsche, since he believes that science is still dependent upon religious premises. This second period (*b*) heralds a rational basis for natural and social reality. Reason is the foundation of the new human world, the real foundation of truth, morality and aesthetics. It is also the basis of meaning and values in life. This is not Nietzsche's reading of the situation at all. For him the modern world has already lost its foundation and its meaning, though it either does not understand this to be the case, or understanding refuses to acknowledge it to be the case. In the third period (*c*) there is an experience of loss of foundation and this is the characteristic of postmodernity. For Nietzsche this is a naïve misreading of the situation. The loss of foundation occurred more than a century ago: its name is nihilism.

There is therefore a complete lack of fit between the two tables, corresponding to a fundamental philosophical disagreement. It is not necessary to agree with Nietzsche's analysis: the point is that he does not prepare the way of the postmodernists. But there is a more important issue which further divides him from them. While they languish in the slough of despond, self-indulgently wallowing in an effete experience of despair and *ennui*, exhibiting the very 'fed-upness'[6] which he despised, Nietzsche refuses to allow nihilism to have the last word. He attacks it with tremendous energy, imagination, originality and commitment. His entire philosophy is directed toward the supersession of nihilism, his life's work is the laying of a new foundation for truth, morality and aesthetics, a new basis for meaning and value in life. A return to Nietzsche is a return to grand theory. And this represents the final alienation between him and the romantic neo-idealist analysis of modernism.

There is nothing in the Romantic neo-idealist analysis to correspond to period 4. in Nietzsche's analysis, empowerment. Nietzsche was critical of those who did not acknowledge the death of God and the consequent loss of foundation. He himself had faced the consequences of nihilism – and his life's work was to supersede it. To begin with he could not see how to proceed, but it was with the revelation at Surlei that he finally made the breakthrough. The transition from 3. to 4. is effected by his belief in the eternal recurrence of the same. This faith constitutes a new world-view, upon which basis he is able to raise up a life of meaning and value, a foundation for truth, morality and aesthetics. The difference between the analyses of Nietzsche and postmodernism depends on whether a constructive, even holistic, project is envisaged, or whether such constructions have lost their attraction and credibility. This is the issue addressed by Jean-François Lyotard in *The Postmodern Condition: A Report on Knowledge*. For Lyotard the term 'modern' designates 'any science that legitimates itself with reference to a meta-discourse ...'[7] This makes it sound ideological and intentional. In fact, as we have seen, according to Nietzsche science is legitimated by religious premises, unconsciously. The religious world-view is the metadiscourse, the 'grand narrative', but science does not even realize that it requires legitimation. This would be true also of moral and aesthetic values. In the modern world, according to Lyotard, 'justice is consigned to the grand narrative in the same way as truth'.[8] On this analysis the transition from the modern to the postmodern world is characterized by the loss of foundation. The agreed picture no longer commands assent. 'Simplifying to the extreme, I define *postmodern* as incredulity toward meta-narratives.'[9] Not that all grand narratives have been explicitly religious. In the modern world there have been at least two other alternatives. One is through speculative philosophy, notably Hegel's phenomenology of the spirit (accepting for the moment that this is not a religious system); the other is through some edifying view of mankind. 'The grand narrative has lost its credibility, regardless of what mode of unification it uses, regardless of whether it is a speculative narrative or a narrative of emancipation.'[10] We have seen that this loss had a devastating effect on Nietzsche. For Lyotard it could have such an effect on people today – but not necessarily. 'Lamenting the "loss of meaning" in postmodernity boils down to mourning the fact that knowledge is no longer principally narrative.'[11] In so far as knowledge is now instrumental, and the quest for truth is no longer an objective of science, then the loss of the grand narrative is a matter of some indifference. 'Most people have lost the nostalgia for the lost narrative.'[12]

Lyotard may well be right. People today may be content with the 'differend'.[13] They may be content with the knowledge which is justified by efficiency and the achievement of immediate ends. They may settle for *ad hoc* judgments about moral behaviour or aesthetic matters. Or Lyotard might be completely wrong. With respect to his 'report on knowledge', his view of science could have been quite out of date even as he wrote, if we are to believe Paul Davies in *Superforce: The Search for a Grand Unified Theory of Nature*.[14] And with respect to moral values, there is an interesting consensus on the relationship between truth and reconciliation developing in such countries as El Salvador, Bosnia and South Africa. There are indications that people cannot live with ad-hocracy, and that there is indeed what Quentin Skinner refers to as 'the return of grand theory in the human sciences'.[15] Fortunately it is not our task to decide between these two scenarios. We are addressing the issue of Nietzsche's relationship to postmodernism. Eternal recurrence is a grand narrative: indeed they do not come any grander. It is not simply that Nietzsche is not the father of postmodernism: rather, he spent his life producing a philosophy which offered a way through and beyond the experience which is the hallmark of this periodization. For Nietzsche the experience described as postmodern is not the very latest and last thing: it already lies in the past. It is not the high-water mark of Western culture, but a low tide which must be overcome if we are not to end up on the rocks of existential futility and moral bankruptcy. It may well be that the majority of people do mourn for the loss of meaning in life. Regardless of this, our conclusion is the even if such nihilism is good enough for Lyotard, it was not good enough for Nietzsche.

And so at last we turn to examine what Nietzsche actually said on the subject. I have reserved this for the end, because what Nietzsche said about postmodernism is an anachronistic question. He can hardly be expected to have a position on a debate the terms of which were not laid out for some eighty years after he finished writing. We noted that Nietzsche and Marx are agreed about the characteristic features of modernity. In *The Communist Manifesto* Marx writes, 'All fixed, fast-frozen relations, with their train of ancient and venerable prejudices and opinions, are swept away, all new-formed ones become antiquated before they can ossify. All that is solid melts into air, all that is holy is profaned ...' Nietzsche observes the same conditions: 'we no longer possess any standard of measurement, everything fixed and rigid begins to grow fluid.'[16] But as with Marx, he has no regrets that 'our social order will slowly melt away ...'[17] Most people who have this experience will be alarmed or depressed by it. Not so Nietzsche. 'One can desire this melting away only if one harbours hope ...'[18] The loss of foundation, solidity, security belong to the modern period, and he (as Marx) looks with faith to the future. The present nihilism must be overcome.

We have noted that Nietzsche's seeming contradictions disappear if we pay attention to their immediate context. This is so in use of the term 'modern'. Sometimes he speaks positively, sometimes negatively. But there is no real contradiction if we pay attention to the context. Again and again he describes himself as a modern man. He is a modern man, disgusted by the romantic idealism of Wagner.[19] He is a modern man suspicious of the constraints of idealism.[20] One of the recurring themes of postmodernist analysis is a carping criticism of the so-called Enlightenment project. But Nietzsche defends the Enlightenment against the Revolution, the free spirit must pursue 'the Enlightenment in himself'.[21] He defends the Enlightenment against the Romantic movement of the earlier part of the nineteenth century: 'this Enlightenment we must now carry further forward ...'[22]

But he can also be critical of the modern age. In this case he is not a modern man. Rather, he looks back to the nihilistic condition from which he has recently rescued himself. *The Antichrist* begins with this Hyperborean polemic. 'It was from this modernity that we were ill – from lazy peace, from cowardly compromise, from the whole virtuous uncleanliness of modern Yes and No.'[23] He, Dr Nietzsche, has wielded the surgeon's knife in curing himself of the views of Schopenhauer and Wagner. 'Nothing is our unhealthy modernity is more unhealthy than Christian piety.'[24] In *Ecce Homo* he describes *Twilight of Idols* as a sustained attack on idols, including those of the modern mind. Nietzsche always presents himself as being against the popular fashion. Is modern fashionable, then he will be against its undervaluing of the tradition. Is tradition fashionable, then he will be against its constraints. *Twilight of the Idols* itself warns that there is no future for conservatism. For one whose philosophy is built upon physiology he sees that 'reversion is impossible'.[25] It is not difficult to see the internal consistency of Nietzsche's position in all this. He evaluates modernity in relation to his own project, the quest for empowerment, the embodiment of the noble values beyond good and evil. The book of this name, *Beyond Good and Evil*, he describes as 'in all essentials a critique of modernity, the modern sciences, the modern arts, not even excluding modern politics, together with signposts to an antithetical type who is as little modern as possible, a noble, affirmative type'.[26] Very often the features which he attributes to modernity are those which others now associate with postmodernism.[27] Chief amongst them is nihilism, in contrast to his philosophy which supersedes it and takes heart in the struggle of life. 'Modern pessimism is an expression of the uselessness of the *modern* world – not of the world of existence.'[28]

Neither in his historical analysis nor in his philosophy of life does Nietzsche deserve to be saddled with paternity of post-modernism, which Erich Heller has described as 'the most unimaginative term of "periodization" hit upon by an enfeebled age'.[29] It was his faith that an enfeebled age could become an empowered age. The reappearance of grand narrative, in the form of eternal recurrence, is the foundation of his faith and therefore of life itself.

Notes

Full bibliographical details are given only when a title is not listed in the bibliography; otherwise short titles are used.

Preface

1. Kaufmann, *Nietzsche: Philosopher, Psychologist, Antichrist*, 117.
2. John 19.5, *The Holy Bible, Revised Standard Version*, Thomas Nelson & Sons 1946.
3. *Ecce Homo*, 134.
4. Jaspers, *Nietzsche and Christianity*, xii.

Introduction

1. *Human All Too Human*, 93.
2. *Ecce Homo*, 69.
3. Ibid., 48.
4. Heller, *The Importance of Nietzsche*, 68.

1. Ecce Homo

1. *Selected Letters of Friedrich Nietzsche*, 334.
2. There are various collections of letters, including *Selected Letters*, ed. Middleton, and *Nietzsche: A Self-Portrait from his Letters*. There are some early sources including Deussen, *Erinnerungen an Friedrich Nietzsche*; Bernouilli, *Franz Overbeck und Friedrich Nietzsche*, and Ludovici, *Nietzsche: His Life and Work*. More recent works include Stern, *A Study of Nietzsche*, and of course Kaufmann, *Nietzsche: Philosopher, Psychologist, Antichrist*.
3. Middleton (ed.), *Selected*

Letters, 293.

4. Ibid., 189.

5. Ibid, 293 n.144.

6. Frenzel, *Friedrich Nietzsche*, 19.

7. A nickname suggested by the impressive intonation of his reading of biblical passages, according to Fuss and Shapiro, *Self-Portrait*, 169.

8. 'From my Life', quoted in Hollingdale, *Nietzsche*, 31–2.

9. Küng, *Does God Exist?*, 353.

10. *Daybreak*, 45.

11. *The Will to Power*, 93.

12. Middleton (ed.), *Selected Letters*, 47.

13. Ibid., 48.

14. Deussen, *Erinnerungen an Friedrich Nietzsche*, quoted in Küng, *Does God Exist?*, 352.

15. *Human All Too Human*, 135.

16. Ibid.

17. *Ecce Homo*, 51.

18. *Human All Too Human*, 330.

19. Kaufmann, *Twenty German Poets*, 143.

20. Middleton (ed.), *Selected Letters*, 7.

21. *The Anti-Christ*, 150.

22. I Corinthians 11.29.

23. Heidegger, *Nietzsche*, Vol. 2, 10.

24. Quoted in Jaspers, *Nietzsche*, 28.

25. Frenzel, *Friedrich Nietzsche*, 36.

26. Middleton (ed.), *Selected Letters*, 92.

27. *Human All Too Human*, 176, a prescription which must have gladdened the hearts of National Socialists sixty years later.

28. Fuss and Shapiro, *Nietzsche: A Self-Portrait*, 12.

29. Middleton (ed.), *Selected Letters*, 41.

30. Ibid, 44.

31. Fuss and Shapiro, *Nietzsche: A Self-Portrait*, 20 n.1.

32. Middleton (ed.), *Selected Letters*, 32.

33. Fuss and Shapiro, *Nietzsche: A Self-Portrait*, 63.

34. Quoted in Jaspers, *Nietzsche*, 72.

35. Tanner, *Nietzsche*, 58.

36. Frenzel, *Friedrich Nietzsche*, 100.

37. *Zarathustra*, 93: the advice of the little old woman to the prophet.

38. Middleton (ed.), *Selected Letters*, 185.

39. Ibid, 141.

40. Middleton (ed.), *Selected Letters*, 346, and Fuss and Shapiro, *Nietzsche: A Self-Portrait*, 180.

41. *Ecce Homo*, 66.

42. *Human All Too Human*, 'conflict with a childish and irritable mother', 156; 'to shake off that motherly watching and warding with which women govern him', 158.

43. Schopenhauer makes observa-

tions about women, fitted in between an essay on suicide and remarks on Sanskrit literature. His knowledge of the last two seems greater than of the first subject. 'Dissimulation is, therefore, inborn in women ... Therefore an entirely truthful and unaffected woman is perhaps impossible.' 'Only the male intellect, clouded by the sexual impulse, could call the undersized, narrow-shouldered, broad-hipped, and short-legged sex the fair sex ...', *Parerga and Paralipomena: Short Philosophical Essays*, Vol. 2, 617, 619.

44. Middleton (ed.), *Selected Letters*, 251.
45. Ibid., 257.
46. Quoted in Küng, *Does God Exist?*, 399.
47. Brandes, *Friedrich Nietzsche*, 3.
48. Ibid., 64.
49. Middleton (ed.), *Selected Letters*, 197.
50. Quoted in Silk and Stern, *Nietzsche on Tragedy*, 117.
51. Quoted in Jaspers, *Nietzsche*, 85.
52. Quoted in Heller, *The Importance of Nietzsche*, 177.
53. Jaspers, *Nietzsche*, 81.
54. Dostoyevsky, *Crime and Punishment*, 47. Zeig, quoted by Gilbert Sigaux in his Introduction. Not that the influence was only one way. See Beermann, 'Nietzsche, Dostoevsky and Russian Symbolism'.
55. Middleton (ed.), *Selected Letters*, 319 n.190.
56. Ibid., 330–44.
57. Ibid, 346.
58. Ibid, 345.
59. Jaspers, *Nietzsche*, 88–115.
60. Quoted in Ludovici, *Nietzsche*, 22.
61. Stern, *A Study of Nietzsche*, 32.
62. Silk and Stern, *Nietzsche on Tragedy*, 42.
63. Kaufmann, *Nietzsche*, 50.
64. Bataille, *On Nietzsche*, 172.
65. *The Times*, quoted in Bataille, *On Nietzsche*, 173.

2. *The Death of God*

1. Quoted by Kamenka, *The Philosophy of Ludwig Feuerbach*, 17.
2. *Die Fröhliche Wissenschaft*, Kritische Gesamtausgabe V.2, 163.
3. Jaspers, *Nietzsche*, 49.
4. Ibid, 140.
5. *Daybreak*, 52.
6. *Twilight of the Idols*, 69.
7. *Untimely Meditations*, 29–30.
8. *Twilight of the Idols*, 69.

9. *The Will to Power*, 147.
10. Jaspers, *Nietzsche*, 194.
11. *The Will to Power*, 423.
12. Heller, *The Importance of Nietzsche*, 48.
13. *Die Fröhliche Wissenschaft, Kritische Gesamtausgabe* V.2, 158.
14. Deleuze, *Nietzsche and Philosophy*, Chapter 4,
'Against the Dialectic'.
15. *The Gay Science*, 279–80.
16. Ibid., 181–2.
17. Heller, *The Importance of Nietzsche*, 5.
18. Heidegger, *Nietzsche*, Vol. 2, 66.
19. Ibid.
20. Heller, *The Importance of Nietzsche*, 3.

3. *The Shadow of God*

1. Warnock, *English Philosophy Since 1900*, 33.
2. Jaspers, *Nietzsche*, 10.
3. *Human All Too Human*, 37.
4. Clark, *Nietzsche on Truth and Philosophy*, 4.
5. Heller, *The Importance of Nietzsche*, 176.
6. Jaspers, *Nietzsche*, 10.
7. *Human All Too Human*, 13.
8. Karl Fortlage, *Materialismus und Spiritualismus* (1856), quoted in Gregory, *Scientific Materialism in Nineteenth-Century Germany*, 10.
9. Heidegger, *Nietzsche*, Vol.1, 200.
10. Ibid., 7.
11. Ibid., 67.
12. Ibid., 68.
13. Schlechta (ed.), *Werke* 3, 953.
14. A. Bogdanov, *Empirio-Monism* (1906), Preface, ix, quoted by V.I. Lenin, *Collected Works*, Vol. XIII, *Materialism and Empirio-Criticism*, Lawrence &
Wishart 1938, 124. I am grateful for this reference to my colleague, the materialist/feminist theologian Dr Marcella Althaus-Reid.
15. *Untimely Meditations*, 184.
16. *The Birth of Tragedy*, 92.
17. Ibid., 93.
18. Ibid., 112.
19. *Human All Too Human*, 32.
20. *Untimely Meditations*, 153.
21. Ibid., 119.
22. *Beyond Good and Evil*, 112.
23. *Human All Too Human*, 18ff.
24. *The Gay Science*, 169.
25. Ibid., 283.
26. Husserl, 'Philosophy as Rigorous Science', in *Phenomenology and the Crisis of Philosophy*, 81.
27. Heidegger, *Nietzsche*, Vol. 2, 112.
28. Jaspers, *Philosophy of Existence*, 101.
29. Jaspers, *Nietzsche*, 194.
30. Quoted ibid.

31. Jaspers, *Nietzsche and Christianity*.
32. *The Gay Science*, 219.
33. *The Will to Power*, 298.
34. *On Truth and Falsity*, 96.
35. Fragmentary draft preface to a new edition of *The Birth of Tragedy*, in *The Will to Power*, 451.
36. *The Will to Power*, 451.
37. *Human All Too Human*, 218.
38. Ibid., 323.
39. *Beyond Good and Evil*, 197.
40. *On Truth and Falsity*, 92.
41. *Thus Spoke Zarathustra*, 285.
42. *The Genealogy of Morals*, 287.
43. Jaspers, *Nietzsche*, 227.
44. *Daybreak*, 206.
45. *The Gay Science*, 288.

46. For further details see Strong, *The Legend and Cult of Upagupta*, 28ff. For this reference I am grateful to my colleague Paul Dundas, Sanskrit scholar, Jain specialist and Hibernian devotee.
47. *The Gay Science*, 167.
48. Wittgenstein, *Philosophical Investigations*, 212.
49. *Twilight of the Idols*, 38.
50. Haar, 'Nietzsche and Metaphysical Language', in *The New Nietzsche*, ed. Allison, 6.
51. Simon, 'Language and the Critique of Language in Nietzsche Studies', 255.

4. Revaluation of All Values

1. *Beyond Good and Evil*, 91.
2. *The Will to Power*, 147.
3. Ibid., 16.
4. Ibid., 331.
5. *Zur Genealogie der Moral*, Kritische Gesamtausgabe VI.2, 385.
6. *The Will to Power*, 9.
7. Ibid., 17.
8. Middleton (ed.), *Selected Letters*, 65.
9. *The Will to Power*, 521.
10. Ibid, 18.
11. Ibid., 3–4.
12. Ibid., 326.
13. *Beyond Good and Evil*, 45.
14. Jaspers, *Nietzsche*, 227.
15. *Daybreak*, 4.
16. *Beyond Good and Evil*, 14.

17. Middleton (ed.), *Selected Letters*, 258.
18. *The Will to Power*, 20.
19. Kaufmann, *Nietzsche*, 142.
20. *The Birth of Tragedy*, 9.
21. *Human All Too Human*, 12.
22. Middleton (ed.), *Selected Letters*, 22.
23. *The Will to Power*, 149; cf. *The Genealogy of Morals*, 155.
24. *Beyond Good and Evil*, 92.
25. *Human All Too Human*, Introduction, xiii.
26. Ibid., 12.
27. *The Will to Power*, 149, cf. *Beyond Good and Evil*, 78.
28. *Beyond Good and Evil*, 45.
29. *Twilight of the Idols*, 55.
30. Feuerbach, *The Essence of*

Christianity, 13.

31. Jaspers, *Nietzsche*, 140.
32. *Thus Spoke Zarathustra*, 191.
33. *The Genealogy of Morals*, 208.
34. *Daybreak*, 60.
35. *The Gay Science*, 169; cf. *Human All Too Human*, 182.36. *The Antichrist*, 124; cf. *Daybreak*, 23.
37. *The Will to Power*, 348–9.
38. *Thus Spoke Zarathustra*, 64.
39. *Menschliches, Allzumenschliches*, Kritische Gesamtausgabe IV.3, 102.
40. *Twilight of the Idols*, 101.
41. *Human All Too Human*, 323.
42. Luke 11.24–26.
43. *The Will to Power*, 148.
44. *Human All Too Human*, 64, 57.
45. *Thus Spoke Zarathustra*, 208.
46. Ibid., 209.
47. *The Gay Science*, 75.
48. Deleuze, *Nietzsche and Philosophy*, 1.
49. Ibid., 98.
50. *The Antichrist*, 117.
51. *Twilight of the Idols*, 45.
52. *The Will to Power*, 243.
53. Ibid., 189.
54. *Ecce Homo*, 34.
55. Ibid., 116.
56. *Human All Too Human*, 7.
57. *Daybreak*, 23.
58. *The Antichrist*, 117.

59. *Twilight of the Idols*, 34.
60. *The Gay Science*, 272.
61. *Ecce Homo*, 34.
62. *Thus Spoke Zarathustra*, 89.
63. *Human All Too Human*, 321.
64. *Daybreak*, 17.
65. *Beyond Good and Evil*, 139.
66. *The Genealogy of Morals*, 160.
67. *Thus Spoke Zarathustra*, 279.
68. Brandes, *Friedrich Nietzsche*, 64. Fortunately Brandes did not add that he thought Nietzsche got the distinction of good and bad from the British moralists, and more immediately from Paul Rée, *Der Ursprung der moralischen Empfindungen* (1877).
69. *Beyond Good and Evil*, 174.
70. *Daybreak*, 219.
71. Deleuze, *Nietzsche and Philosophy*, 34.
72. *Beyond Good and Evil*, 175ff. Nietzsche discusses good and evil, the morality of master and slave as early as 1878, in *Human All Too Human*, 34ff.
73. Magnus, *Nietzsche's Existential Imperative*, 154; cf. Zeitlin, *Nietzsche: A Re-examination*, 59.
74. Zeitlin, *Nietzsche: A Re-examination*, 46.
75. *Beyond Good and Evil*, 108. chapter on 'Art and 5.Ibid.,

5. Lest the Bow Break

1. *The Antichrist*, 151.
2. *The Will to Power*, 423.
3. *The Gay Science*, 168.
4. *The Will to Power*, 435.

5. Ibid., 423.
6. *Ecce Homo*, 61.
7. *The Will to Power*, 61.
8. *The Nietzsche-Wagner Correspondence*, ed. Förster-Nietzsche, 7.
9. Middleton (ed.), *Selected Letters*, 180.
10. *The Birth of Tragedy*, 17.
11. Schacht, in his excellent chapter on 'Art and Artists', makes the important distinction between 'the kinds of transfiguration involved, rather than in terms of a division of the various art-forms', *Nietzsche*, 489.
12. *The Birth of Tragedy*, 24.
13. *Truth and Falsity*, 94.
14. *The Birth of Tragedy*, 9.
15. Ibid., 42
16. Ibid.
17. *Twilight of the Idols*, 81.
18. *Untimely Meditations*, 34–5.
19. Ibid., 212.
20. Ibid., 254.
21. Ibid., 213, cf. *Human All Too Human*, 243.
22. *The Will to Power*, 520–1.
23. *Nietzsche Contra Wagner*, 74.
24. *Untimely Meditations*, 215.
25. Ibid., 229.
26. *Ecce Homo*, 82.
27. *Twilight of the Idols*, 110.
28. *The Case of Wagner*, 1.
29. Middleton (ed.), *Selected Letters*, 340.
30. *The Case of Wagner*, 41.
31. *Nietzsche Contra Wagner*, 8.
32. Ibid., 5.
33. *The Case of Wagner*, 16.
34. Pütz, 'Nietzsche: Art and Intellectual Inquiry', 24.
35. *The Case of Wagner*, 1–2.
36. *The Will to Power*, 422.
37. *The Case of Wagner*, 10.
38. Ibid.
39. Ibid., 45.
40. Ibid., 68.
41. Ibid., 28.
42. Ibid., 16.
43. Ibid., 18.
44. *Ecce Homo*, 119.
45. Middleton (ed.), *Selected Letters*, 188.
46. *The Case of Wagner*, 7.
47. Middleton (ed.), *Selected Letters*, 223.
48. *Ecce Homo*, 90.
49. *Nietzsche Contra Wagner*, 82; cf. *Human All Too Human*, 211; *Beyond Good and Evil*, 171.
50. *Ecce Homo*, 93.
51. Ibid.
52. *The Case of Wagner*, 58.
53. *The Genealogy of Morals*, 237.
54. *The Case of Wagner*, 56.
55. Pütz, 'Nietzsche: Art and Intellectual Inquiry', 6.
56. *Nietzsche Contra Wagner*, 67 (italics added).

6. Decadence

1. *Human All Too Human*, 204.
2. *Twilight of the Idols*, 35.
3. Jeremiah 2.7.
4. Philippians 2.7.
5. I Corinthians 1.26.
6. Frend, *Martyrdom and Persecution in the Early Church*, 97, referring to Romans 16 and I Corinthians 16.19.
7. Sobrino, *The True Church and the Poor*, 23.
8. Ibid., 8.
9. De Santa Ana, *Good News to the Poor*.
10. Kee, *Constantine versus Christ*.
11. *The Antichrist*, 184.
12. Ibid., 186.
13. Ibid., 185.
14. Ibid., 186, cf. *Ecce Homo*, 121; *The Genealogy of Morals*, 187.
15. *The Birth of Tragedy*, 138.
16. Ibid., 140.
17. Ibid., 139.
18. *The Antichrist*, 168.
19. *Beyond Good and Evil*, 178.
20. *The Genealogy of Morals*, 260.
21. *The Birth of Tragedy*, 11.
22. *Daybreak*, 159.
23. *The Antichrist*, 127.
24. Ibid.
25. Genesis 1.25–26.
26. Deleuze, *Nietzsche and Philosophy*, 13.
27. *The Gay Science*, 272.
28. Deleuze, *Nietzsche and Philosophy*, 122.
29. Ibid., 119.
30. *The Antichrist*, 117.
31. Ibid., 121.
32. Ibid., 131.
33. Ibid., 186.
34. Karl Marx and Frederick Engels, 'Contribution to the Critique of Hegel's Philosophy of Right: Introduction', *Collected Works*, Vol. 3, Lawrence & Wishart 1975, 175.
35. *The Will to Power*, 139.
36. *The Gay Science*, 99.
37. Middleton (ed.), *Selected Letters*, 271.
38. *The Antichrist*, 162–3.
39. *The Birth of Tragedy*, 11.
40. *Human All Too Human*, 73.
41. *The Genealogy of Morals*, 280.
42. *The Will to Power*, 483.
43. Ibid., 389.
44. *The Antichrist*, 116.
45. *Thus Spoke Zarathustra*, 226.
46. Ibid., 113.
47. *Nietzsche Contra Wagner*, 89.
48. Pütz, 'Nietzsche: Art and Intellectual Inquiry', 23.
49. *Nietzsche Contra Wagner*, 90.
50. Ibid., 87.
51. Ibid., 90.
52. Ibid., 92.
53. Hegel, *Logic*, 9; cf. *Philosophy of Right*, 10.
54. *Ecce Homo*, 56.
55. Ibid., 92.
56. Ibid., 56.

57. *Thus Spoke Zarathustra*, 233.
58. *The Will to Power*, 452.
59. *Thus Spoke Zarathustra*, 177,
60. *Ecce Homo*, 45.
61. *The Gay Science*, 223.

7. The Will to Power

1. Freud, in his *Introductory Lectures on Psychoanalysis,* separated the self-preservation instinct from the narcissistic libido, a distinction which he later abandoned in *Beyond the Pleasure Principle.*
2. *Thus Spoke Zarathustra*, 138.
3. *The Will to Power*, 148. Ironically, there is little discussion of the will to power in the collection entitled *The Will to Power.*
4. Clark, *Nietzsche on Truth and Philosophy*, 206.
5. *Beyond Good and Evil*, 49.
6. Schacht, *Nietzsche*, 220.
7. *The Will to Power*, 550.
8. It might be said that 'Nietzsche, by uttering the term "will to power", did re-enact the traditional move of metaphysics', Haar, in *The New Nietzsche*, ed. Allison, 8.
9. Magnus, *Nietzsche's Existential Imperative*, 25.
10. *Thus Spoke Zarathustra*, 136.
11. Heidegger, *Nietzsche*, I, 46.
12. Ibid., 52–3.
13. Ibid., 61.
14. Haar, in *The New Nietzsche*, ed. Allison, 11.
15. Magnus, *Nietzsche's Existential Imperative*, 31.
16. Deleuze, *Nietzsche and Philosophy*, 85.
17. *The Antichrist*, 115.
18. Ibid., 127.
19. Ibid., 117.
20. Ibid.
21. *Human All Too Human*, 229.
22. Ibid., 322, cf. pity as 'unworthy of a strong, dreadful soul', *Daybreak*, 16.
23. *The Antichrist*, 118; 'Pity is praised as the virtue of prostitutes', *The Gay Science*, 88.
24. *Thus Spoke Zarathustra*, 272.
25. Ibid., 276.
26. Ibid., 277.
27. *Daybreak*, 86.
28. *The Will to Power*, 397.
29. Ibid., 7.
30. *Thus Spoke Zarathustra*, 397.
31. Ibid., 110.
32. E.g. Taylor, *Hegel*, Ch. 15, 'Reason and History'; Kee, *Marx and the Failure of Liberation Theology*, Ch. 5, 'Historical Materialism as Religion'.
33. *Untimely Meditations*, 100–6.
34. Ebeling, *Word and Faith*, 363.
35. *Human All Too Human*, 302. 'Overshoot' *(Nachtrieb)* might be better translated here as 'propensity', *Menschliches, Allzumen*

schliches, Kritische
Gesamtausgabe IV.3.

36. *The Antichrist*, 186.
37. *Untimely Meditations*, 66.
38. Ibid., 72.
39. *Daybreak*, 98.
40. Hegel, *Philosophy of Right*, 13.
41. *Thus Spoke Zarathustra*, 104.
42. *Unzeitgemässe Betrachtungen*, ed. Schlechta, I, 270.
43. Hayek, *Law, Legislation and Liberty*, Vol.1, *Rules and*

Order, 24.
44. *The Gay Science*, 305.
45. *The Will to Power*, 344.
46. Ibid., 363.
47. *Untimely Meditations*, 111.
48. *Human All Too Human*, 29.
49. *Thus Spoke Zarathustra*, 65; 'Not "mankind" but overman is the goal!', *The Will to Power*, 519.
50. *Thus Spoke Zarathustra*, 143.
51. Ibid., 42.
52. Ibid., 104.

8. Eternal Recurrence

1. *The Gay Science*, 210.
2. Heidegger, *Nietzsche*, Vol. 2, 107.
3. The sub-title of *Twilight of the Idols*.
4. Marais, *History of Philosophy*, 27.
5. *Ecce Homo*, 81.
6. Deleuze, *Nietzsche and Philosophy*, 29; cf. Magnus, *Nietzsche's Existential Imperative*, 48.
7. *Ecce Homo*, 56.
8. *Twilight of the Idols*, 104.
9. *The Gay Science*, 167.
10. Ibid., 168.
11. *The Will to Power*, 548.
12. Ibid., 549.
13. *Thus Spoke Zarathustra*, 234.
14. *The Will to Power*, 549.
15. Jaspers, *Introduction*, 364.
16. Middleton (ed.), *Selected Letters*, 193 n. 67.
17. Clark, *Nietzsche on Truth and*

Philosophy, Ch. 8.
18. Ibid., 247; *The Will to Power*, 36.
19. *The Will to Power*, 35.
20. Ibid., 36.
21. Magnus, *Nietzsche's Existential Imperative*, 140.
22. Ibid., 142; cf. Clark, *Nietzsche on Truth and Philosophy*, 248–54.
23. Deleuze, 'Nomad Thought', in *The New Nietzsche*, ed. Allison, 86.
24. *Thus Spoke Zarathustra*, 178.
25. Heidegger, *Nietzsche*, Vol.1, 120.
26. Ibid.
27. *Thus Spoke Zarathustra*, 178.
28. Ibid., 179.
29. Quoted Magnus, *Nietzsche's Existential Imperative*, 60.
30. *Ecce Homo*, 98; *The Gay Science*, 74. In a letter to Peter Gast, September 1884,

he hopes to see the creation
of such a brotherhood in
Nice, where he was at the
time, Middleton (ed.),
Selected Letters, 230.

31. *The Gay Science*, 273–4.

32. '... in bad faith it is from
    myself that I am hiding the
    truth', Sartre, *Being and
    Nothingness*, 49.

33. Löwith, *From Hegel to
    Nietzsche*, 196.

34. Deleuze, 'Nomad Thought',
    in *The New Nietzsche*, ed.
    Allison, 100.

35. Magnus, *Nietzsche's
    Existential Imperative*, 143.

36. Clark, *Nietzsche on Truth and
    Philosophy*, 269.

37. Heidegger, *Nietzsche*, Vol. 2,
    Ch.18.

38. Deleuze, *Nietzsche and
    Philosophy*, 47.

39. Magnus, *Nietzsche's
    Existential Imperative*, 157.

40. Ibid., 139.

41. *Thus Spoke Zarathustra*, 237.

42. Ibid., 180.

43. Ibid., 235.

44. Ibid., 236.

45. Ibid., 78, 326. '"Was that
    life?" Perhaps. But here is
    death. And your conversion
    takes place only when the
    turn of your wheel is over',
    Irigaray, *Marine Lover of
    Friedrich Nietzsche*, 8. In this
    Irigaray has missed the exis-
    tential point. She has lost the
    plot, she or her mermaid. A

curious mechanism. 'This
amorous sexual relationship
seems unlikely: what, after
all, is a subtle feminist, who
until this point stressed the
pleasure of lesbian love-mak-
ing, doing in a relationship of
amorous sexuality with a
moustachioed misogynist like
Nietzsche?', Oppel,
'"Speaking of Immemorial
Waters": Irigaray with
Nietzsche', 88.

46. *Ecce Homo*, 101.

47. Ibid., 102–3.

48. Ibid., 99.

49. Ibid.

50. From Sils-Maria, 14 August
    1881, quoted in Klossowski,
    'Nietzsche's Experience of
    Eternal Return', in *The New
    Nietzsche*, ed. Allison, 106.

51. Birault, 'Beatitude in
    Nietzsche', in *The New
    Nietzsche*, ed. Allison, 230.

52. Heidegger, *Nietzsche*, Vol.2,
    12–13.

53. Klossowski, 'Nietzsche's
    Experience of Eternal
    Return', in *The New
    Nietzsche*, ed. Allison, 108.

54. Katz, 'Language,
    Epistemology, and
    Mysticism', 22–74.

55. Otto, *The Idea of the Holy*,7.

56. Clark, *Nietzsche on Truth and
    Philosophy*, 265.

57. Jaspers, *Nietzsche*, 352.

58. Furness, 'Nietzsche, the
    Madman and the Death of

God', 15.

59. *The Birth of Tragedy*, 139, italics added.
60. Magnus, *Nietzsche's*

Existential Imperative, 192.
61. John 10.7–8.
62. Quoted Heidegger, *Nietzsche*, Vol.2, 201.

9. *Nietzsche's Faith*

1. Hayek, *The Road to Serfdom*, Ch.1.
2. *The Will to Power*, 542.
3. Jung, *Selected Writings*, 45.
4. Zelechow, 'Nietzsche's Theology of History and the Redemption of Postmodernism', 128.
5. Heller, *The Importance of Nietzsche*, 11.
6. Quoted Haar, 'Nietzsche and the Metamorphosis of the Divine', 157.
7. Ludovici, *Nietzsche*, 39.
8. Deleuze, *Nietzsche and Philosophy*, 214.
9. Brandes, *Friedrich Nietzsche*, 86.
10. Jaspers, *Philosophy*, Vol. 1, 84.
11. Quoted Heller, *The Importance of Nietzsche*, 143.
12. Jaspers, *Philosophy*, Vol.1, 20.
13. Kee, 'Transcendence and God: A Critique of Religious Objectivism'.
14. Jaspers, *Philosophy*, Vol. 1, 20.
15. See especially Jaspers, *Philosophical Faith and Revelation*.
16. *Daybreak*, 1.
17. Feuerbach, *The Essence of*

Christianity, 64.
18. Kierkegaard, *Concluding Unscientific Postscript*, 91.
19. Heidegger, *Nietzsche*, Vol.2, 129.
20. Kierkegaard, *Concluding Unscientific Postscript*, 51.
21. *The Gay Science*, 340.
22. E.g. Matthew 11.21; Mark 6.12; Luke 13.3; Revelation 9.21.
23. *Ecce Homo*, 99.
24. Heidegger, *Being and Time*.
25. Karl Marx, 'The Critique of Hegel's Philosophy of Right: Introduction', in *Karl Marx: Early Writings*, 58. For a discussion of the German text (Marx/Engels, *Werke*, I, 390), see Kee, *Marx and the Failure of Liberation Theology*, 285 n.42.
26. Castro, 'In Tribute to Che', 26.
27. *Untimely Meditations*, 162.
28. *Thus Spoke Zarathustra*, 161.
29. Ibid., 163.
30. Ibid., 162.
31. Ibid., 161.
32. *Ecce Homo*, 110.
33. Jaspers, *Nietzsche*, 352.
34. Valadier, 'Dionysus Versus the Crucified', in *The New*

Nietzsche, ed. Allison, 253.

35. Löwith, *From Hegel to Nietzsche*, 373.
36. Haar, Michel, 'Nietzsche and Metaphysical Language', in *The New Nietzsche*, ed. Allison, 30.
37. Ibid.
38. Ibid.
39. Küng, *Does God Exist?*, 403; cf. Jaspers, *Nietzsche*, 365.
40. Quoted by Jaspers, *Nietzsche*, 363.
41. Jaspers, *Nietzsche*, 430.
42. *The Genealogy of Morals*, 162.
43. Revelation 22.20.
44. Heller, *The Importance of Nietzsche*, 53.
45. *The Genealogy of Morals*, 230.
46. *The Gay Science*, 255.
47. *Thus Spoke Zarathustra*, 41.
48. Ibid., 42.
49. Ibid., 43.
50. Ibid., 44.
51. Ibid., 110.
52. Clark, *Nietzsche on Truth and Philosophy*, 272.
53. Haar, *The New Nietzsche*, ed.

Allison, 7.
54. *The Gay Science*, 131.
55. Deussen, quoted in Jaspers, *Nietzsche*, 36.
56. Deleuze, *The New Nietzsche*, ed., Allison, 147.
57. *The Will to Power*, 452.
58. Tanner, *Nietzsche*, 27.
59. Ibid.
60. Quoted in Küng, *Does God Exist?*, 401.
61. *Ecce Homo*, 104.
62. *The Gay Science*, 255.
63. Hollingdale, 'Commentary' to *Beyond Good and Evil*, 216 n. 25.
64. *Untimely Meditations*, 213.
65. Otto, *The Idea of the Holy*, 20.
66. Magnus, *Nietzsche's Existential Imperative*, 192.
67. *Ecce Homo*, 126.
68. Ibid.
69. Quoted in Tanner, *Nietzsche*, 60.
70. *Human All Too Human*, 233.
71. *The Will to Power*, 219.
72. Ibid, 229.

10. *Jesus of Nazareth*

1. *Beyond Good and Evil*, 162–3.
2. *The Genealogy of Morals*, 295.
3. Quoted Löwith, *From Hegel to Nietzsche*, 423.
4. *The Genealogy of Morals*, 294.
5. *Human All Too Human*, 175.
6. *Beyond Good and Evil*, 163.
7. Ibid.
8. *The Gay Science*, 291.

9. *Daybreak*, 125.
10. Ibid.
11. *The Genealogy of Morals*, 281.
12. *Zur Genealogie der Moral*, Kritische Gesamtausgabe, VI.2, 412.
13. *Beyond Good and Evil*, 62.
14. *The Gay Science*, 187.
15. Ibid., 188.

16. *Beyond Good and Evil*, 100.

17. *The Genealogy of Morals*, 168.

18. *Daybreak*, 39.

19. *The Antichrist*, 155.

20. *The Will to Power*, 101.

21. Ibid., 100–1.

22. Ibid., 124–5.

23. Ibid., 98.

24. Reimarus, *Fragments*, 151.

25. Ibid., 249.

26. Ibid., 254.

27. Schweitzer, *The Quest of the Historical Jesus*, 13.

28. Harris, *David Strauss and his Theology*, xi.

29. Ibid., 51.

30. Quoted ibid., 77.

31. Stern, J.P., 'Introduction' to *Untimely Meditations*, xi.

32. *The Antichrist*, 140.

33. *Untimely Meditations*, 30.

34. *The Antichrist*, 141.

35. Renan, *The Life of Jesus*, 22, 28, 51, 63, 70, 73, 75, 102, 120.

36. *The Antichrist*, 144.

37. Ibid., 146.

38. Ibid., 147.

39. *The Will to Power*, 98–9.

40. Ibid., 102.

41. *The Antichrist*, 148; *The Will to Power*, 103. Philologists fare no better.

42. *The Antichrist*, 151.

43. Ibid., 150.

44. *King Lear*, Act 1, Scene 1: Cordelia: "I am sure my love's more

ponderous than any tongue."

45. *The Will to Power*, 145.

46. Quoted Heidegger, *Nietzsche*, Vol. 1, 160: 'How little Nietzsche had outgrown Christianity ...', Löwith, *From Hegel to Nietzsche*, 373.

47. *The Will to Power*, 125.

48. *Daybreak*, 36.

49. Fuss and Shapiro, *Nietzsche: A Self-Portrait*, 55. The same sentiments are expressed in a letter to Gast. "It is still the best bit of ideal life that I have ever come to know: from my childhood on I have followed it into many nooks, and I believe in my heart I have never been vicious against it," quoted in Jaspers, *Nietzsche*, 434.

50. *Daybreak*, 37.

51. *Human All Too Human*, 135.

52. *Ecce Homo*, 48.

53. *The Antichrist*, 139.

54. Ibid., 148: 'repudiation of maintaining one's rights of self-defence', *The Will to Power*, 102.

55. *The Will to Power*, 100.

56. *The Antichrist*, 141; *idios* in Liddell-Scott-Jones, *Greek-English Lexicon*, Oxford University Press [9]1968.

57. *The Will to Power*, 125.

58. *Ecce Homo*, 69.

59. Ibid., 53.

60. *The Will to Power*, 513.

11. The Noble God

1. Tille, 'Introduction', *The Case of Wagner*, xvi.
2. Brandes, *Friedrich Nietzsche*, 98.
3. Quoted Kamenka, *The Philosophy of Ludwig Feuerbach*, 15.
4. *The Antichrist*, 162–3.
5. Feuerbach, *Essence of Christianity*, 29–30.
6. Exodus 3.2–6; Freud, 'Moses and Monotheism', 306.
7. Otto, *The Idea of the Holy*, 19.
8. *Human All Too Human*, 101; *Menschliches, Allzumenschliches*, Kritische Gesamtausgabe IV.3, 180.
9. Joshua 6.21.
10. *Human All Too Human*, 267.
11. Ibid.
12. II Samuel 6.6–7.
13. *Thus Spoke Zarathustra*, 68; *The Will to Power*, 535.
14. II Samuel 6.14; cf. Eldad, 'Nietzsche and the Old Testament'.
15. *The Will to Power*, 7.
16. Ibid., 36.
17. *The Genealogy of Morals*, 282.
18. *The Antichrist*, 126.
19. Cf. Irigaray's treatment of castration in 'Veiled Lips', *Marine Lover of Friedrich Nietzsche*, 80–1.
20. *The Antichrist*, 127; cf. the words of Queen Morgan le Fay of the land of Gore, half–sister to Arthur, addressing Lancelot of the Lake: 'I tell you, in a world of power, weakness is a sin, the only sin, and it is punished with death,' Steinbeck, *The Acts of King Arthur and His Noble Knights*, 240.
21. *Nietzsche contra Wagner*, 92.
22. *The Antichrist*, 127.
23. Ibid., 136.
24. Neumann, 'The Case Against Apolitical Morality: Nietzsche's Interpretation of the Jewish Instinct', 32.
25. Kofman, *Nietzsche and Metaphor*, 55. Zeitlin contrasts the egalitarian Decalogue with the Mesopotamian Code of Hammurabi, in which the penalties for nobles injuring nobles are different from those for nobles injuring the common people. However, the Decalogue was not originally addressed to all, certainly not women and slaves. It may itself have been a code for the nobility of Israel (ibid., 61–9).
26. *The Antichrist*, 138.
27. *The Will to Power*, 401.
28. Ibid., 534.
29. Ibid.
30. *Human All Too Human*, 323.
31. Ibid.
32. *The Antichrist*, 164.

33. Genesis 2.17.
34. Nietzsche returns to this theme in *Ecce Homo*, 113, where he conceives of God as the serpent. 'The Devil is merely the idleness of God on that seventh day.'
35. *The Will to Power*, 533.
36. *The Birth of Tragedy*, 9–10.
37. *The Will to Power*, 534.
38. Ibid., 95.
39. Ibid, 534.
40. Ibid.
41. Ibid.
42. Philippians 2.7.
43. *The Will to Power*, 497.
44. I Timothy 2.2.
45. *The Birth of Tragedy*, 60.
46. *Ecce Homo*, 45.
47. *The Will to Power*, 457.
48. Cf. *Ecce Homo*, 77.
49. Irigaray, *Marine Lover of Friedrich Nietzsche*, 72.
50. 'Klage der Ariadne', *Dionysos-Dithyramben*, Kritische Gesamtausgabe V 3, 396.

12. *Nietzsche Contra Lyotard*

1. *Ecce Homo*, 126.
2. Kee, *Marx and the Failure of Liberation Theology.*
3. Marx, 'Economic and Philosophical Manuscripts', *Collected Works*, Vol. 3, First Manuscript, *passim*.
4. Marx, 'The Communist Manifesto', *Collected Works*, Vol. 6, 487.
5. Shakespeare, *The Tempest*, Act 4, Scene 1.
6. *The Genealogy of Morals*, 257.
7. Lyotard, *The Postmodern Condition*, xxiii.
8. Ibid., xxiv.
9. Ibid.
10. Ibid., 37, 60.
11. Ibid., 26.
12. Ibid., 41.
13. Lyotard, *The Differend.*
14. Davies, *Superforce*; see also Connor, *Postmodern Culture*, 31.
15. Skinner, *The Return of Grand Theory in the Human Sciences.*
16. *Untimely Meditations*, 224.
17. *Human All Too Human*, 163.
18. Ibid.
19. Ibid., 211.
20. *The Gay Science*, 337.
21. *Human All Too Human*, 367.
22. *Daybreak*, 118.
23. *The Antichrist*, 115.
24. Ibid., 119.
25. *Twilight of the Idols*, 96.
26. *Ecce Homo*, 112.
27. *The Will to Power*, 42.
28. Ibid., 23.
29. Heller, 'Introduction', *Human All Too Human*.

Bibliography

1. *Nietzsche's Works*

'On Truth and Falsity in Their Extramoral Sense', *Philosophical Writings*, ed. Reinhold Grimm and Caroline Molina y Vedia, Continuum Publishing Co 1995

The Birth of Tragedy from the Spirit of Music, translated by Francis Golffing, Doubleday 1956

Untimely Meditations, translated by R.J. Hollingdale, Cambridge University Press 1988

Human All Too Human, translated by R.J. Hollingdale, Cambridge University Press 1986

Daybreak: Thoughts on the Prejudices of Morality, translated by R.J. Hollingdale, Cambridge University Press 1989

The Gay Science, translated with commentary by Walter Kaufmann, Vintage Books 1974

Thus Spoke Zarathustra, translated with introduction by R.J. Hollingdale, Penguin Books 1971

Beyond Good and Evil, translated with introduction by R.J. Hollingdale, Penguin Books 1973

The Genealogy of Morals: An Attack, translated by Francis Golffing, Doubleday 1956

The Case of Wagner, translated by Thomas Common, T. Fisher Unwin 1899

Twilight of the Idols, translated with commentary by R.J. Hollingdale, Penguin Books 1971

The Anti-Christ, translated with introduction and commentary by R.J. Hollingdale, Penguin Books 1968

Ecce Homo: How One Becomes What One Is, translated with introduction and notes by R.J. Hollingdale, Penguin Books 1979

The Will to Power, translated by Walter Kaufmann and R.J. Hollingdale, Vintage Books 1968

Nietzsche Contra Wagner, translated by Thomas Common, T. Fisher Unwin 1899

Nietzsche Werke: Kritische Gesamtausgabe, ed. G. Colli and M. Montinari, Berlin: Walter de Gruyter & Co 1967ff.

Nietzsche: Werke in drei Bänden, ed. Karl Schlechta, Munich: Carl Hanser 1954–6

Selected Letters of Friedrich Nietzsche, edited and translated by Christopher Middleton, University of Chicago Press 1969

Nietzsche: A Self-Portrait from his Letters, edited and translated by Peter Fuss and Henry Shapiro, Harvard University Press 1971

2. Secondary Works

Allison, David B. (ed. and introduction), *The New Nietzsche. Contemporary Styles of Interpretation*, The MIT Press 1985

Altizer, Thomas J.J., 'Eternal Recurrence and the Kingdom of God', in *The New Nietzsche*, ed. D.B. Allison

Bataille, Georges, *On Nietzsche*, translated by Bruce Boone, Paragon House 1992

Beermann, René, 'Nietzsche, Dostoevsky and Russian Symbolism', *Co-Existence*, Volume 20, no.1, April 1983, 85–103

Bernouilli, Carl, *Franz Overbeck und Friedrich Nietzsche: eine Freundschaft*, Jena: Diedrichs 1908

Birault, Henri, 'Beatitude in Nietzsche', in *The New Nietzsche*, ed. D.B. Allison

Biser, Eugen, 'The Critical Imitator of Jesus: A Contribution to the Interpretation of Nietzsche on the Basis of a Comparison', in *Studies in Nietzsche and the Judaeo-Christian Tradition*, ed. J.C.O' Flaherty et al.

Blanchot, Maurice, 'The Limits of Experience: Nihilism', in *The New Nietzsche*, ed. D.B. Allison

Blondel, Eric, 'Nietzsche's Life as Metaphor', in *The New Nietzsche*, ed. D.B. Allison

Brandes, George, *Friedrich Nietzsche*, William Heinemann 1914

Castro, Fidel, 'In Tribute to Che', in Che Guevara, *Reminiscences of the Cuban Revolutionary War*, Penguin Books 1968

Cayfill, Howard, 'The Return of Nietzsche and Marx', in *Nietzsche, Feminism and Political Theory*, ed. Paul Patton

Clark, Maudemarie, *Nietzsche on Truth and Philosophy*, Cambridge University Press 1990

Connor, Steven, *Postmodern Culture*, Blackwell 1997

Conway, Daniel W., *Nietzsche's Dangerous Game: Philosophy in the*

Twilight of the Idols, Cambridge University Press 1997

Davies, Paul, *Superforce: The Search for a Grand Unified Theory of Nature,* William Heinemann 1984

Deleuze, Gilles, 'Nomad Thought', in *The New Nietzsche,* ed. D.B. Allison

–, *Nietzsche and Philosophy,* translated by Hugh Tomlinson, The Athlone Press 1996

Derrida, Jacques, 'The Question of Style', in *The New Nietzsche,* ed. D.B. Allison

Deussen, Paul, *Erinnerungen an Friedrich Nietzsche,* Leipzig: Brockhaus 1901

Dostoyevsky, F.M., *Crime and Punishment,* J.M. Dent & Sons, Everyman ed., nd

Ebeling, Gerhard, *Word and Faith,* translated by J.W. Leitch, SCM Press 1963

Eldad, Israel, 'Nietzsche and the Old Testament', in *Studies in Nietzsche and the Judaeo-Christian Tradition,* ed. J.C. O' Flaherty et al.

Feuerbach, Ludwig, *The Essence of Christianity,* translated by George Eliot, reissued Harper & Row 1957

Förster-Nietzsche, Elizabeth (ed.), *The Nietzsche-Wagner Correspondence,* translated by Caroline V. Kerr, Duckworth & Co. 1922

Frend, W.H.C., *Martyrdom and Persecution in the Early Church,* Blackwell 1965

Frenzel, Ivo, *Friedrich Nietzsche: mit Selbstzeugnissen und Bilddokumenten,* Reinbek: Rowohlt Taschenbuch Verlag 1966

Freud, Sigmund, 'Moses and Monotheism', in *The Pelican Freud Library, Vol.13,* Penguin Books 1986

Furness, R.S., 'Nietzsche, the Madman and the Death of God', in D.W.D. Shaw, *Dimensions: Literary and Theological,* St Mary's College: University of St Andrews 1992

Gal, Yves Le, 'Unzeitgemass: Out of Season', in *Nietzsche and Christianity,* ed. C. Geffré and J.-P. Jossua

Geffré, Claude, and Jossua, Jean-Pierre (eds), *Nietzsche and Christianity, Concilium 145,* 1981

Goedert, Georges, 'The Dionysian Theodicy', in *Studies in Nietzsche and the Judaeo-Christian Tradition,* ed. O' Flaherty et al.

Granier, Jean, 'Nietzsche's Conception of Chaos', 'Perspectives and Interpretation', in *The New Nietzsche,* ed. D.B. Allison

–, 'Thinking With and Against Nietzsche', in *Nietzsche and Christianity*, ed. C. Geffré and J.-P. Jossua

Gregory, F., *Scientific Materialism in Nineteenth-Century Germany*, Dordrecht: Reidel Publishing Co. 1977

Gustafsson, Lars, 'Dr Nietzsche's Office Hours are Between 10 am and 12 am', in *Reading Nietzsche*, ed. R.C. Solomon and K.M. Higgins

Haar, Michel, 'Nietzsche and Metaphysical Language', in *The New Nietzsche*, ed. D.B. Allison

–, 'Nietzsche and the Metamorphosis of the Divine', in *Post-Secular Philosophy*, ed. Philip Blond, Routledge 1998

Harris, Horton, *David Strauss and His Theology*, Cambridge University Press 1973

Hayek, F.A., *The Road to Serfdom*, George Routledge & Sons 1946

–, *Law, Legislation and Liberty, Volume 1, Rules and Order*, Routledge & Kegan Paul 1973

Hegel, G.W.F., *Logic*, The Clarendon Press 1982

–, *The Philosophy of Right*, Oxford University Press 1967

Heidegger, Martin, *Nietzsche*, Volume 1 translated with notes and analysis by David Farrell Krell, Routledge & Kegan Paul 1981; Volume 2 translated by David Farrell Krell, Harper & Row 1984

–, *Being and Time*, translated by John Macquarrie and Edward Robinson, SCM Press 1962, reissued Blackwell 1966

Heller, Erich, *The Importance of Nietzsche*, University of Chicago Press 1988

–, 'Introduction' to *Human All Too Human*

Henry, Martin, *Franz Overbeck: Theologian?*, Frankfurt am Main: Peter Lang 1995

Hollingdale, R.J., *Nietzsche*, Routledge & Kegan Paul 1973

–, 'Commentary' to *Beyond Good and Evil*

Husserl, Edmund, *Phenomenology and the Crisis of Philosophy*, translated with notes by Quentin Lauer, Harper 1965

Irigaray, Luce, *Marine Lover of Friedrich Nietzsche*, translated by Gillian C. Gill, Columbia University Press 1991

Jasper, David (ed.), *Postmodernism, Literature and the Future of Theology*, Macmillan 1993

Jaspers, Karl, *Nietzsche: An Introduction to the Understanding of his Philosophical Activity*, translated by Charles F. Wallraff and Frederick J. Schmitz, University of Arizona Press 1965

–, *Nietzsche and Christianity*, translated by E.B. Ashton, Henry

Regnery Co. 1961

–, *Philosophy of Existence*, Basil Blackwell 1971

–, *Philosophy*, University of Chicago Press 1969

–, *Philosophical Faith and Revelation*, Collins 1967

Jung, Carl G., *The Collected Works of C.G. Jung*, Volume 6, *Psychological Types*, Princeton University Press 1977

–, *Selected Writings*, selected and introduced by Anthony Storr, Collins Fontana 1983

Kamenka, Eugene, *The Philosophy of Ludwig Feuerbach*, Routledge & Kegan Paul 1970

Katz, Steven T., 'Language, Epistemology and Mysticism', in *Mysticism and Philosophy*, ed. Steven T. Katz, Sheldon Press 1978

Kaufmann, Walter, *Nietzsche: Philosopher, Psychologist, Antichrist*, New York: Vintage Books 1968

–, *Twenty German Poets*, edited and translated, Random House 1962

Kee, Alistair, *Constantine versus Christ: The Triumph of Ideology*, SCM Press 1982

–, *Marx and the Failure of Liberation Theology*, SCM Press 1990

–, 'Transcendence and God: A Critique of Religious Objectivism', in *Being and Truth*, ed. Alistair Kee and Eugene T. Long, SCM Press 1986

Kierkegaard, Søren, *Concluding Unscientific Postscript*, Princeton University Press 1941

Klossowski, Pierre, 'Nietzsche's Experience of the Eternal Return', in *The New Nietzsche*, ed. D.B. Allison

Knight, G. Wilson, *Christ and Nietzsche: An Essay in Poetic Wisdom*, Staples Press 1948

Kofman, Sarah, 'Metaphor, Symbol and Metamorphosis', in *The New Nietzsche*, ed. D.B. Allison

–, *Nietzsche and Metaphor*, translated with introduction by Duncan Large, The Athlone Press 1993

Krell, David Farrell, and Wood, David, *Exceedingly Nietzsche: Aspects of Contemporary Nietzsche-Interpretation*, Routledge 1988

Küng, Hans, *Does God Exist? An Answer for Today*, Collins 1979 reissued SCM Press 1984

Ledure, Yves, 'The Christian Response to Nietzsche's Critique of Christianity', in *Nietzsche and Christianity*, ed. C. Geffré and J.P. Jossua

Lenin, V.I., *Collected Works*, Lawrence & Wishart 1938

Lewis, Charles, 'Morality and Deity in Nietzsche's Concept of Biblical Religion', in *Studies in Nietzsche and the Judaeo-Christian Tradition*, ed.J.C. O' Flaherty et al.

Lingis, Alphonso, 'The Will to Power', in *The New Nietzsche*, ed. D.B. Allison

Ludovici, Anthony M., *Nietzsche: His Life and Work*, Constable & Co. 1910

Lyotard, Jean-François, *The Postmodern Condition: A Report on Knowledge*, Manchester University Press 1984

–, *The Differend: Phases in Dispute*, translated by Georges Van Den Abbeele, Manchester University Press 1988

Magnus, Bernd, *Nietzsche's Existential Imperative*, Bloomington: Indiana University Press 1978

–, 'Jesus, Christianity and Superhumanity', in *Studies in Nietzsche and the Judaeo-Christian Tradition*, ed.J.C.O' Flaherty et al.

–, and Higgins, Kathleen M., *The Cambridge Companion to Nietzsche*, Cambridge University Press 1996

Marais, Julian, *History of Philosophy*, Dover Publications 1967

Marx, Karl, *Early Writings*, translated and edited by T.B. Bottomore, Watts 1963.

–, and Engels, Friedrich, *Collected Works*, Lawrence & Wishart

Neumann, Harry, 'The Case against Apolitical Morality: Nietzsche's Interpretation of the Jewish Instinct', in *Studies in Nietzsche and the Judaeo-Christian Tradition*, ed. J.C.O' Flaherty et al.

O' Flaherty, James C., Seliner, Timothy F., and Helm, Robert M. (eds), *Studies in Nietzsche and the Judaeo-Christian Tradition*, University of North Carolina Press 1985

O' Hara, Daniel (ed.), *Why Nietzsche Now?*, Indiana University Press 1981

Oppel, Frances, '"Speaking of Immemorial Waters": Irigaray and Nietzsche', in *Nietzsche, Feminism and Political Theory*, ed. Paul Patton

Otto, Rudolf, *The Idea of the Holy*, Oxford University Press 1925

Pasley, Malcolm (ed.), *Nietzsche: Imagery and Thought*, Methuen 1978

Patton, Paul (ed.), *Nietzsche, Feminism and Political Theory*, Routledge 1993

Penzo, Giorgio, 'The Influence of Nietzsche in Literature and

Philosophy up to Heidegger', in *Nietzsche and Christianity*, ed C. Geffré and J.-P. Jossua

Pütz, Peter, 'Nietzsche: Art and Intellectual Inquiry', in M. Pasley (ed.), *Nietzsche: Imagery and Thought*

Reimarus, H.S., *Fragments*, ed. Charles H.Talbert, SCM Press 1971

Renan, Ernst, *The Life of Jesus*, J.M. Dent & Sons 1934

Rosen, Stanley, *The Mask of Enlightenment. Nietzsche's Zarathustra*, Cambridge University Press 1995

Salaquarda, Jorg, 'Dionysus versus the Crucified One: Nietzsche's Understanding of the Apostle Paul', in *Studies in Nietzsche and the Judaeo-Christian Tradition*, ed. J.C.O' Flaherty et al.

Sallis, John, 'Dionysus – In Excess of Metaphysics', in *Exceedingly Nietzsche: Aspects of Contemporary Nietzsche-Interpretation*, ed. D.F. Krell and D. Wood

Santa Ana, Julio de, *Good News to the Poor: The Challenge of the Poor in the History of the Church*, Geneva: World Council of Churches 1977

Sartre, Jean-Paul, *Being and Nothingness*, Philosophical Library 1956

Schacht, Richard, *Nietzsche*, Routledge & Kegan Paul 1983

Schiffers, Norbert, 'Analysing Nietzsche's "God is Dead"', in *Nietzsche and Christianity*, ed C. Geffré and J.P. Jossua

Schopenhauer, Arthur, *Religion: A Dialogue and Other Essays*, selected and translated by T.B. Saunders, Swan Sonnenschein & Co. 1889

–, *Parerga and Paralipomena: Short Philosophical Essays*, translated E.F.J. Payne, The Clarendon Press 1974

Schutte, Ofelia, *Beyond Nihilism: Nietzsche without Masks*, University of Chicago Press 1884

Schweitzer, Albert, *The Quest of the Historical Jesus*, A. & C Black [3] 1954 reissued SCM Press 1981

Shapiro, Gary, 'The Writing on the Wall: *The Antichrist* and the Semiotics of History', in *Reading Nietzsche*, ed. R.C. Solomon and K.M. Higgins

Shaw, D.W.D., *Dimensions: Literary and Theological*, St Mary's College, University of St Andrews 1992

Silk, M.S., and Stern, J.P., *Nietzsche on Tragedy*, Cambridge University Press 1981

Simon, Josef, 'Language and the Critique of Language in Nietzsche Studies', in *Studies in Nietzsche and the Judaeo-Christian Tradition*, ed. J.C.O' Flaherty et al.

Silverman, Hugh J., 'The Autobiographical Textuality of Nietzsche's

Ecce Homo', in O' Hara (ed.), *Why Nietzsche Now?*

Skinner, Quentin, *The Return of Grand Theory in the Human Sciences*, Cambridge University Press 1985

Sobrino, Jon, *The True Church and the Poor*, SCM Press 1984

Solomon, Robert C., and Higgins, Kathleen M. (eds.), *Reading Nietzsche*, Oxford University Press 1988

Stambaugh, Joan, '*Amor dei* and *Amor fati*: Spinoza and Nietzsche', in *Studies in Nietzsche and the Judaeo-Christian Tradition*, ed. J.C. O' Flaherty et al.

Steinbeck, John, *The Acts of King Arthur and His Noble Knights*, William Heinemann 1979

Stern, J.P., *A Study of Nietzsche*, Cambridge University Press 1979

–, 'Introduction' to *Untimely Meditations*

Strong, John S., *The Legend and Cult of Upagupta*, Princeton University Press 1992

Tanner, Michael, *Nietzsche*, Oxford University Press 1994

Taylor, Charles, *Hegel*, Cambridge University Press 1975

Tille, Alexander, 'Introduction' to *The Case of Wagner*

Uhl, Anton, 'Suffering from God and Man: Nietzsche and Dostoyevsky', in *Nietzsche and Christianity*, ed. C. Geffré and J.P. Jossua

Valadier, Paul, 'Dionysus Versus the Crucified', in *The New Nietzsche*, ed. D.B. Allison

Warnock, C.J., *English Philosophy Since 1900*, Oxford University Press 1969

Wittgenstein, Ludwig, *Philosophical Investigations*, Basil Blackwell 1963

Woo, David, 'Nietzsche's Transvaluation of Time', in *Exceedingly Nietzsche: Aspects of Contemporary Nietzsche-Interpretation*, ed. D.F. Krell and D. Woods

Zeitlin, Irving M., *Nietzsche: A Re-examination*, Polity Press 1994

Zelechow, Bernard, 'Nietzsche's Theology of History and the Redemption of Postmodernism', in *Postmodernism, Literature and the Future of Theology*, ed. D.Jasper

Index